THE LAND AND THE DAYS

The Land and the Days

A Memoir of Family, Friendship, and Grief

TRACY DAUGHERTY

UNIVERSITY OF OKLAHOMA PRESS : NORMAN

This book is published with the generous assistance of the Wallace C. Thompson Endowment Fund, University of Oklahoma Foundation.

Library of Congress Cataloging-in-Publication Data

Names: Daugherty, Tracy, author.
Title: The land and the days : a memoir of family, friendship, and grief / Tracy Don Daugherty.
Description: Norman : University of Oklahoma Press, [2022] | Includes bibliographical references. | Summary: "Combines reminiscence, history, and meditation to create a probing portrait of a developing self, from a childhood in Texas and Oklahoma—steeped in the mysteries of politics, race, and class—to the challenges of maturity, bringing inevitable confrontations with mortality"—Provided by publisher.
Identifiers: LCCN 2021028332 | ISBN 978-0-8061-7623-9 (paperback)
Subjects: LCSH: Daugherty, Harry Tracy, 1898–1978. | Daugherty, Tracy. | Dougherty family. | Businessmen—Oklahoma—Walters—Biography. | Politicians—Oklahoma—Walters—Biography. | Walters (Okla.)—Social life and customs—20th century. | Walters (Okla.)—Biography. | Midland (Texas)—Biography.
Classification: LCC F702.C75 D38 2022 | DDC 976.6/49—dc23
LC record available at https://lccn.loc.gov/2021028332

The paper in this book meets the guidelines for permanence and durability of the Committee on Production Guidelines for Book Longevity of the Council on Library Resources, Inc. ∞

For Debra and Margie,
for Joey and Hannah

Each of us finds that in [our lives] every moment of time is completely filled. [We are] bombarded every second by sensations, emotions, thoughts, which [we] cannot attend to for multitude, and nine-tenths of which [we] must simply ignore. A single second of lived time contains more than can be recorded . . . By far the greater part of . . . teeming reality [has] escaped human consciousness almost as soon as it occurred . . . At every tick of the clock, in every inhabited part of the world, an unimaginable richness and variety of "history" falls off the world into total oblivion.

—C. S. Lewis, "Historicism"

CONTENTS

We have all had dreams that felt like visitations or prophecies of the future, and we have all, in dreams, projected ourselves into other worlds. In dreams, chronology and continuity, finality and place have no meaning. I remember, from readings assigned to me in college, that Mark Twain had a powerful premonitory dream three days before his brother Henry died in a boiler explosion aboard a steam-powered paddle-wheeler on the Mississippi River. In sleep, Twain saw his brother's coffin straddling two chairs in a bare room, covered with white roses. Three days later, in a Memphis hospital, he witnessed precisely this scene. Twain also famously predicted he'd die with the return of Halley's Comet, and he did, just as his birth had coincided with the visitor's sparkling appearance in western skies seventy-five years earlier. "These two unaccountable freaks," he said, referring to himself and the comet. "They came in together, they must go out together."

In college I learned just how strange and dreamlike American literature can be. The oddest book I encountered in my undergraduate years was required reading in a seminar I took on the James family—William, Henry, Alice, and their decidedly freakish father, Henry Sr. When William, the eldest child, was still an infant, Henry Sr. experienced what he later called a "vastation," a waking dream state revealing to him hidden worlds. He described the experience this way, in the volume the seminar teacher asked us to read, *Society the Redeemed Form of Man:*

> One day . . . having eaten a comfortable dinner, I remained sitting at the table after the family had dispersed, idly gazing at the embers in the grate, thinking of nothing, and feeling only the exhilaration incident to a good digestion, when suddenly—in a

lightning-flash as it were—. . . some damnèd shape squatt[ed] invisible to me within the precincts of the room . . . raying out from his fetid personality influences fatal to life. The thing had not lasted ten seconds before I felt myself a wreck, that is, reduced from a state of firm, vigorous, joyful manhood to one of almost helpless infancy.

I remember that my copy of *Society the Redeemed Form of Man* was a thick hardback with a grainy green cover missing a dust jacket. It felt grim and weighty in the hand, exactly the way its dense contents snuggled into the mind. It was the first book I bought that embodied for me the *college experience*, or more accurately, the *activity of learning:* the challenge, alternately thrilling and futile, of grappling with elusive ideas.

The teacher wanted his students to read the book so we could understand the thinking of Henry James Sr. and trace his influence on the works of his remarkable sons, William and Henry Jr. (Alice, every bit as brilliant as her older brothers, was physically and emotionally infirm most of her life, and so was prevented from achieving as much professionally.) James Sr.'s "vastation" convinced him of humankind's estrangement from God, of the individual's vulnerability to unfathomable forces, and the need each of us has, in our stumbles from grace, to be redeemed by America's well-organized democratic society. Collective democracy, James wrote, would lift us from our individual wreckage. "That's the central message you must take from Mr. James," our teacher lectured us.

I took from him something else entirely, especially when I learned that Mr. James also claimed to speak to angels, and when I read, in another class, the account of Mark Twain's spooky brother-dream. From that point on, I carried the conviction that American literature was not as grounded in the principles of realism—that is, chronology and continuity—as most of my teachers insisted it was. Moreover, it occurred to me to question the nature of realism—in fact, to interrogate *reality*—prompted not by angels and dreams, but by my physical encounter with *Society the Redeemed Form of Man*. The feel of the book in my hand, its texture and weight, paled next to my mental intimacy with it.

I suppose I had been aware before this time that internal life could rage and storm more powerfully than the external events shaping our experiences, at least in our usual telling of them, but I had never considered the matter consciously. I didn't know it yet (I'd not yet taken a philosophy course), but I was entering the *mind-body problem*, the problem of *duality*. I accepted that whenever I opened a book, my brain, controlling my eyes (or working in concert with my eyes), considered the print on the page. But it seemed that some-thing else—my mind, for lack of a better word, or my self—was mulling the *import* of the print, the book's concepts, its spirit, so to say, clothed in the flesh and bones of paper, fiber, leather-embossed cardboard. Were brain and mind the same? The state of conscious-ness was—*what*?

The nature of learning became a source of intense curiosity for me. I knew the body could learn, pleasure and pain its primary instruc-tors. As a kid, growing up in Texas and Oklahoma, I'd danced to rock and roll and taken up drumming; ever since, muscle memory had been of crucial interest to me. Usually, if I thought too hard about circling my drumsticks in a rhythmic pattern from the rim of the snare drum to the floor tom to the ride cymbal, I'd mess up the beat. But if I gave myself to the music, let my body *enter* the rhythm without contemplating the pattern, I'd lock the moves down cold.

But the brain and the mind . . . was my brain like my hand grip-ping a stick: the propulsive muscle required for learning? If so, then what was the mind? The rhythm (of what? of life?) to which the brain must submit if it hoped to ride a solid groove?

Immediately, the trouble with this line of questioning became clear to me. Brain and mind occupied different spaces in such a con-ception. Did they really exist apart from one another (like dreams and "reality")? Did the brain produce the mind the way the body manufactured hormones—or in some other, more complicated fashion? Could the mind survive the loss of the brain, and vice versa? Was the mind, in fact, what some folks called the soul?

In volume after volume of American literature, *soul* has often been linked to *land*. Recently, critic A. O. Scott published in the *New York Times* a lengthy reappraisal of Wallace Stegner's body of work—Stegner, the grand scribe of the modern American West and a pragmatist like William James. Scott suggested it was a writer's job to locate the elements of individual self in the regional landscapes from which a writer springs: the claims of place and finality (that is, burial in the soil of a place). He called his piece "Wallace Stegner and the Conflicted Soul of the West." Stegner invited such scrutiny. "I was shaped by the West," he wrote. Further, he insisted that consciousness was not "implanted by divine act" but was rather the product of "tradition and the society which has bred us." From earliest childhood, he said, we absorb the contours of the land we walk; our walking rhythms establish metabolisms of body and mind, what we call consciousness; *where* we choose to walk forms our behavior toward others.

Stegner believed it was the bonds of body and land that laid the foundations of tradition. For him, as for Henry James Sr., society, the repository of collective consciousness, strengthened individuals by giving them a structure on which to base their character.

He admitted the limits of his beliefs. He would have nothing to do with metaphysics. Concerning the relationship of consciousness to greater realms—the realm of Twain's restless comets, say—he said, "I simply do not know; I don't think I *can* know." He left this age-old puzzle to another great American writer partly shaped by the West. Willa Cather was as reticent as Stegner to trace a direct line from individual self-awareness to the infinite. But in a book of stories entitled *Obscure Destinies*, about the hard lives of poor Americans living off the land, she hinted at such a link. In the book's first story, a farmer observes a pretty country graveyard, "sort of snug and homelike, not cramped or mournful,—a big sweep all round it,"

Cather writes. The farmer reflects on his fondness for the world—
"He wasn't anxious to leave it." But when the time came, "it was
a comfort to think that he would never have to go farther than the
edge of his own hayfield. The snow, falling over his barnyard and
the graveyard, seemed to draw things together": an image of endless expanse, the hayfield serving as the outer (inner?) perimeter of
what little we may know, on this good green earth, of Forever.

"May your days and the days of your children be many in the
land," says the poet of Deuteronomy, inscribing our lives between
two poles, that of time (the days) and that of substance (the land).
Whether we choose to believe in a soul, whether we believe the soul
resides in the contours of "reality" or in dreamlike fragments of
worlds beyond imagining, we live our lives seeking meaning, pur-
pose, destinies we hope against hope will not be obscure. We never
stop learning.

In the following pages, eager for new discoveries, I walk through
my land and my days—step by slow, halting step, clutching my
writer's pen like an Oklahoma dowser waving a divining rod,
scratching at the mysteries of *self, mind, soul.*

I begin with the premise that, encompassed by the land, we are all
shaped by the rituals of our regions, by family and friends. In "Cotton County" I consider these apparently straightforward facts. I say
"apparently" recalling Mark Twain's strange vision of his brother.
It doesn't take most of us long to discover that the facts of our lives
rarely offer the clarity they promise. They are just fragments of the
story. The body stumbles bravely ahead.

At some point, stunned by the passing of days (if we survive long
enough), we are shaped by grief, and by mourning's grip on our
perceptions of time. "Death is a convention, a certification to the end
of pain, something for the vital-statistics book, not binding upon
anyone but the keepers of graveyard records," Stegner wrote, by
which he meant to affirm that the dead remain ever alive to the living. In "The Unearthly Archives," documenting a *mind's* stumbles in

the face of grief, I consider ultimate destinies: the passage, through time, of a self bound for silence.

In these modest sketches, I have tried to trace the progress of an individual, hoping for a collective portrait. In the spirit of Cather's American elegies, I have followed a narrow "stretch of dusty white road drinking up the moonlight beside a blind wall," where I hesitate now and feel an "old uneasiness"—a sense that "the truths we want to keep" will elude us if we ever quit walking.

Cotton County

I remember, as a boy of five or six, watching the American flag wave stiffly in gusts of dusty wind above the front lawn of the Cotton County Courthouse in Walters, Oklahoma, a small cattle and oil town located in the southwest part of the state, a few miles north of the Red River and the border with Texas.

I'm sure my grandmother Zorah had taken me to the courthouse to see the county clerk's office, where my grandfather used to work. She'd hung on her living room wall a framed black-and-white photograph of my grandfather from the 1930s. He was sitting behind a massive wooden desk in the courthouse in front of a silver wall radiator, staring at an Underwood typewriter. The typewriter was big, black, and bulky. He wore a dark suit and buttoned vest. A watch chain was just visible beneath the lapels of his coat, and the caps of two bright fountain pens poked above his breast pocket. His wavy short hair was parted in the middle. Even as a child, I could see my father's face, as well as my own, in his features: the thick, quizzical brows; the tight smile suggesting a touch of whimsy beneath an air of grave seriousness. He leaned back, comfortably but formidably, in his chair, fingering an official document. A row of fat leather books, legal tomes, rose in a stack on the desk next to the typewriter, beneath a wrinkled map of the county tacked to the otherwise bare plaster wall.

By the time I was five or six, in the early 1960s, neither wall radiators nor old-fashioned typewriters were still in use—at least not where I lived, with my parents in West Texas—and I was fascinated with these objects in the picture.

The photograph hung on my grandmother's wall next to a loud clock. Each *click* of the second hand sounded like a snare drum's rim shot. The timepiece's rectangular face was the type you'd see atop a grandfather clock, but it was free-hanging, without a pendulum or weights. Its *tock-tock* carried me steadily through the nights whenever my mother and father, my sister, and I visited my grandparents. I associated the clock's comforting regularity with the typewriter and the radiator in the picture, displayed at a tilt over the pink daisy wallpaper. No such items existed in my world. All the clocks I saw in Texas, for sale in the hardware department at Sears, were round, modern-sleek; some of them even had numbers that glowed in the dark. Photographs screamed in gauzy Kodachrome. My grandparents' house belonged to another realm of existence—to another time, certainly, but concepts of time were far too abstract for me then; to my childhood sensibility, old-fashionedness translated most immediately into exotic tastes, smells, and textures: fried okra, mothballs, cotton batting—radiators and ancient typewriters—things I experienced only in Oklahoma.

I don't know how my grandmother's ritual with me started, but at a certain point, trips to the Cotton County Courthouse became a regular part of my visits north of the Red River. The office that my grandfather had occupied in the 1930s still served the county clerk and his staff. The space benefitted now from electric heating, but the old radiator, fixed to the wall, still hunched beneath the drawn paper shade, stained with coffee drops and cigarette burns, on the window. The Underwood no longer sat on the desk; years ago, someone had stored it on a shelf above a filing cabinet in a corner, next to a pale blank rectangle on the rough plaster where the county map had hung. Useless, the typewriter remained one of the first things you noticed when you walked into the room. Zorah took me there—the clerk and his staff tolerated our brief visits—because she knew the objects gave me pleasure. I was an easy child to please.

I would sit behind the massive desk, just as my grandfather had, backed by the ponderous radiator. It was like a guardrail, protecting me—from what, I wonder now. My fears consisted of . . . the uncertainty of change, even at that innocent age? Passing time? A sweet odor of old wax rose from the scuffed floorboards. I stared out the window at the flag fluttering on the lawn.

My grandfather's name was Harry Tracy Daugherty. I was chris-
tened after him. His father had taken the name Harry Tracy from the
masthead of a nineteenth-century North Texas newspaper devoted
to socialist causes. A young man called Harry Tracy was the paper's
managing editor. My great-grandfather Andy owned a furniture
and hardware store in Walters, which my grandfather inherited and
ran until he retired in the 1970s. Before opening the store, Andy had
been a small farmer, at a time when land laborers in the American Southwest were often fairly radical in their politics, convinced
that big government and corporate monopolies had aligned against
them and their only hope was collective action, including violence.
It was not the Oklahoma we know today.

Andy admired Harry Tracy's populist rhetoric and the paper's
socialist vision, so he named his boy after the inflammatory editor. From the first, then, my grandfather was directed toward public
service. County clerk was only one of a number of official positions
he held; while becoming a successful businessman, he would rise
to prominence in state politics, eventually serving two terms in the
Oklahoma House of Representatives in the 1950s and early 1960s.
Framed on my study wall at home, I have a letter from Senator John
F. Kennedy, dated January 24, 1959, congratulating my grandfather
on his election to the Oklahoma House and his "participation in
the extensive Democratic victory. We in the Democratic Party have
every reason to be proud of the results of the election, and I look
forward to working with you for our party and our country."

One day several years ago, I sold my IBM computer with its flaccid
floppy discs, along with my cumbersome filing cabinets, to make
more room in my study. PCs connected to the cloud had become a
better storage system than the monstrous cabinets, and the Internet
promised swifter access to information than the newspaper clippings I hoarded.

I became curious to know if the algorithmic universe retained anything of my grandfather's life and career. I positioned my slumped

and aging back at my desk and Googled "Harry Tracy Daugherty, Walters, Oklahoma." Several bold ads appeared onscreen claiming, "We found Harry Tracy Daugherty." None of the names related on those lists had the remotest connection to my grandfather, who, thirty years dead, was beyond finding, anyway. "Updates" on his furniture and hardware store, shuttered now for over thirty-five years, appeared, apparently based on decades-old license requests he had filed with Oklahoma business associations. How these counted as updates was not clear to me.

On a website cataloguing "precedential" court cases, my grandfather's name popped up in a 1935 lawsuit filed in Cotton County by the father of a boy who had been married by a justice of the peace at five o'clock one late November morning at the Walters courthouse. The father sought to annul the marriage on the grounds that "(a) at the time of the marriage he (the appellee) was a minor, 14 years of age, (b) that as such he had no express authority either in person or in writing from parent or guardian sanctioning his marriage, and (c) that at the time of the marriage appellee was under the influence of intoxicants to such an extent that he did not and could not understand the effect of a marriage contract and a marriage ceremony."

Furthermore, the suit alleged that section 1670 of the Oklahoma Statutes had been violated, in that "no application for a marriage license in writing, signed and sworn to before the judge or clerk of the county court, was ever made or filed." The license "had been issued and signed in blank by the county clerk of Cotton County, Oklahoma, acting through a deputy clerk." The evidence was indisputably "to the effect that the deputy clerk, F. T. Wagner, signed 'Tracy Daugherty, County Clerk,' by himself, to the license, and that the contents of said license had not been written in."

The young woman (the appellant) who'd accompanied the boy to the justice of the peace insisted the marriage was valid. She was seventeen years old. She "denied that the appellee was intoxicated." Further, she "pleaded that the union was sufficient as a common-law marriage." The court ruled against her.

On the website, a lengthy discussion followed the ruling, explaining why this case had become "precedential"—it had to do with definitions of common-law marriage in Oklahoma—but my attention remained caught on why my grandfather had allowed his deputy clerk to forge his name on a blank marriage license to be used one cold November morning by a drunk fourteen-year-old. I could not get past these obscure details in an obscure document that may have had a profound effect on many lives going forward.

The couple's names—Heamon and Tassoday—were unfamiliar to me. Nothing in the document shed any light on their family circumstances, financial situations, social class, or potential criminal pasts.

Possibly, the deputy clerk, Mr. Wagner, had acted on his own without Tracy's knowledge. I have never entertained this option, and I wonder why: perhaps for the simple reason that I don't believe anything ever got past my grandfather. Walters was, and is, a very small town; he knew everyone and, to hear him talk, knew every single thing that ever went on, even behind closed doors.

And there was something—I'm not entirely sure what—about his expression in the county clerk's office in the picture on Zorah's wall: maybe the hint of mirth and mischief lurking just beneath the impression of gravity, his awareness of the absurdities of daily life undermining all our attempts at dignity.

My father's older brother, James Clay, told me a story about Tracy one Thanksgiving after dinner, when he'd nearly emptied a bottle of Jack Daniel's. I was twelve years old. He said that after his return from military service in Europe in the 1940s—during which he saw heavy combat at Normandy—he had moved back into his old bedroom in Zorah and Tracy's house in Walters. For months he did nothing but sleep all day and drink homemade 'shine with his buddies all night. One morning around dawn, he pulled the family Ford into the driveway after a long debauch, and promptly passed out on his bed. Tracy woke him, whispering urgently, at around seven o'clock. He had glimpsed a pair of panties in the front seat of the car when he'd gone out to pick the morning's *Walters Herald* up off the lawn. J. C. blinked and sputtered, preparing for a tongue-lashing, but all Tracy did was wave the panties in the air. Gently, he said, "So, what are we going to tell your mother?"

Whatever happened between the appellee and the appellant at five A.M. in late November 1935, I believe Tracy was well aware of it and had signed off on the plan.

At a glance, it appears to be a mighty unethical business. Generally speaking, Tracy was a staunchly ethical man. The dapper county clerk has a face you can trust: he will do the right thing. On the other hand, as J. C.'s Thanksgiving story suggests, he was no J. Edgar Hoover, eager to punish the slightest weakness. To the contrary, he could be empathetic and quite forgiving of personal failings.

I try to imagine him padding privately through his house early in the morning, before he has put on his dark suit and vest, before he has assumed his public expression. It was a house I always loved, and often at night I still dream of returning to it, buying it, and living my final days in Walters among my grandparents' untouched furnishings, though of course the furniture was sold off after they died, and the house was remodeled—essentially demolished—sometime in the 1980s.

In gray light going gently yellow through lace curtains, my grandfather passes the clock and the picture of himself in the county clerk's office hanging on the wall. The pink daisies etched into the wallpaper glow nearly purple in the early morning light. He goes into the kitchen to pour himself a cup of coffee. The kitchen is small and square, and where the eastern wall should be, a wide arch opens up into a dining room distinguished by a café-style red leather booth running in a semicircle round the table in the center of the room.

Tracy dresses in dim bathroom light, beneath a typed sheet he's tacked to the wall: "A friend is not a feller who is taken in by sham, a friend is one who knows our faults, and doesn't give a damn!—

from the writings of J. P. McEvoy." This is one of the first texts I ever learned to read.

Tracy moves through the kitchen into a darkened space, the walls painted burgundy and white, where tall oak hutches store Zorah's silver and her beautiful bone china. His law books are here as well, inside glass-covered cherrywood bookcases. (He is self-taught, having never finished high school.) Down a short hallway to the right of the bookcases are the small bedrooms where his boys sleep. What year is this? In my mind, it can be any year I want it to be.

As a child, I liked the bedrooms best when they were empty.

It was on a summer afternoon when I was five or six and the bedrooms were empty—the windows open, horseflies batting against the dusty screens, the curtains blowing mildly across the muslin bedcovers—that I discovered the giant horned frog painted inside a cabinet in the bathroom my father used as a boy. The frog stared at me with black pop-eyes. He was sitting in a lush green field. He was fifty times taller than people. He dwarfed the trees. The painting was signed in childish letters at the bottom of the cabinet door, "Don Eugene," my father's name. Excited, I scrambled onto the tile counter next to the sink so I could reach other cabinet doors. Behind each one was a fanciful creature painted in vivid colors: an orange dinosaur; a unicorn, hoofs tufted purple; a two-headed dog the dark green of stormy seas. The cabinets smelled of mothballs and calamine lotion.

I knew my father was a gifted Sunday painter—he had built his own easel and set it up in our living room in West Texas—and I was delighted to discover these early examples of his art, pleased to know that my grandmother had deemed them worth keeping.

Now my grandfather pulls a red and beige leather volume from a bookcase, tucks it beneath his arm, and steps carefully onto his dew-soaked verandah. He adjusts his vest. The wooden porch swing, dangling on long silver chains, sways lazily in the morning breeze. He nods politely to his neighbor, a full-blooded Comanche to whom he has never spoken. He turns, locks the door, makes his way down the concrete steps, past Zorah's bluebonnets blooming in big red pots, and walks the seven blocks under noisy robin song in the elms to the Cotton County Courthouse with its vigorously waving American flag.

— 2 —

My parents' marriage license, dated December 26, 1950, appears nearly blank now because the ink has faded after so many years. I found the license in a box in a closet in my father's assisted living space a week or so after he died at the age of eighty-nine in 2015. My mother, three years younger than he was, had died two years earlier.

This is a story about them, and before them, and after them. It's a story about my grandfather, the town he served, and the lives, including mine, swirling from the center of Cotton County, Oklahoma.

That day in my father's place, I found in the box old driver's licenses, voter registrations, Social Security cards. And two photographs. In the first one, my mother and father, both in their early twenties, stand together holding hands in a small meadow in Walters's Sultan Park, in front of a placid creek and a round-topped white Oldsmobile. They have known each other all their lives. My father is wearing a short leather jacket and wide cotton pants; he looks confident, arrogantly so, an attitude I never associated with him. It's an expression I don't recognize, and it makes me wonder if something happened to him in later years. He was never weak or timid, but in my presence, at least, he was not cocky, either. My mother, curly-haired, wearing a wool sweater down to her hips and a black ankle-length skirt, leans into his chest, her pointed chin tucked into the crook of his shoulder. She looks dreamy and content—again, a mood I would not typically ascribe to the woman I knew. In the second photograph, taken a few years later on their wedding day, they are leaning against the Oldsmobile, in which they had driven from the First Methodist Church in Walters to their new apartment in Wichita Falls, Texas. My father had just secured a job in Wichita Falls as a junior geologist with the Sinclair Oil and Gas Company. My parents look surpassingly happy—somewhat unrecognizable to me—as they gaze at the darkening North Texas sky, daring it to rain.

Two years after they'd settled in Wichita Falls, my father was transferred to Midland, nearly three hundred miles farther south and west, at the edge of Texas's arid Permian Basin. My sister Debra and I were born there. At Thanksgiving, at Christmas, and in the summers when my father got two weeks off, we'd drive the six and a half hours from Midland to Walters, always in an Oldsmobile, the brand my father swore by. Every mile along the way reminded us why we lived where we lived: Pumpjacks and derricks peppered the flat red-sand plains. Caliche pits pocked the sagebrush fields beneath swaybacked blue mesas northwest of Sweetwater. Coming home from Oklahoma, I always knew we were nearing Midland when we passed the steaming vast petroleum refinery at Big Spring. The air smelled like a thousand skunks. The plant's spidery towers glowed with vivid yellow lights at night so low-flying airplanes could spot them. My sister and I called the complex the "Light Bub Place."

Once, on the way back from Walters early in the month of August, my father drove us through Wichita Falls so Debra and I could see where he and our mother had lived before we were born, in the first years of their marriage. I was maybe ten. The city sat, flat and sprawling, just across the river from Oklahoma, but I remember thinking how terribly different Texas seemed from the lushness we had just left: much less moist and green, hotter, more humid. Fireflies, which I loved to chase at dusk in Walters, popping them into cleaned-out honey jars with holes punched in their thin tin lids, making lamps of living creatures—these magical beings seemed to have stopped their migration at the river's north shore. Texas appeared barren by contrast with Cotton County, and the farther west we traveled, toward the Light Bub Place and then on to Midland, the worse it got.

In memory now, our afternoon in Wichita Falls survives as a tour through a city of mud. I can only see various shades of brown: buildings, cars, people. But perhaps this is because, at about this time, my father made an oil painting using only umber, darkened or lightened with dabs of white mixed in varying densities, and this project struck me as miraculous: a new way of seeing, or a new way of *thinking* about seeing—viewing the world through filters of vision other than "normal." In any case, I now consider that day in Wichita Falls the beginning of a new awareness for me, a fresh perspective; specifically, I imagined myself an Oklahoman rather than a Texas native. This may sound like a minor mental shift, but in that part of the nation, where tribal affiliations are tight, enacted in sports contests that often fray into bruising brawls, it was no small thing.

My parents' first apartment was located in a one-story ranch-style building that operated now as a rent-by-the-hour motel just off the interstate to Dallas. Young as I was, I remember being fully aware of how difficult it would be for two people to live together in such a claustrophobic space and continue to find life joyous. A warehouse stocked with oil field equipment ran along the south side of the motel's parking lot. Semi cabs circled it. A mercury-vapor lamp emitting a weak glow the color of clabber (a sour milk concoction Zorah liked to drink with a spoonful of molasses each night) lighted a square of the aluminum-sided warehouse in the late afternoon sunshine. The wall's washed-out hue, like notebook paper eroding in dirty water, made me unaccountably lonely. August: tornado season on the High Plains. The sky was turning green toward evening. Fierce winds buffeted mistletoe nests in the trees. Newly aware in the world, I understood how easily all of this—everything—could blow away.

As a petroleum geologist, my father was neither the Fat Cat Oil King portrayed in Edna Ferber's *Giant* nor the hard-hatted rough-neck stomping around in heavy boots, dancing in crude-oil sprays from gushers in the desert. George H. W. Bush moved to Midland the year my father did, to prospect for oil. Dad *worked* for men like Bush; he didn't run in their rarified circles. Something in him would always be just an old Okie. Every morning he'd put on a coat and tie, drive his Olds to a high-rise office building—one of only a handful in downtown Midland, which nevertheless fancied itself the "Tall City"—and spend his days poring over seismographs and charts, so the Fat Cats and George Bushes would know where to dispatch their drillers.

It gave me great pleasure to visit his office. His walls were covered with floor-to-ceiling maps of the Permian Basin, eastern New Mexico, southern Oklahoma. Square magnets the size of my twelve-year-old palms, placed on the maps' numbered lots, indicated dry holes or reasonable drilling risks. County lines ran like rivers across my father's splendid walls; farm roads and highways branched in every direction.

Soon after my father was promoted to district geologist and given a hefty raise, he bought a second car—not another Oldsmobile, but a "little thing to putter around town in": a blue Volkswagen Beetle. Years later, this would be the car I learned to drive in, always killing the engine in intersections, unable to shift the stick fast enough.

It seems to me now that several key moments in my relationship with my father occurred in that purring blue Bug. One Saturday afternoon, shortly after my sixteenth birthday, Dad handed me the key and said I could "open the Beetle up a little" on the nearly deserted farm-to-market road west of town. He slid into the passenger seat next to me. I still remember the sweet scent of Old Spice on his skin. The road took us past Sinclair oil tanks squatting like flying saucers in the low mesquite, behind rows and rows of tumbleweeds snagged on barbed-wire fences. Red cows, some as large and hunched as our car, watched us chug down the road. It soon became clear that my father had something he wanted to show me.

We passed the Odessa Meteor Crater, filled nearly to its rim with paper cups and old hamburger wrappers. The big, uneven divot prompted my father to talk about his brother in Europe in the war, surrounded by falling shells and ruined landscapes. "J. C. swore that if he ever got out of France alive, he was going to devote his life to pure pleasure, because—why not?" he said. Was this ragged hole in the earth the surprise he wanted to show me? What was he asking me to consider? J. C.'s drinking? Why?

In fact, what the crater had raised in me was a sudden fear of obliteration. At any moment, a flaming rock hurled from the stars could come crashing out of the sky.

In the years since then, reminiscing with my sister and former West Texas buddies, I have learned it was not uncommon for the harshness of our surroundings to plant permanently in us a melancholy nervousness.

My father directed me onto a dirt road. The rough path seemed poised to plunge off the edge of the earth. We passed cable-tool rigs and discovery wells abandoned, he said, since the 1920s—the ancient ruins of his profession. *This* had been his destination. Somehow, I felt it was tied to the recklessness he'd just been discussing and J. C.'s bargain with pleasure and death.

He tried to explain to me the Permian Basin's history so I'd understand what rooted him, *us*, there: "Two hundred million years ago, a salt sea swamped all this. Then a limestone seabed formed. *That* was eventually overlaid by dolomites, anhydrites, tons more salt . . . "

These terms meant nothing to me. He might as well have been listing the mysterious features of the female reproductive system— which I'd *never* got straight, in spite of his help.

A few years back, when he'd decided it was time for me to "learn the facts of life," he'd driven me in the Beetle one evening a week to the local YMCA to watch clinical sex films. Afterward, we'd drive home mostly silent—he was embarrassed; I was embarrassed and confused. "Does Mom still *bleed* like that?" I asked him one night. He nodded and then, to end the interrogation, pulled over at Hank's Superette so I could buy a "Silver Surfer" comic book.

"When the Spraberry Field came in, toward the end of '49, and started pumping 112 barrels a day, that's when I knew we'd live the rest of our lives in Texas. There'd always be plenty of work," he said that Saturday afternoon on the road at the edge of the world.

I recall one other mystifying incident while driving with my dad in the Beetle—it may have been after one of our nights at the Y. We were turning into our neighborhood on an unusually dark evening when the temperature had dropped into the twenties, according to the radio, and we spotted a young man, maybe fourteen years old, slogging through a day-old snowdrift along the curb. (Snow was rare in Midland, but when it came, it could pile high.) The boy wore no shoes, and his light cotton shirt was unbuttoned all the way down to his waist. His eyes were glassy—I could tell this even in the dark, in the headlights' quick sweep—and his breath came hard, in thick vapor-streams. In retrospect, this moment seems to foretell all that would soon split American families like ours, a glimpse beyond the "normal" vision of the world as it had existed.

Frightened, I asked my father what was wrong with the boy. He didn't answer right away. He rolled down his window and called to the kid, who either couldn't hear or chose not to respond. He just kept walking, freezing, in the dirty snow. My father shouted and shouted at him. Then he zipped around the block several times. "Where's a cop when you need one?" he said, craning his head left and right. Someone in the neighborhood must have seen the damaged walker and made a phone call, because on our third or fourth spin around the block, we saw a patrol car park in front of the boy, blue and red lights turning the snowbanks a sickly citrus color. Two officers took the boy in hand. He flailed, screaming. I asked my father again, "What's the matter with him?" Though I'm certain Dad had never witnessed anyone tripping on LSD, which I think now is what we saw, this was the first time I'd heard the word "intoxicated."

Because of Dad's promotions, we moved into three different houses in nine years, adding plenty of square footage each time. Each time, Dad said we had "bettered" ourselves—and by implication, socially surpassed our former neighbors. Through the years, those lessons in social class taught me a good deal about Cotton County as well as West Texas.

The first house, a boxy two-bedroom made of loblolly pine, sat on a dirt lot just north of Highway 20, the road we took to Walters, on Midland's south side. It was shadowed in the late afternoons by a massive water tank looming at the end of the block, and bathed at night in a deep red glow cast by KCRS's radio towers ("The Voice of Rock and Roll!").

The second house, a rather bland brick affair with a big picture window, was located in an aspirational neighborhood, as evidenced by the street name—Princeton. Running parallel, in the next few blocks, were Dartmouth, Auburn, and Clemson. Despite their pretensions, each street was characterized by dirt yards and no trees, or racks of sticks *referred* to by the neighbors as trees but fooling no one. My mother told me I was old enough now (seven or eight) to look after my sister, who was four years younger. I remember Halloween our first year in that house. I wore a Quick Draw McGraw mask, a cardboard contraption squeezing my head like a hatbox in the shape of a horse. Debra went as Huckleberry Hound. The masks were too big for us; neither of us could see through our eyeholes. Holding hands on the pebbled sidewalks, clutching our trick or treat bags, Debra and I jostled one another, unable to find where we were going. She broke away from me. From somewhere behind us, my mother called, "Tracy, watch your sister!" I turned in circles, trying to see. I recall thinking, "She's gone. I've let her get away." I can say without hesitation: from that moment on, I have never shed the fear that I cannot keep my sister from harm.

The third house was the last house I lived in with my parents, and it is the one I consider my true childhood residence. It's the one in which my dad built a grandfather clock from a kit he had ordered, styled like the clock on Zorah's wall. It ticked with satisfying constancy, the pendulum unerring. I felt comfortable in that house, despite the electrical power lines running straight overhead—which even then we joked would give us all cancer someday—but I didn't love it the way I loved my grandparents' home in Walters.

In each of these houses, on the weekends my father would set up his easel, a thick wooden tripod, put big band music on the hi-fi—Tommy Dorsey, Glenn Miller, and his favorite, Gene Krupa, jungle drums rumbling through the house—and make oil paintings based on family photographs or photographs he'd taken from *Life* magazine. He was a superb draftsman, but he didn't trust himself to imagine scenes. He needed a model to copy. His most memorable early paintings were a self-portrait, wavy hair, eyes big and brown; a Spanish beach scene from *Life* featuring an old fisherman coiling rope; and the Artful Dodger from a shot of the Broadway production of *Oliver!* I always thought this was a self-portrait, too: the boy's mischievous smile reminded me of Dad; his wry expression said he knew dignity was a sham, no matter *how* tall your top hat was.

For my birthday one year, Dad painted a sad clown based on a photo he'd found of a Mardi Gras parade. Confetti and streamers whirled around the bright red face. My father hung the painting in my bedroom, above my toy box, and it scared me witless in the dark. I dreamed the clown would come alive at night and turn my toys against me, especially the Rock 'Em Sock 'Em Robots. It is perhaps too easy to believe now that what I really feared were my father's secret layers, unveiled by the jester. My father had depths to be tested and might not always have been the man I thought I knew.

When my sister was a baby, I'd wake at night to the *tink-tink* of bells in the house—at the far end of the front hallway, in the kitchen, by the back porch door. Leather straps tied the bells to my mother's fuzzy blue house shoes. *Tink-tink, tink-tink* went the bells as she paced the darkened rooms holding my sister, hoping to stop her from bawling.

Throughout her life, my mother would *never* be able to settle my sister. Debra had the soul of an "Okie Sooner," Mom said—always recklessly one step ahead of everyone else.

In that pine house, my father bought us our first television set, a black-and-white Crosley. It was as big as a washing machine—my first window onto a larger world beyond the desert and the rivers of Cotton County. The Pioneer Furniture Company, a local establishment, sponsored a live show on KOSA on Saturday nights, featuring a peculiar pale singer and his band: Roy Orbison and the Teen Kings. Orbison's slick hair, his dark glasses, fascinated me, and his rendition of "Ooby Dooby" sent me into ecstasy. I shimmied in front of the Crosley wearing a red felt cowboy hat and strumming a plastic guitar. Orbison came from Wink, Texas, a tiny hellhole in the larger perdition of West Texas, and I must have sensed that music— art in general, after my father's example and Krupa's roaring tom-toms—offered escape from aridity and despair.

In this first house, too, my "Sooner" sister introduced me to the thrill of rebellion. My mother had warned me to stay out of her kitchen when she was not in it, but one afternoon while she was hanging laundry in the back yard, I got into her cabinets and found a bucket of Crisco. Debra kept straining for the bucket, crying, and wasn't satisfied until I'd slathered greasy white clumps across her face and arms. My mother walked into the house and screamed. I remember how delighted Debra was when she realized we had done something wrong.

It pleased her, as well, to search for Salon la Vida on Highway 20, on the outskirts of town, whenever we returned to Midland from an Oklahoma visit. We'd pass the Light Bub Place in Big Spring, and then, forty minutes later, hit Midland's "wrong side of the tracks," Dad said, a stretch of road clotted with bail bondsmen, wrecking yards, used auto parts stores, and bodegas. The Salon la Vida was a cube-shaped bar, half wood, half brick, draped year-round with Christmas lights, most of which didn't work. It dazzled Debra. She always asked about it. "It's a scary place," Dad said. "Lots of bad men go there. Sometimes fights break out and someone gets really, really hurt. You never want to go into a place like that." On our trips home from Walters, Debra gazed out the Oldsmobile's grimy back windshield, waiting to spot the blinking red lights. "I *dare* not go into the Lonna da Vita," she'd say, wide-eyed, but the bar held a powerful allure for her.

When we had lived in our third house for about five years, I wondered if the power lines above us were altering the chemistry of our brains by zapping them with odd electrical impulses. It was almost easier to accept this as an explanation for why my body was changing than to believe that I was morphing from the inside out, a mutating monster, sprouting hair where hair had never grown before, talking in an entirely different register, experiencing painful yet pleasant sensations. My sister's body, even at a very young age, appeared to bubble beneath her blouses. What was *happening* to us? For a while, I even thought the humming currents might be affecting the weather. One summer day, a hailstorm pounded the house, stones as big as baseballs. I'd never seen anything like that. Later that year, after five full days of rain, flash floods made rivers of the neighborhood's streets. My father had to leave work early in the Beetle and rescue me at school because I couldn't walk home. Near the spot where we had seen the boy trudging through snow, waves of undrained rain nearly swallowed the car. Frantically, my father fought the steering wheel to keep the Beetle from washing away. That image of him trying to maintain control summed him up for me during this period—we're talking '67, '68—because of everyone in the family, he seemed to be changing the most.

Granted, he'd been on the move for a while. Like his father, he'd always voted Democratic in national elections. I remember him expressing his love for Adlai Stevenson. But in 1964 he voted for Barry Goldwater. I was too young at the time to grasp the importance of this shift. For me, his most significant alteration was his switch from painter to golfer. At a certain point, once he'd advanced several notches in the oil company, he rarely touched the easel anymore. Instead, he'd load his brand-new golf clubs in the back of the Beetle and "hit the links," he said—usually with a colleague of his, a loud, burly man he'd grown up with in southern Oklahoma. This man, a fellow named Bob Hearon, had also gone to work for Sinclair Oil and Gas in Midland. Whether Bob was the one who first encouraged my father to take up golf, I don't know, but I do remember him standing in our living room one morning pulling on a pair of beige leather golf gloves and staring at a half-finished canvas of my father's—a portrait of our family that he never completed. Bob laughed. "Still doodling, eh?" he said to my dad. "I thought you'd outgrown that stuff by now." After that, the easel remained tucked in my father's bedroom closet.

I confess the incident set me against Bob Hearon. It seemed to me he had abducted part of my father, an important part, a part that I loved, but this couldn't have been the case, not really—they'd known each other all their lives. Whatever influence Bob Hearon had on my dad, it had been established long before in Cotton County, Oklahoma. And my dislike of Bob had been immediate, from my earliest awareness: he was a bully, especially to his family. He always smelled funny, like rubbing alcohol. Frequently, he'd show that glassy look I'd seen on the boy in the snow.

By default, his son Bobby was my first close friend. Because of Bob's long friendship with my dad, Bobby and I—the same age— were thrown together early and often in life. Ours was not an easy alliance. He looked like his father: broad shoulders, big head round as a bowling ball. He wore a burr haircut (my own hair was curly like my mother's; charmed by the curls, she let me wear it long).

Bobby's front teeth were stained dark brown ("Too much fluoride in the water from their well," my mother said—the Hearons lived on a small ranch just outside of town). He carried a BB gun—I don't remember ever seeing him without the slender rifle as a kid—and he shot pigeons. The bloody hunks of feathers, begrimed with dirt and twigs, horrified me. He liked to wrestle and always punched me in the shoulder as a greeting. I didn't share these enthusiasms.

My delight in rock and roll music, sparked by the Teen Kings, expanded after the Beatles' first appearance on the Ed Sullivan Show. Slack-jawed in front of the screen, I recognized their long hair as a form of rebellion, tweaking adults who considered themselves better than kids. I recognized in the group's rhythms the same heartbeat pumping through Roy Orbison's cowboy songs, and experienced another new awareness (though I didn't have the language for it then, and wouldn't for many years)—namely, that art was renewal through re-immersion in the past. My love of history, of literature, must have started then, encouraged later by my grandfather.

My father—apparently abandoning *his* interest in art—couldn't stand the music. Grudgingly, he admitted Ringo might have a smidgen of talent. Drummers he always respected. I think now his attachment to clocks and to big band beats had to do with steady time management—the illusion that regular patterns would keep his family safe.

The Fabs were a burst of joy after months of gloom following John F. Kennedy's murder. Whether it was my father's opinion of Ringo or my sense that no one *ever* had as much fun as this boy, I cast aside my "Ooby Dooby" guitar. In the garage next to the parked Volkswagen, I found a pair of dowel pins that my father had saved from a woodworking project. They looked like little dowsing rods. With the heavy sticks, I beat the hell out of an orange footstool my mother loved until its stuffing spilled onto the floor. This moved Mom to buy me a cheap snare drum.

Bobby hated rock and roll and my repetitive drumming. This was surprising, since his mother, Natalie, also a Walters native, a close childhood friend of my mother's, was a middle school music teacher in Midland. She taught me one day to hold a pair of drumsticks properly, not in a straight "hammer grip" like Ringo, but at an angle—"In the left hand, it's like clutching a fork," she said—to enhance the wrist's flexibility.

Natalie was a small, gaunt woman with an engrossing smile. It didn't look like a smile; her lips didn't curl, but when she turned your way, you felt her genuine warmth. Maybe it was the tenderness in her eyes. I always liked her, and I cringed whenever Bob or Bobby shouted her name across a room. Their voices were harsh, grating, lacking patience and kindness. I have an early memory of my mother saying Natalie was ill, an "ongoing battle" with breast cancer. Naturally, as a child I had no grasp of the magnitude of this information or any sense of Natalie's day-to-day experience.

Sometimes the Hearons visited their families in Walters when we did. I was forced to play with Bobby. Usually this meant marching with his BB gun through muddy creek beds and marshy bluffs in Sultan Park, hunting pigeons. I didn't want Bobby linked to Oklahoma. I wanted Cotton County to be a retreat from Midland's ugliness. I preferred to sit in my father's Oldsmobile, parked at Zorah and Tracy's house, listening to "Please Please Me" on the radio. I wanted to visit the courthouse. I wanted to lie on the dewy lawn, next to Zorah's goldfish pond, and watch the fireflies sparkle at night.

A Comanche family lived across the street. We didn't know them—never even bothered to speak to them—but I loved to sit on the porch swing and watch their little girls. They'd dance in their yard, barefoot, wearing thin print dresses.

Or I'd sit in Zorah's living room, beneath the loudly ticking clock, reading books from my grandfather's shelf. Mark Twain. *Joe Hill* and *The Big Rock Candy Mountain* by Wallace Stegner. *Prairie City*, a plainspoken history of Oklahoma by Angie Debo, which ended with a line from Plutarch: "As for me, I live in a small town, where I am willing to continue, lest it grow smaller." I remember, in particular, appreciating the narrator's gentle patience in *The Education of Henry Adams,* the "classic story of an American family," said the dust jacket.

My father and his brother golfed in the mornings with Bob Hearon. Walters had a nine- hole course out by the town cemetery, an abandoned pumpjack, and a small trailer park ("Drunken Indians," Bob Hearon said of the trailer park whenever he passed it). Plastic American flags flew near some of the tombstones in the graveyard, placed there every Veterans' Day by the Chamber of Commerce. Before each golf round, J. C. insisted on stopping at the cemetery and saluting the flags.

While my father was hitting the links, secretly I'd be opening Zorah's bathroom cabinets, reacquainting myself with the horned frog, the dinosaur, and the unicorn. In time, even more than my father's old artworks, Tracy's political tracts snagged my attention: campaign posters announcing his speeches in Waurika or Oklahoma City, drafts of addresses he had written to deliver at Rotary Club meetings around the state. I'd become an avid reader. But I was less interested in the contents of those documents than in seeing his name, *my* name, on the pages, a solid, unchanging presence in the world.

Noting my interest in his papers, Tracy called me "the professor." "Maybe you'll grow up to be the family historian," he said. He gave me his old fountain pen whenever he bought a new one. He showed me his letter from John F. Kennedy and correspondence he'd received from other notable politicians: Fred Harris, Carl Albert, Lyndon Johnson.

At holidays, Zorah, my mother, and my Aunt Barbara cooked turkey, greens, and vegetable stuffing. Sometimes these dinners included the Hearons. Barbara I never knew well, and she has little to do with the story I am trying to tell, but she made a strong impression, and merits a glance. She died when I was young, of complications following a hysterectomy.

Mostly, she is memorable to me for the shouting matches she had with J. C. in one of Zorah's back bedrooms. What they argued about, I have no idea, but during each of these fights J. C. sloshed a large drink in his hand. Always Jack Daniel's from his favorite "cheap" liquor store in Holdenville, east of Walters, where he and Barbara lived, and where he worked as a criminal defense lawyer. After J. C.'s Thanksgiving story, I wondered if Barbara was the girl whose panties Tracy had found in the Ford.

I remember her haughtiness with my mother. Nothing overt: indirect reminders that *she* had finished college, while my mother had barely made it through high school.

She spooked me. One night she cornered me in a hallway—she had been drinking J. C.'s bourbon; I could smell it on her breath—and said, "You're a smart and curious young man. There's a hunger in you for the truth, I can tell . . . and one day this hunger will lead you to the Roman Catholic Church." The Daughertys were Methodists (in name, not practice); I'd always heard it whispered, as if it were a shameful secret, that J. C. had married a "reckless daughter of the pope."

Zorah, firm and stoic, steered clear of her daughters-in-law's tensions, stayed out of her son's fights with his wife, and never said a word about Catholicism, Methodism, or any religious "nonsense." Christmas, however, she celebrated with glee because it meant she could spruce up her house. She'd string white lights on the verandah. She'd hang a wreath wrapped in red ribbons on the front door and place wooden dolls—angels, wise men, the nutcracker—on the mantels. Bubble lights were her crowning glory: long glass tubes, lighted blue and yellow and filled with bubbling water, clipped to the branches of her Christmas tree. Where she bought them I don't know, but I never saw them anywhere but in Zorah's warm, glowing home.

The Christmas I was ten—the year was 1965—Bobby Hearon told me Santa Claus didn't exist. The conversation occurred in Zorah's back yard after a muddy day in Sultan Park bloodying pigeons. I was already mad at him. I heard the adults laughing in the house, Bob Hearon louder than anyone. Natalie I couldn't hear at all. Nor my mother. Bobby was just being mean because he knew I still believed in St. Nick, and I *knew* he was just being mean. I glanced at the sky. A meteor streaked through the Dipper. I wished I'd never see this awful kid again.

– 3 –

In the fall of 1966, the Hearons moved to a small ranch just west of Roswell, New Mexico. My dad said Bob had been fired from Sinclair. He didn't say why. That November, we phoned Tracy and Zorah and told them we wouldn't be sharing Thanksgiving with them in Oklahoma this year: we'd promised to celebrate with friends. We changed the oil in the Oldsmobile, bought a new set of tires, and drove half a day from Midland to stay with the Hearons over the long holiday weekend. On the way, my father—always insistent that I learn the history of the land—pointed out the "Bottomless Pits," deep craters in a limestone escarpment worn away over time.

I hadn't seen Bobby for several months, since his family had moved. A plaster cast wrapped his right arm. He'd fallen from a horse. His neck looked wider, redder from days in the sun, and his shoulders were muscular and taut. Our interests had diverged even further. I still played the snare drum, but my love of rhythm was shifting more to language, to the musicality of words. With my grandfather's old fountain pens, I wrote, on legal pads, my father's geology lessons, labeling them "West Texas History." My mother, always sensitive to my passions, bought me a portable typewriter, and I took it everywhere, even to the Hearons' that autumn, teaching myself to hunt and peck.

I'd also developed an interest in astronomy—inevitable, I suppose, given the landscape's barrenness and the sky's immensity in all that flatness . . . though Bobby was no more concerned with comets and stars than he was with rock and roll. He was riding horses, camping, baling hay. It surprised me that he couldn't wait to get back on his black colt, even though the creature had thrown him into a boulder and broken his arm. "Cain't be a scaredy-cat all your life," he said to me. "Got to *face down* your fears. That's what Dad always says." This was Bobby's reminder to me that I wasn't nearly as tough as he was. Before he'd left Midland, he'd teased me about the "lady doctor" my mother took me to—Dorothy Wyvell, a crusty old boot with a face like a marmot. "I'd never let an old woman poke around on *my* body," Bobby said. I went to Dr. Wyvell nearly every week because I suffered from asthma and had frequent ear infections as a kid. I never told Bobby how much I liked her waiting room, because I knew he'd make fun of me: on the wall she'd hung a map of "Fairy Land," featuring drawings of elf huts (toadstools with steep thatched roofs) and princes' castles glittering like sparklers. "Fairy Land's" yellow brick roads resembled the county lines on the maps in Dad's office.

The doctor astonished me one day: she said she didn't own a television set. How could she live without Roy Orbison?

Like my grandfather's speeches and the poem on his bathroom wall, her prescription pads stirred in me an early interest in words. One of the first sentences I ever learned to read was typed at the top of her referrals, next to the *Rx* symbol: "Government big enough to give you everything is big enough to take it away." A quote from Thomas Jefferson. When I asked my father what it meant, all he said was, "Oh, that crazy old woman . . . she may be a good doctor, but she's a darned John Bircher."

The Hearons' ranch, twenty acres sloped against a cactus-spiked mesa, was an ocean of sand, red clay, and rock. While Bob and Natalie and my mother and father started dinner in the house, Bobby and Debra and I stood in a pasture watching Bobby's colt run in circles along a sagging oak fence. Natalie looked thinner than before. Her hair was grayer, sparser. Her eyes looked tired. Bob was meaty, red-faced—his belly had grown. A slab of flesh, like a leg of lamb, jiggled above his belt. He opened wine for the ladies and poured my father some whiskey. "I'll just have half a jigger," he said, reaching for the bottle. I saw the look my father gave him—a flicker of uncertainty—and wondered why.

While sauces simmered in the kitchen, the adults moved onto the back deck with their drinks. They lighted cigarettes, except for my dad, who'd quit smoking. They shared memories of Cotton County. "Girl, you could have had your pick of *any* boy at Walters High School," my mother teased Natalie.

"Yeah, but *I* was the handsomest devil she'd ever seen, right, hon?" Bob bellowed, reaching for the whiskey again. "And *you*, Annie"—he addressed my mother—"you were lucky to get any dates at all." He laughed, signaling it was just good fun. I didn't believe it. He was *mean*, like his son. "Your mother's old house—I swear, it was like a corn patch after the hogs had come through! And your scroungy brothers . . . Bill looking like some Cherokee chieftain . . ."

It was true, I thought: to me, my mother's older brother Bill resembled an Indian. He had dark red skin and layers of folds around his eyes.

" . . . he coulda been kin to ol' Ray Tasuda, right, Gene?"

My father nodded, quiet. I knew Ray Tasuda was a childhood friend of his. I'd heard the name, but that was all.

"Instead, lookee here, Annie—you hit the jackpot! Snagged the big basketball star!" Bob said. He slapped my father's back. "Leading high school scorer? Two years in a row? Now, how in the hell did you manage to pull *that* off, you ol' son of a bitch?" By now, Bob had emptied a third of the bottle. Natalie pretended not to notice. I thought I knew, then, why the oil company had fired him.

Bobby said to Debra and me, "C'mon out to the pasture." He pulled a big wool blanket out of the barn. It was pink and covered with hay. He said he'd show us how to make a tent. He draped one edge of the blanket over the top of a barbed-wire fence, pulled it tight at a forty-five-degree angle to the ground, and staked the opposite side with heavy stones in the dirt. The three of us crawled into the space beneath the blanket and huddled around a candle Bobby had snagged in secret from his mother's dining room table. He'd pocketed a book of matches.

Now he lighted the wick. "If we's up in the mountains, we wouldn't have no frills," he said. "We'd have to rub sticks together to start a fire."

"Show us!" Debra said.

"No, stupid. It takes a long time."

He was showing off. He irritated me. I wanted to run to the car and pull my typewriter from the trunk, to demonstrate *my* knowledge and skills, but my mother just waved me away when I asked for the keys. She was laughing on the deck. Her face was flushed and her eyes were bright. I'd never seen her high on liquor. Natalie and my dad were also happily relaxed, but Bob was a different story. Loud and lurching. The turkey was taking a long time to cook in the oven. He had opened a second bottle of whiskey. I'd seen J. C. drink a lot at holidays and yell at his wife, but my uncle had never seemed out of control—not the way Bob appeared to me now, a reckless spiral.

The setting sun's light spread like slow liquid among scattered clouds. Venus rose in the west. I pointed to a darkening blue patch in the south. "Keep your eyes right there and soon you'll see Mars," I told Bobby. He snickered to show me he didn't give a damn. Debra joined his laughter. She resented Mom encouraging my interests when all she ever got were orders to "behave like a proper little girl." "You think you're better than I am!" Debra sometimes said to me.

The hay covering the blanket made her sneeze. Suddenly, I couldn't breathe. Smoke filled my mouth. The blanket had sagged near the ground where the stones held it. It had touched the candle. The wool had caught fire. Now the thick awning was collapsing. We were about to be engulfed in the flames. Debra screamed.

Hands hoisted me into the air. I grew dizzy. My ribs ached. It took me several minutes to understand that Bob Hearon had heard Debra scream. He'd sprinted to the tent. He'd pulled us out of the smoke while the rest of the adults stood thoroughly dazed, rooted to the deck.

"What the hell were you thinking?" Bob yelled at his son, stamping the blanket in the dirt. "What kind of dumb stunt was *this*? You'll get no supper, boy!" It took nearly an hour for Natalie to calm Bob and convince him to let Bobby sit at the table with us when dinner was ready. "And where the hell *is* this food, hmm? What's taking so damn long?" Bob shrieked at his wife. "Our *guests* expect a *feast*!"

I remember the meal as a very silent occasion. We had reason to be thankful, but no one said as much.

Afterward, Bob opened a sweet dessert wine. He let us kids have a sip, reserving most of the drink for his glass. "Lyndon's a damn *weakling*!" he shouted. He poked my father in the chest. "Now, Goldwater—he'd have bombed those Viet Cong back to the caves, am I right?"

"You're right," my father said.

They agreed they'd have to meet sometime in Ruidoso, a resort town near Roswell, to play a round of golf.

Bobby had disappeared into his bedroom after the wine. We didn't see him again that night. I walked out into the dark to gaze at the Dipper, Cassiopeia, the Northern Cross. A fat horned toad scurried in the dirt at my feet, and I remembered my father's fanciful creature painted inside Zorah's cabinet. I heard Bob Hearon roaring, wheezing with laughter in the ranch house. Why was my father friendly with this horrible man? The part of Dad that used to "doodle" seemed to have vanished altogether, especially when Bob was around.

− 4 −

To his final days, Tracy voted for the Democratic Party in national elections, and lamented the fact that in Oklahoma, the party could hardly be considered a "beacon of progress." I don't know what he thought of my father's increasingly conservative outlook (though Dad never went so far as to become a "darned John Bircher"). Perhaps Tracy simply accepted, as I have come to accept, that my father adopted the persona necessary to survive as a West Texas oilman. A West Texas oilman didn't paint pretty pictures. Or vote for Adlai Stevenson.

Before he'd become the clerk of Cotton County, Tracy had served as deputy sheriff. It's an aspect of my grandfather I found, and still find, appealing. I have his badge (with *my* name on it) and a spring-loaded leather blackjack he carried. To my knowledge, he never used it on anyone. I have a photograph of him wearing his uniform: khaki pants, leather jacket, cowboy hat. At his feet sits a favorite family dog, Blackie, a spotted mutt. "Blackie was a good little patrol dog," Tracy used to say. "He could smell fear on a man two miles away."

Prohibition was in full swing when Tracy was charged with keeping the peace. I know, from stories he told me, that he busted plenty of stills in the woods outside of Walters, but I also know he wasn't above sipping a little Choctaw beer with bootlegging buddies whenever he went off duty. (Zorah used to swear she'd collected her beautiful silver by making a deal with Tracy early in their marriage: every night he came home with bootleg liquor on his breath, he had to buy her a serving knife or a fork or a spoon.)

He was part of the statewide manhunt for Pretty Boy Floyd. On orders from the county, he forced a few tenant farmers off their land. He attended an electrocution in McAlester—two fellows, a Black man and an Apache, accused of murdering a filling station attendant. Later, he publicly chided a judge who'd said he'd "enjoyed" witnessing this "act of justice." The man must have been imbibing "Oklahoma Mountain Dew," Tracy said, to take pleasure in watching men die.

As a law officer, he mopped up petty crimes, usually late at night when his little boys were asleep in their beds. Invariably, the crime scenes smelled of corn liquor. Among his papers—Zorah passed them all to me when he died in 1978—is a copy of a trial transcript from December 18, 1924, typed on flaking onionskin. "The substance of the testimony on behalf of the state shows the prosecuting witness, Sam Byerly, was running a café in the city of Walters, that he slept in the café each night, and that some time around 3:30 the morning of the 20th of November, 1924, Byerly was robbed of $5," the transcript begins. "During the course of the robbery, Byerly was struck with a piece of lumber about 3 feet long, 4 inches wide, and ½ inch thick, the wound necessitating hospital treatment by a physician."

Later that morning, an examination of the café turned up a bloodied hat crumpled on the floor in a back bedroom where Byerly slept, as well as a piece of wood fitting the description of the assault weapon. According to the transcript, at "about 6:15 A.M., the defendant was arrested at the home of a man by the name of Richards, where the defendant's sweetheart lived."

Tracy was the arresting officer. He testified, "At the time of the arrest, the defendant had blood on his shoes and shirt, and he was intoxicated. He tried to explain the blood on his clothing, claiming he had been hit on the side of the jaw causing his mouth to bleed."

From details in the transcript, and from memories of the tales Tracy told me, I can imagine the early morning of November 20, 1924, in Walters: at his home, Tracy sleeps next to Zorah in a small bedroom just off the living room. By now, he is so used to the loudly ticking clock on the living room wall that it no longer keeps him awake. At around four A.M., the bedside telephone rings. The all-night operator, an insomniac named Laverne who has clearly found her role in life, tells him he is needed at the hospital. "Injured man, suspected robbery," Laverne says, a little less laconic than usual. Tracy kisses Zorah's cheek. She murmurs, "Be careful," and he rises to dress quietly in the dark. His movements excite Blackie. The dog wags his tail. He turns in swift circles at the foot of the bed, preparing for a bracing walk, the pleasure of chilly morning air, a crime to sniff out. Tracy reaches for his blackjack. He pokes his head into Gene's bedroom, and then he looks in on J. C. His boys are sleeping soundly.

It's a four-block walk to the eight-room hospital, and Blackie takes the lead. The dog dislikes but accepts the fact that he'll have to sit by the curb while Tracy goes into the building for an unspecified length of time.

"What happened, Sam?" Tracy asks the bandaged man in the bed. A malarial-yellow bulb, bare above the unshaded window, lights the room.

"Hell, they got five bills from the watch pocket in my pants, Tracy. And they made off with a jug of whiskey, too."

"Where were you hiding the whiskey?"

"You ain't gonna—"

"I don't care what you tuck away, Sam. But the location'll help us with our investigation."

Tracy then asks him if he knows who the suspects were. "Oh, you betcha," Byerly says. "Sons of bitches."

A half hour later, Blackie scratches at the front door of a man named George Beard. The smell of fear—it's strong in there, Blackie's tongue tells Tracy with wagging, wet certainty.

Beard pretends to have been roused from a profound sleep by Tracy's knocking, but his jitters lead my granddad to suspect the man's been up all night. He's fully dressed, in overalls and a red flannel shirt. "I swear, it was *Jack*," Beard says. "I's down at Clark's Restaurant having myself a bowl of four-alarm chili—"

"What time was this?"

"Oh, 'bout one o'clock."

"This morning?"

"Yeah. Jack was there. He said he was goin' to take a roast beef sandwich and some milk to someone, and he left. 'Bout thirty minutes later I start to head for the house, and Jack catches up with me on the street. He says, 'You know, I hear tell ol' Sam keeps some 'shine behind his café counter. What say we check it out?' I told him I wanted nothin' to do with it, and that was that. I come back here and went to bed. Next thing I know, hell, here *you* are."

Tracy tells Beard to sit tight. Blackie ducks down an alleyway, turning his head every thirty seconds to make sure Tracy's still behind him. The dog comes to a shotgun shack next to the town's rodeo arena. This is it, Blackie signals Tracy with his tail. The house belongs to Howard Richards, a no-good wildcatter whose older sister, Ruby, is rumored to be turning tricks in an attic room there, though the sheriff has never caught her at it. It's the younger sister, Rachel, Tracy has come to see. "Now, Rachel, you tell me the truth," Tracy says to her. She's standing in the nearly bare kitchen, shivering in a brown cotton bathrobe. Her black hair is slightly mussed, but not from tossing on a pillow. She's not been sleeping, either.

She's unmarried, but she has a three-year-old boy. The child is fast asleep beneath a sheet on a couch in the chilly front room.

"I swan, Tracy," Rachel says. "I just don't know what it could be that you're after."

Tracy notices a half-eaten roast beef sandwich left on a cracked plate on the table. Blackie sits patiently at his feet, head down, on the alert. Clearly, the dog doesn't trust this woman. "Did Jack drop by?" Tracy asks.

"Yeah, he come to see me. He brought me this here sandwich and a bottle of milk."

"Was George tagging along? George Beard?"

"No."

"Did Jack look like he'd been in a fight? Anything like that? Blood on his shirt?"

"No!"

A low little rumble waggles Blackie's throat. "Rachel. Is Jack here now?" Tracy says quietly.

"He left 'bout . . . I don't know . . . 'bout two hours ago."

"Where's Howard? Where's Ruby?"

"Oh, they's visiting our ma over by Lawton. Been away all week."

"I think I'll have a look around," Tracy says.

Blackie stands abruptly, a warning to the woman not to protest or to try anything funny. The trail of fresh blood drops on the pine-wood floorboards in the back hallway is impossible to miss, and it leads to a closed closet door in a small bedroom. Tracy stands in the middle of the room. He pulls the blackjack from his belt and grips it firmly in his right hand. "Come on out of there, Jack. I want to talk to you," Tracy says.

"He ain't here!" Rachel calls from the doorway.

"Jack, we can do this the hard way or you can make it easy on yourself."

Suddenly, thudding erupts from the back of the closet, a persistent pounding. Tracy rushes to the door and pulls it open. A big man is banging his shoulder against the closet's plywood backing. The wood cracks; through the rip, dawn light floods the house. The smell of horse dung, from the rodeo lot. The man has already set one foot in the alley. Tracy reaches past empty hangers and faded cotton dresses to grab the man's shirt collar. The shirt, dirty white, is spattered with dried blood. Tracy lifts his blackjack into the air. "Don't make me use this, Jack. Come on out of there." The man is much bulkier than the slender deputy sheriff, but the blackjack makes him cower. Meekly, he steps into the bedroom. Tracy still has a grip on his collar. Without being asked, the man blurts, "I didn't take nothin' from nobody, all right? I's just walkin' down the street, takin' a sandwich to my girl, when Sam Byerly starts yellin' at me for no reason from the doorway of his place, and then he comes at me swingin'. Busts my jaw. Maybe he's drunk or somethin'. I hear he keeps some whiskey . . ."

"Rachel here says you weren't bleeding when you got home with the sandwich."

"Well, I's . . . I started bleedin' later, maybe . . . you know, I got a slow damn heart."

Tracy discovers five one-dollar bills in the man's front pocket. Jack's breath smells of hops. Blackie stares exultantly at the woman shivering in her robe.

The transcript: "This case is circumstantial but every circumstance connected with the robbery points toward the defendant as being the guilty party. The record discloses that the defendant knew the prosecuting witness, knew the location of his business. He encountered George Beard on a street in the vicinity of the witness's café and made remarks to the effect, 'I wonder if he has any dough. I hear he's got some whiskey.' Beard admitted he suggested they go find out.

"The evidence and the logical inferences to be drawn from it are sufficient to convince the jury beyond a reasonable doubt of the guilt of the defendant, and this court will not disturb the verdict for insufficiency."

The defendant's full name was Jack Leslie Hearon. Bob's father. Bob was the three-year-old sleeping on Rachel's couch. These facts only became known to me when I inherited Tracy's papers in 1978.

A look through the papers reveals that Tracy endured several more run-ins with Jack Hearon. To begin with, Jack claimed he'd not gotten a fair trial in the Byerly matter. A second transcript: "Defendant argued that the court prevented him from an impartial hearing as the court did not instruct the jury on his theory of his defense." Jack appealed his verdict, but the new judge saw no warrant for a reversal: "The defendant's contention that he was struck by the witness is not a defense to a charge of robbery, therefore he had no theory upon which the court could predicate an instruction."

Jack tried a second appeal on the grounds that two of the jurors were former deputy sheriffs, friends and colleagues of the arresting officer, but the court ruled, "The fact that a man tapped for jury service has at some point held a law enforcement commission does not disqualify him to serve on the jury." The "judgment of the trial court" was "affirmed," and Jack Hearon held a grudge against my grandfather for the rest of his life.

Three times in the decade following Jack's brief jail term for the café robbery, Tracy was summoned to the shotgun shack in the middle of the night by a phone call from Rachel, whom Jack had finally married. She wanted Tracy to "cart the bastard away." Jack had beaten her—Tracy could plainly see the bruises on her face and arms—but each time, in the end, she'd change her mind, return to Jack in tears, and refuse to press charges.

When I was a child, wondering why my father was so friendly with Bob Hearon, I was unaware of Bob's early circumstances (I doubt that knowing them would have changed my mind about him). I didn't know what he'd witnessed in his house between his mother and his father, didn't grasp the danger he'd faced.

Now, sitting in my study, fingering the rough onionskin of the transcripts, I imagine Bob, a boy of nine or ten, lying in the dirt in the middle of the rodeo arena near his house, having slipped out of his room. He's watching stars appear, enjoying the warm summer breeze touching his skin: a temporary respite from the anger fouling his home, his mother's life, his future prospects. No, he thinks. *My* path will be different. Glancing about, at the empty track, at the cattle pens and the hay stalls for the horses, perhaps he contemplates owning his own ranch someday in the high desert of New Mexico.

He will ride free, in the open air, at the top of blue mesas.

As he lies dreaming in the dirt, maybe Blackie, on one of his evening walks, with or without Tracy, pauses at the arena's wire fence just long enough to determine that the boy is okay, that he's not hurt or sick, that he's just enjoying the night.

"Oklahoma is a land of timbered mountains, treeless plains, mesquite and sage brush, cypress and pine, massive buildings and small homes, of pioneer newness and old tradition. Within its boundaries is found nearly everything that we think of as genuinely American," begins *The WPA Guide to 1930s Oklahoma*, originally published in

1941 as *Oklahoma: A Guide to the Sooner State*. Neither this volume nor *The WPA Oklahoma Slave Narratives*, a collection of oral histories compiled by New Deal writers then left to rot in an Oklahoma City basement, acknowledges my grandfather, but he was essential to the projects in Cotton County, stopping the Ku Klux Klan from kidnapping, torturing, and even killing some of the WPA field workers. Tracy's involvement with the Writers' Project, and thus with artists and musicians of the New Deal, began with the Tasuda family. As I would discover from his papers, his devotion to the Tasudas occasioned further trouble with Jack Hearon.

This will take some explaining.

Charley and Lucy Tasuda were Kiowa. They lived in a one-room cottage overlooking rich cotton fields out by East Cache Creek. Their boy, Ray, was born the same year my father was, and he'd become my dad's best friend. Ray's sister, Mollie, was three years older than he was.

Tracy met the family sometime in the early 1920s—the papers aren't clear on dates. He got a ring from Laverne one morning at dawn just as she was set to go off shift. She told him about some Indian fellow over by the Cache. He'd put in a call to the sheriff's office asking to speak to someone "official." The sheriff ordered Laverne to get Tracy out there, see what he wanted.

He drove the Ford across the swinging bridge and pulled up when he saw a skinny man waving to him about fifty yards from the cottage, in a raggedy corn patch. The leaves were burned to flinders: like charred tamales. It had been a rough summer. The man introduced himself as Charley. He had thin black hair, long— past his shoulders to the middle of his back. He wore a blue work shirt sweated all the way through, though it was early in the day. "I's out here seeing if I could save any of this old stuff"—he ruffled the dying stalks—"when I found this." With the toe of his boot, he nudged something toward Tracy out of the hard-packed dirt. "It just sort of . . . upended, I guess, when the soil got to cracking so much."

Tracy knelt. He was staring at a black and desiccated human hand.

"Now, my family, we been working this land since before the Civil War," Charley said. "It was a odd situation . . . we was slaves, basically, to a Chickasaw family that'd owned Negroes, but their Negroes all passed away, so *my* kin became indentured to 'em. These Chickasaws didn't mind ownin' *other* Indians, long as they considered them . . . well, lesser people, you know what I mean. Anyhow, I figger *this*" — he toed the hand — "it's my great-great aunt Clarinda."

"How do you reckon that?" Tracy asked.

Charley recounted for him an old family story, "kind of a legend, but we's always told it was true." One day, Clarinda's master, dissatisfied with her work in the cotton fields, tried to frighten her with a hatchet. She grabbed the ax from him, laid her hand on a log, and whacked it off. Then she picked up the bloody hunk of flesh and threw it in the man's red face. She walked off into the woods. Charley squinted across the fields. "Maybe there's more of her out there somewhere. I don't know."

One by one, the members of the Chickasaw family died, leaving no heirs, Charley explained. Finally, in the 1890s, the Tasudas managed to purchase a few acres there from the county.

Tracy removed his hat. Rubbed the back of his neck. Lit a cigarette. "We'll get the coroner out here, but if what you say is true, this incident is generations old. Everybody's dead. What do you want me to do about it?"

"I don't know," Charley said. "Seems like there ought to be some fairness . . . you know, the way this poor old woman got treated . . ."

"What kind of 'fairness' you have in mind?"

"I'm just saying it don't seem right, even after all these years. I guess it's just a harsh old world. I guess that's it."

Tracy asked him if his family was going to be able to eat comes the cold if their crops didn't make. Charley said nothing.

The coroner—a "sloppy man, always about half-pickled," Tracy said—determined the hand was "very old," but that was all. The story of Clarinda Tasuda came to an inconclusive end, but that winter Tracy crossed the swinging bridge once a week in his Ford, delivering to Charley, Charley's wife, and their kids baskets of Zorah's homemade cornbread and apple pies, and an occasional ham hock. Sometimes my father went with him, holding Blackie in his lap, and that's how he got to know Ray.

Tracy's attitude toward Indians always puzzled me. He embraced the Tasudas, but he wouldn't speak to the Comanche family living across the street from him. He was never impolite to his neighbors, nodded hello across the lawn, but he didn't try to get to know them. I assume, now, he was comfortable with the Tasudas because they were in need and he could help them; his role as an authority figure, as a community businessman and benefactor, was clear.

The Comanches had declared themselves his equal, buying a house in town. Abstractly, I don't imagine this perturbed Tracy, who was a generally enlightened man, but he was also a man of his place and time. Indians living across the street was no abstraction. His discomfort with the situation was palpable to me as a child. I learned from him to act courteously, but to remain distant from the neighbors.

In the 1930s, when the Roosevelt administration dispatched writers to construct state histories as part of its works program, Tracy remembered Charley Tasuda's call for "fairness." WPA field workers went county to county, collecting local lore. Tracy made every attempt to keep Clarinda Tasuda's story from getting lost. He drove two young writers to the cottage so they could interview Charley. With Tracy's help, Cotton County led the charge collecting slave narratives. Tracy knew every family in the area, including the Black families down by the river bottoms. He helped young men and women from the WPA earn these families' trust enough to record a few stories before the elders were gone. He told me about one afternoon—he'd driven a girl, a college teacher from Oklahoma City, to a shack in a floodplain crazy with mayflies and bees. She'd hired on with the New Deal that summer. He introduced her to an old man he knew named Hosea Williams. Dutifully, the young teacher brought out her notebook and fountain pen. Hosea looked her over. He said, "When I's ten years old, I watched my overseer strip my mama's clothes to her waist and whip her till the ground was a river of blood. I don't want nobody asking me 'bout that." He turned and walked into his shack.

The girl stared at Tracy. "What am I supposed to do with *that*?" she asked. "That's your story," Tracy said. "Tell it as it happened just now."

It didn't take long for the *Walters Herald* to spread the notion that Negroes were telling horror tales to young white kids coming into the county, stirring up trouble. The paper published editorials denouncing President Roosevelt's "communistic" programs. In Oklahoma, the WPA Writers' Project had been placed under the direction of William Cunningham, a proletarian novelist whose books Tracy had read: *The Green Corn Rebellion*, about a tenant farmers' uprising, and *Pretty Boy Floyd*, lauding bank robbery as an act of patriotic heroism. Banks had fleeced the poor for years, Cunningham wrote, so now, at the hands of Pretty Boy, they were getting what they deserved. Tracy thought this a naïve and sentimental portrait of the murderer, but in general he appreciated Cunningham's sympathy for Oklahoma's dispossessed, and he heartily approved of the project's story-gathering.

Each week, the *Herald* berated Roosevelt and Cunningham. The WPA was "coddling" freeloaders "willing to take government money regardless of how they get it," the paper said. In Cotton County, the Klan was active, burning crosses on the courthouse lawn and arranging "night rides" to terrorize Black families in the bottomlands. Tracy had always been at odds with the Klan. It was an unspoken tenet that local businessmen had to be members of the secretive group if they hoped to thrive in Walters. Tracy had made a point of not joining. His store had never suffered because he was so well liked in town. As a deputy sheriff, he had more than once stood guard all night in front of river-shore shacks, against possible Klan attacks.

And now word went round that he was helping Negroes spread lies to communists invading Cotton County, "professor types" from sinful cities in the East (the *Herald*'s editor was a Klan member). Hell, the Daugherty family had *always* been a bunch of stinking socialists—wasn't that the case? One night, Tracy's father, Andy, woke to a flaming cross in his pea patch. It was a story he'd never stop telling—I heard it thirty years later, standing one afternoon in that very same patch. By then, Andy was eighty-seven. He loomed above me, gripping a garden hoe. He'd lost his right eye to cancer. The black, cold-looking hole in his head frightened me more than the story he told.

The Klan threatened to abduct WPA field workers and leave their burned bodies by the roadside if they didn't stop their subversive activities. At this point, Tracy no longer served as deputy sheriff— he'd become the county clerk—but he escorted the writers into the woods to collect slave tales. Once or twice, he told me, he played chicken on the highway with carloads of hooded figures.

Jack Hearon reenters our narrative now.

He was a 'shine-drinking buddy of the *Herald*'s publisher. He became one of the most vocal editorialists in the paper against Tracy's involvement with the WPA. He may have been a Klan member—I don't know—but he needn't have been a Grand Dragon to go after my granddad. He'd never forgiven Tracy for the jail time he'd served. He still claimed his trial was unfair. He was probably humiliated after all those nights Tracy ran him in for pounding his wife. Now the *Herald* gave him space to rail against Tracy every week, impugning his character, questioning his loyalty to the town. These public attacks went on for years, even after William Cunningham had been fired from the Writers' Project as too "radical." Roosevelt made a conciliatory speech, promising his critics that "political" content would not "infect" the state histories. The WPA suspended the controversial slave history project; the transcripts were tossed into the basement of the Oklahoma Historical Society in Oklahoma City and forgotten until researchers rediscovered them in the 1990s. Still, Jack tore at my grandfather.

William Cunningham's sister, Agnes, always known as Sis, became an activist singer alongside Woody Guthrie and Pete Seeger. She called for art to be the voice of collective action, fighting economic oppression. In the *Herald*, Jack used this information against Tracy, smearing him by association with these "reds."

In fact, Tracy never really warmed to Woody's songs. Though still "on the side of the people," he became, as he got older, more conventional in his politics. Nevertheless, when I was a kid, he'd quote, with obvious pleasure, Woody's line "I ain't a communist necessarily, but I been in the red all my life."

The Tasuda family was a particular source of bile for Jack Hearon. Somehow he'd got hold of Clarinda's story. He knew of Tracy's participation in its dissemination (before the details vanished, along with the other histories, in the Oklahoma City basement). Jack wrote in the *Herald* that the Tasudas were savages spreading hate to undermine Christian society, and Tracy Daugherty, working with the United States government, had aided their treasonous campaign.

One afternoon, my father—he would have been nine or ten— motored across the swinging bridge in the Ford with Tracy and Blackie. They were taking a basket of cornbread to Lucy Tasuda. Already, Dad was tight with Ray. He also knew Bob Hearon from school. "Why is Bob's dad so mean to you in the paper?" he asked my grandfather. Tracy smiled. "Because I can take it," he said.

Later, in Tracy's papers, I found these lines from J. P. McEvoy, whose poem about friendship Tracy had tacked to his bathroom wall: "If you can hear the whispering about you / And never yield to deal in whispers too . . . / . . . then have no fear / That anything in all the world can hurt you."

It always surprised me how little my father seemed to know about Tracy's political past. Even before I inherited my grandfather's papers, Tracy let me read them. In a small back room in his store, Zorah upholstered used furniture. She'd framed pictures of her grandbabies and hung them on soft fir posts in the room — my sister, red hair tied in a bow, playing with my mother's wallet; me in diapers, wearing an Oklahoma Sooners T-shirt and one of Tracy's vests. Zorah's worktable, littered with hammers and with tattered recliner seats, braced a couple of filing cabinets Tracy had kept in the county clerk's office. In their drawers, he'd stuffed his old documents into folders, alongside floppy leather books displaying Zorah's fabric patterns, swatches of paisley, red velvet, brown corduroy. Tracy gave me permission to inspect the file drawers — I think, now, to keep me from rearranging his product displays. When I was very little, I loved to upend the boxes of colorful fishing lures on the front shelves. His papers, disorganized, out of context, confused me, but I did savor the posters proclaiming Tracy Daugherty a "stirring public speaker" and a "man for our time." I learned that Andy had taught Tracy socialist catchphrases, and that as a boy, my grandfather had stood on street corners, quite literally on soapboxes, delighting crowds with his incendiary rhetoric. As a child, he'd attended country revival meetings and even delivered speeches onstage with Eugene Debs, Oscar Ameringer, and Kate O'Hare. When I was old enough to grasp the significance of these names, I asked my father about this period in Tracy's life. My dad drew a blank.

Across Main Street from Daugherty Hardware were a bowling alley, the Cotton Bowl; a cinema house — mostly, in the early 1960s, it showed 007 movies for weeks at a time; and the post office, a marble edifice with tall leaded windows and two large murals in the lobby, next to a bank of pewter mail slots. In one of the murals, men in shirtsleeves, necks long and taut as if they were ponies in a field, squatted by rivers of molten steel. In the other scene, women wearing sweaty rags on their heads bent painfully above depleted cotton rows. The figures were blocky and elongated, a style that appeared to fit the subject of labor, an embodiment of motion and strain. I saw in this style a visual cousin of the train rhythms Roy Orbison had borrowed from the blues, from cotton pickers working next to Southern Pacific railroad tracks.

My father didn't like the paintings—he said they "weren't realistic." I didn't mention his fifty-foot frog. One day as we stood in line together waiting to mail some Christmas packages, I asked him, "Why don't you paint anymore?"

"Not enough time."

"You don't have to golf so much."

He laughed.

"What if I got you some canvases for Christmas?"

He ruffled my long, curly hair. "For a while, people wanted *this* kind of stuff." He waved at the murals. "And nowadays, lord . . . all that psychedelic hoo-ha." Sadly, he shook his head.

"These pictures," I said. "They're like the speeches Granddad used to give, right? All about the workers and stuff?"

He said he didn't know.

What *was* he aware of, growing up in Walters? In the last two years of his life, after my mother died, I'd drive him to Oklahoma City, where J. C. had retired, so the brothers could sit and reminisce about the past. Every story they told concerning their teenage years began "Oh, [so-and-so] was a good-lookin' gal" and ended with "and then we crashed the car."

As they relived their exploits, I remembered Bob Hearon telling crash stories, too, Thanksgiving night on the ranch in New Mexico when Bobby and Debra and I nearly burned ourselves to death. That night, Bob and my father had laughed about a juke joint called Some Other Place north of Walters, on the road to Lawton, where they'd do their underage drinking, sometimes in Tracy's Ford. "Did Granddad *know* you had his car?" I asked them.

"Sometimes," Dad said.

"Well, he *sure* knew we had it when we brought it back all twisted up after a night in a ditch or a cotton field," Bob said. "More often than not, right? We'd pull up in front of the courthouse in the morning . . . hell, that flag always made my hangover so much worse, red, white, and blue waving this way and that . . . we'd sit in the front seat of that ol' car and say, 'Okay, which one of us is going to tell him *this* time?'"

It was my father's late-life visits with his brother that rendered Bob Hearon differently for me (I was in my fifties then, living and teaching in Oregon). I'd always thought Bob was nasty to my mother, telling her that night at the ranch she was lucky to get any dates as a girl. He had been dead twenty years when J. C. and my father got together in 2015 to talk about Cotton County. In contrast to *my* memories, they remembered Bob acting quite gentlemanly toward Mom. "He was *always* good to Annie," J. C. said one evening. "Wasn't he sweet on her before you were?"

"They never went out together," my father said. "But yeah, he liked her family an awful lot. He kidded her brother Bill about how much he looked like a damned old Cherokee warrior . . . but, you know, that's the way he was with Ray, too. Gave him no end of hell for being a stinkin' Indian. But he loved Ray. Would have done anything for him."

"He *competed* with Ray," J. C. said.

"No, no, he wasn't at all like his pop . . ."

"Oh, I know. I remember him sneaking around with Ray, 'cause if his dad knew he had *anything* to do with the Tasudas . . . no, what I mean is, he competed with Ray for *you*. He knew how tight the two of you were. *Bob* wanted to be your best friend."

"Well, me and Ray had basketball in common. The team went to the state championships two years in a row. I just didn't *see* Bob as much."

As the brothers spoke, J. C. sipped Jack in a yellow coffee mug (between shallow pulls of oxygen from a steel tank—by then, he suffered from congestive heart failure). I learned that one summer, Bob Hearon had gone to live with the Tasudas in their creek-side cottage. Ray had invited him to stay for as long as he needed to after seeing Jack beat Rachel and Bob one night in a blackout rage.

"Was this while Jack was attacking Tracy and the Tasudas in the paper every week?" I asked.

"I don't know," Dad said. "Probably. We were around thirteen, fourteen at the time."

He couldn't recall how long Bob stayed at the cottage, "but he and Ray got closer than ever that summer—always out fishing in the Cache—and I remember Bob and Mollie, Ray's sister, holding hands at the movies."

Dad said he worked that summer as a film projectionist in the cinema house—the same place I'd watch James Bond in the 1960s, though the building was entirely made over. My father had burned it down. One evening in late August, he'd been showing a slapstick two-reeler when a filmstrip got stuck in the heavy machine. The light bulb ate through it, fueled by the filmstrip's emulsion layer, and the tiny projection booth went up in flames. My father scrambled down the back stairs, yelling into the darkened auditorium for everyone to get out.

The theater was insured. Tracy grounded my father anyway, just for good measure. "Got to learn responsibility," he said. "What if the fire had spread across the street, to the store?"

"I remember standing in the alley that night, watching the smoke clear after the volunteers had got the fire under control," Dad told J. C. and me. "Bob and Mollie had been to the pictures together like sweethearts, up in the balcony, back row, and they stood there behind the post office, shivering, holding hands. And then Jack came along with some buddies of his . . . they'd been drinking down at Clark's . . . Bob and Mollie, well, they scattered . . ."

"I just can't figure those two," J. C. said. "Mollie Tasuda? Bob Hearon?"

"What it was," my father said, "was the same reason he was so good to Annie. The branches their families sat on . . . they were fixed pretty nearly at the same level."

"Yeah," said J. C. "Not too high, you mean."

You think you're better than I am.

No one could say to you anything more vicious than this in Walters, Oklahoma, during the Great Depression, but people said it a lot. Because it was true a lot.

My mother's mother, Janie, lived on a dirt road on the north edge of town across the highway from a filling station known to the sheriff's department for holding high-stakes poker games in its garage on the weekends. My step-granddad, Pop, came into Janie's life seven years after her husband, Jim, a wildcatter for Skelly Oil, ran off with a prostitute. Until then, Janie raised four kids on her own. My mother was the youngest by several years. Simply put, my mother's family was what people in Walters called "oil field trash."

"Ever' damn one of them," Janie said to me one day at her kitchen table. I was just a boy. She was sipping coffee; I was staring at a plate of scrambled eggs. Said to *me*? No. Said to herself. Lonely and distracted. If she'd been talking to me, she wouldn't have said "damn." "Ever' damn one of the fellows in my life—my father, my husband, my new husband, and my sons—they've all gone to work in the oil fields. *Hellholes*. I just don't see the attraction."

A year or so later, I had good reason to remember Janie's morning reverie. I'd dropped by my father's office in Midland. I happened to catch him in a contemplative mood. It was late in the afternoon, after I'd finished school for the day. He leaned back in his rolling chair against a map of the Permian Basin. Quietly, he told me, "When you drill, it's hard at first—the formation, I mean. You just can't believe the power of the earth. But you keep pushing, and soon it gets softer, not exactly spongy, but *sort* of like a sponge, soft enough to soak in oil, at any rate, porous, you know . . . so you start moving faster, spinning the drill a little . . . you're into old salt water then, an ancient sea, and new energy born from dead animals and eons of pressure and layers of rocks and silt . . . oh, there's nothing like it. The odds are always against you, which is why it's such a thrill to find it, that *accumulation* of what the planet's tried so hard to hide." On his face I read confidence and pride, but I believe his confession—*the odds are always against you*—explains why he never acted cocky, though "cocky" was the coin of the realm for West Texas men. In any case, I wanted to rush back to Janie's kitchen after hearing my father rhapsodize that day, and share with her the romance of oil as he'd laid it out for me. Maybe it would help her understand her men.

But there was no question that on the surface of the earth, among the red clay and limestone bluffs where men *aimed* those diamond-like drills, life was hard. Often as a kid, I heard my mother's two brothers, Bill and Bud, recount their wildcatting adventures: how the torqueing and screaming of the drill could bust your damn eardrums if you weren't careful; how sometimes you got so thirsty in the field, waiting on the log trucks, you'd want to gulp the salt water pumped from the anticlines, and then you'd be sick as a dog; how you could easily break a toe, even through a thick, heavy boot, dropping a core sample on your foot; how sometimes it turned so cold, even in southern goddamn Oklahoma, that no gas came hissing through your pipes—frozen solid, mixed with little drops of water in the flow line.

The worst was how lonely it got on a prairie lease underneath the waning moon. It's why I never knew my mother's father, Jim. By the time I was born, he'd vanished with his "oil field woman." "The earth is just so damn big," Bud said one night, sitting at Janie's table, wearing an oily shirt, drinking a can of beer. "But somehow you got to find a way to stand up against it anyway."

Bud got so lonely one summer, working a wildcat at Kilgore, in East Texas, he found his own "oil field woman," a sixteen-year-old café waitress named Doreen (Bud was just a year older than she was). Together they had a child, my cousin Philip, two years before Janie bore Mom.

My mother was the last of Janie's brood, an accident, born just before Jim lit out. By the time she came along, both her brothers and her sister Fern had left Janie's house. Mom worshipped Fern. Fern moved to Lawton on her eighteenth birthday to sell women's shoes in a clothing store. She'd always been a sucker for fashion. She spent her afternoons after school thumbing through fancy magazines in the downtown Rexall's drugstore (a block north of Daugherty Hardware, by the courthouse), staring at ladies' plush hats. A girl with few attractive prospects in Walters, Fern felt, more than Janie's other children, the shame of being "oil field trash." She was determined to break that cycle. Photographs of her sitting with my mother and Janie on their front porch show a tight-lipped woman whose smile doesn't hide the pain in her eyes. She leans away from Janie, already investing her affections, her ambitions, elsewhere. (Janie knows it, too; thick-waisted and tired, she barely smiles.) Fern wears a sleek black dress, immaculately pressed, a string of pearls, and starry silver earrings. She's a magazine model, like the ladies she's admired in Rexall's, but her problem is this: my mother, in a raggedy skirt, her hair all a-muss, is the pretty one, the one with the soft, round face, the tender smile (her chin tapering to a delicate point), the one unafraid to look directly at the camera and say, "Here I am."

I'm sure it was that soft, round face that caught the eye of the middle school basketball star, Gene Daugherty, the youngest son of a well-respected Walters businessman and public servant; just as I'm sure it was her direct and challenging gaze that made Gene look twice, even though it was a social mistake to do so.

You think you're better than I am. But you're not.

And he believed her.

When I was learning to talk, I couldn't say "Janie." I called my grandmother Deenie. I knew my mother's name was Annie, but Deenie often slipped and called her Fern. My mother, I think, never got past knowing she was an afterthought in the family. My awareness of this made Deenie's house feel sad.

It was plain to me as a boy that Deenie's house was not as nice as Zorah's (no pretty wallpaper, no china, no lovely clocks). The only thing tacked to Deenie's wall was a commendation Pop had received from the U.S. government for being gassed in the First World War.

It was plain to me that J. C. and my father were better-mannered than Bill and Bud, plain that Bill was pudgy and swarthy like many folks in town about whom I received decidedly mixed signals. ("Yes, I imagine somewhere back in the family line, we've probably got some Indian blood in us," Deenie said to me one day—a common belief among white families in Oklahoma.)

When I was old enough to walk around Walters on my own, without adult supervision, I'd pop into the Cotton Bowl. With the quarters my mother had given me, I'd bowl a round or two. A big Comanche managed the facility. I never knew his name. Kids called him Butterball. He didn't seem to mind. The way people felt about Butterball, as opposed to my father's friend Ray, who had the advantage of being handsome and slender, confused me but starkly exposed class tensions in town (my schoolteachers claimed class prejudice had never existed in the United States). It was a complicated business. I loved my mother's family but, like Fern, I always put some distance between Deenie's house and me. Bill's "Indian" look didn't bother me . . . and yet it *did*, in that mixed Walters way. He used to ask me if I'd like to go with him to the tracks and watch the stock car races. I always turned him down. I was into rock concerts. I couldn't imagine anything more boring than a bunch of muddy old cars screeching in endless circles. I'm sure he took my "no" as a class snub as well as a personal rebuke.

Pop used to shoot squirrels, skin them, and fry them up in a pan, a ritual that always made me squirm.

Things *really* got bad in Deenie's house when Bud died in a car wreck. He and his son Philip were coming home from a juke joint one night after a day in the oil fields. Philip was driving. He was drunk. He spun off the road and hit an oak tree, killing Bud instantly. Philip lost an eye in the accident. I was nine at the time. For a year after the wreck, Philip sat quietly at Deenie's kitchen table each morning, where Bud used to sit nights drinking cans of beer. Philip stared at the yard. The missing eye did not leave a gaping hole in his head, like Great-Grandpa Andy's; instead, doctors had fitted Philip with a glass eye, a milky marble-like insert, poised, always, to pop out and hit me in the face. It terrified me. I spent even more time out of the house, in town, bowling, watching the flag on the courthouse lawn, following processions of wide black limousines pulling away from the Hart-Wyatt Funeral Home, heading for the cemetery.

The implications of "oil field trash" bore on me when Philip's mother, Doreen, remarried eighteen months after Bud died. Her new man was an "alcoholic tool-pusher," according to Deenie. Philip couldn't stand him. They'd drink and fight—verbal and physical standoffs. One night, in an alley behind the Cotton Bowl, Doreen's new husband pulled a pistol from his coat pocket and shot Philip dead. (I always wondered what happened to that creepy fake stare—did it roll behind the movie house, shatter, get snatched by a rat?) Doreen refused to press charges. The couple moved to Texas.

For a while, I couldn't *put* enough distance between my mother's family and me.

Bob Hearon. *He* was Oklahoma trash. "It's why he was so good to Annie," my father told his brother.

And *like* my mom, Bob managed to slip across Walters's social barriers, befriending my dad, a boy from a prominent family in town; befriending Ray Tasuda in spite of Walters's ambivalence about its Native population and his father's animosity toward the family.

"What did Bob do during the war?" J. C. asked my father one night, setting aside his oxygen mask and filling his mug with more bourbon.

"The army didn't take him. He was flat-footed."

"That's what I thought," J. C. said. "He hung around town, raising hell, while you and I fought the good fight, that right?"

"I suppose," Dad said.

My father served as a gunner's mate on the USS *New Orleans* toward the end of the war. He was luckier than J. C. He got to sail round the world, but he didn't see any combat. He landed back in Walters in the spring of 1946, four months before J. C. returned from Europe. He looked spiffy in his sailor suit, "more prince-like than ever," Mom said. "Then when his brother got home, and *both* the Daugherty boys hit town in their uniforms, well, Katie bar the door, and that was all she wrote! They were heroes. And so handsome! I figured Gene was out of my league for sure at that point, especially when he started Cameron in the fall—the little junior college in Lawton. He scored just as much on the basketball court there as he did as a high school player."

Initially, J. C. didn't strut much at home. He'd sit for hours in Zorah's back garden, drinking beer by the goldfish pond and the mound where Blackie was buried. (The old dog, who'd developed cataracts and arthritis, had simply collapsed, causing Tracy to close shop and weep for a day.) J. C. would talk to my dad and no one else about the horrors he'd seen at Normandy. To others, he'd repeat gentle stories: he said he'd helped fat priests in the small towns of France remove stained glass from the windows of Gothic cathedrals. They'd do this in advance of German attacks so the glass would survive the bombings. "We'd wrap the pieces in newspapers or cloth," J. C. said. "We'd set them in crypts in church basements. Sometimes a ray of sunshine would filter through a grate near the basement's ceiling, touch a chip of glass, and waves of blue or green would spin around the arches in the room."

(Years later, Aunt Barbara told my mother these details were the reason she'd married J. C.: "I think maybe he witnessed the Holy Spirit in those old cathedrals—something *I* hope to do someday." The poor woman never got to Europe.)

After his fifth or sixth beer, sitting in Zorah's back yard, J. C. would finally respond to my father. "Come on. We'll take Tracy's Ford out to Some Other Place," Dad said. "Ray and Bob'll be there."

J. C. said, "What the hell. Nothing but good times from here on out, eh?" And that's how someone's panties wound up in the front seat of the car.

In the meantime, my father had gotten another glimpse of my mother's soft, round face. No matter how skilled he was on the basketball court, he was too small to succeed as a professional athlete. At Cameron, he encountered an inspiring young geology teacher; he finished up at the University of Oklahoma with a degree in petroleum science. If Zorah or Tracy fretted about his "trash" girlfriend, they never said anything. (Much worse for them was their son's move, later, across the Red River to Wichita Falls. Goddamn *Texas*!) They genuinely liked my mother.

Bob Hearon and Ray Tasuda had lost some ground with the Daughertys. They weren't war heroes. They didn't wear spit-shined shoes or carry stripes on their shoulders. They scrounged for work. They'd show up at the juke joint on Friday nights to drink with J. C. and Gene, but the boys' closeness had eroded some.

Ray got a summer job painting ads on signboards for display at public events inside the rodeo arena: "Doan's Pills," "Dr. Scholl's Foot Powder," "Ezra's Magic Elixir—Good for Whatever Ails You!" He wasn't the draftsman my father was (Dad taught him a few tricks about mixing colors), but he was competent enough for the work, and he talked his boss into hiring Bob as his assistant. Eventually, Ray's experience hanging the signboards earned him more sophisticated construction jobs; by the time my dad finished his degree in Norman, Ray had established himself as a site foreman with a local housebuilding crew.

Bob drifted. He'd always dreamed of becoming a rancher, but that seemed economically impossible. Then my mother introduced him to her friend Natalie Cox. Natalie was already working as a music teacher at the Walters Elementary School. After falling out with Mollie Tasuda ("Bad business," Dad told J. C. "I never knew what it was"), Bob hadn't spent much time with girls. But now he and Natalie double-dated with Annie and Gene—in Gene's new Oldsmobile. When Gene was home from college (bless the GI Bill!), they'd spend days picnicking in Sultan Park and long nights dancing to Glenn Miller acetates at Some Other Place.

My father appears to have *fully* renewed his friendship with Bob Hearon as a result of Tracy's kindness. For two years Tracy hired Bob as a salesclerk, though at no other time in the store's history did he place anyone but Zorah on the payroll. It seems he was helping Bob raise money for college. My father told Bob the oil companies couldn't hire fast enough, as long as you had a degree. In Dad's senior year at the University of Oklahoma, he roomed off campus with Bob, who'd started as a freshman. Eventually, Bob would follow my father to Midland.

"You know, you don't always have to drill straight down," my father told me in his office the day he shared with me his romance with oil. "Sometimes it's best to hit a seam from the side, slanting in at an angle. You never know what you'll find."

Though nothing in this narrative has been exactly *straight* so far, I realize that from here on out, the story I have to tell will be the rough equivalent of a slant well.

– 6 –

Three more times in my life, after burning the tent, I'd see Bobby Hearon. Our most recent encounter occurred last year. I was walking down a gentle grass bluff in the Walters Cemetery, going to visit my parents' graves. My mother and father lie near the western edge of the lot, next to a chain link fence on the other side of which a dirt road leads to the nine-hole golf course. These days, three new pumpjacks work the ground near the fence, a fact that would amuse and perhaps gratify my father: the leaching of his bones for America's energy.

At the bottom of the bluff, one of three small lakes winds around private mausoleums and a pleasant pink rose bed. I had nearly circumscribed the lake when I came upon a tombstone I hadn't noticed before: Natalie Cox Hearon, 1926–2015. Gentle Natalie. I touched the warm granite. The same year my father died . . . and I hadn't known.

I looked out across the graveyard, one of the prettiest places I know, and the one stretch of Walters that hasn't changed except to spread. And then there occurred one of those serendipitous moments that often appear in stories but rarely grace us in life. A figure loped toward me from the other side of the bluff, moving among sprays of nosegays stuck in the ground, among plastic U.S. flags. He carried three white roses: an old man, hunched and gray (what little hair he had), and I recognized him instantly.

"Bobby," I said.

He stood, bowlegged, looking me up and down, puzzled. "Tracy," I told him. "Tracy Daugherty."

He squinted, shifted the roses in his arms, glanced at his feet, then turned back to me. "Well, I'll be," he said. Forty years had passed. "How the hell are you?"

He was confronting an old man, too: hair still long but wiry, streaked with white. "I'm sorry," I said, touching his mother's stone. "I didn't realize . . ."

He nodded. He groaned as he bent to place the flowers in the dirt; the soil was still fresh, but it was beginning to sprout pink nettles. When he straightened back up, we stood face to face. He wore a khaki jacket with a thin, furry collar, dirty jeans, dusty work boots. His skin was tough. Toasted. He'd lived in the sun. I watched him appraise my face (I knew it was pale—a lifetime of General Electric lighting), my pressed cotton shirt, gray slacks. When he grinned at me, I noticed his teeth were still brown. Decades, and thousands of miles, had collapsed for us to be standing there together, and yet in the most important ways we still stood far apart.

Before that day last year, our fathers had brought us together in the summer of 1970. Bobby and I were fifteen. It was four years after the night we'd torched the tent at the ranch. Bob had invited my dad for a golf weekend at the Inn of the Mountain Gods in Ruidoso, New Mexico. One afternoon, on the first fairway, Bob and Dad took off in a golf cart, chasing their tee shots (Bob's had landed in the rough; he was already fuming). My mother and Natalie followed in a second cart, chatting, laughing, shaking their heads at their husbands' boyish antics. Bobby, Debra, and I were allowed to drive a third cart as long as we stayed out of the fairways and hushed whenever the men made a shot.

The course nestled among twittering pine trees, in the cool shadows of the Sierra Blanca mountain range. Strings of mist unspooled among granite rock faces in the distance, curling around sunlit crags and lingering drifts of snow in the highest elevations. The fairways were mildly hilly, an unreal green—a green you might see in Disney animations—bordered here and there by tiny lakes and streams. Bob cursed the sand traps, but still they were beautiful, smooth, startling white in vivid contrast to the green slopes. I could see, at last, why my father loved this game. Arching your back, swinging your arms: an ecstatic dance for the gods so they'd grant you entry into paradise.

On the drive from Midland to Ruidoso, my mother had told my sister and me that Natalie had undergone surgery for her breast cancer: a double mastectomy. When Mom explained what that meant, I pictured Great-Grandpa Andy's missing eye, cousin Philip's glassy stare. I tried to imagine the absence beneath Natalie's blouse. PARTS AND LABOR said a sign in the mechanic's shop where Dad took the Beetle every six months for a tune-up. So *that's* what our bodies are, I thought: parts and labor. Mucus and bone.

By the third hole, Bob was openly drinking Scotch from a pocket flask he'd brought. One by one, he cussed his clubs. "Call that a pitching wedge? Hell, I could *kick* the ball better than that . . . What kind of putter is this? Acts like a damn four wood!" I overheard snatches of his talk with Dad whenever Bobby gunned our cart past the men. Bob complained that the ranch was leaking money. Beef prices had dropped. Did my father know of any independent oil drillers looking for roustabouts in the field?

By contrast, Bobby had nothing but praise for ranch life. He'd found his calling. Calving, sheep shearing, roping in the rodeo. I remained unsure about the future. A science teacher at school had lauded my curiosity about the stars but warned me that most modern astronomers were engineers or mathematicians. All I really wanted to do was track Mars across the zodiac with a big reflecting telescope and see the Northern Lights someday. I loved the drums, but I was reaching the limits of my talent. With steady practice, I might become good but never great: Gene Krupa had convinced me of that, and my father didn't have to say a word about it. The only thing I felt certain of—I'd known it since watching "Ooby Dooby" on TV—was that *art*, in some form or another, would be my savior. My father's abandonment of painting persuaded me of this. It was either art or the oil field.

Now I know my choices were never quite that stark. With the example of my mother's family in mind, and the harshness of the West Texas desert, I understand I was simply making class distinctions.

This was not something I could kick around with Bobby—nor would he have cared. We rode in the golf cart at the Inn of the Mountain Gods, he in his "shit-kicking" boots, me in my bell-bottom pants, pretending ease with each other. Debra was only eleven years old, but Bobby kept ogling her "boobies." "You've got little boobies!" he'd say. She laughed. I felt ashamed of them both. I tried to find common topics with Bobby, recalling our days together in Walters, but even *those* memories stirred tensions: standing in Rexall's at the magazine rack, staring at celebrity photos, "John Lennon's nothing but a long-haired freak," Bobby would say. Watching a gourd dance on Sunday afternoon at the Comanche Nation Pow Wow in

Sultan Park, Bobby would shout, "Drunken Indians!" One day, in a dumpster behind a medical clinic near the Cotton County Courthouse, we found boxes of used syringes, old oxygen masks, empty medicine bottles. Bobby wanted to take them back to Deenie's house so we could play with them in the yard. "You can be Dr. Wyvell, dispensing *girlie* pills," he teased me. My mother heard us through an open window, rushed into the yard, and promptly scolded us: "These things are unsafe! You know better than that!" I *did* know better than that. I never forgave Bobby for getting us into trouble. I didn't want to be the boy I became whenever he showed up—like my father with Bobby's dad.

On the back nine in Ruidoso that day, Bob Hearon reverted to trash. That's how I saw it. I became sternly judgmental, and not a little frightened. He was weaving in the fairways, belching, cursing, laughing too loudly, falling in the sand traps. The contrast of his behavior with the beautiful surroundings only made him that much more embarrassing. Natalie grew paler. Quieter. My mother, frowning, driving the cart, lagged farther behind the men. At the tee box on seventeen, she announced that she and Natalie were heading for the clubhouse "for a sandwich and some tea." Bobby was muted, too. His stiff shoulders warned me not to say anything.

On the seventeenth green, Bob missed an easy putt. He slammed his putter on the ground, making a vertical gash: the head of the club sank into the earth like a drill bit. Then he flung the putter into the trees, scattering mist among the needles and cones. When the club landed, it nearly hit my father in the head.

"I bogeyed that one," Bob said.

"*Double* bogey," Dad said.

"Bogey!" Bob shouted. "You put that down, all right? Bogey! You hear me?"

Six months later, back in Midland, we heard that Natalie had locked Bob out of the ranch house and gotten a restraining order against him. Shortly after that, they divorced.

During this period, my mother spoke with Natalie on the phone nearly every night. All she would say to me was that "Bob has not treated her nicely, and she needs love and support if she's going to fully recover from her medical ordeal."

It pains me to say I don't remember worrying about Bobby. I didn't try to get in touch with him. I went to school each day, and at night played my rock and roll in my room.

For a long time, I thought Bob and Natalie were the only divorced couple I knew. Divorce was not something that *happened* to people like us. But one day my mother surprised me, mentioning casually and in passing that Fern had married and divorced when she was eighteen, her first year out of Deenie's house.

"Wait a minute," I said. We were standing in my mother's kitchen. A West Texas sandstorm was brewing outside. The sky became a big red wall. The air smelled of dust. "Fern had a husband before Uncle Al?"

Al was a nice man, a man in the habit of avoiding family get-togethers. He was, and remains, stubbornly resistant to being remembered by anyone.

"She did. Not a very good fellow, I'm afraid."

"What do you know about him?"

"Not much. I was too little. He ran whiskey, I know that. He owned a big black Dodge."

"How did Fern meet him?"

"He sold fluoroscope machines to shoe stores."

I remembered those bizarre contraptions. Fern had shown me one once: a large wooden box into which a person would slip a bare foot. At the top of the box were two dark lenses, like eyepieces in a pair of binoculars. The salesclerk would peer into the lenses to see an X-ray of the customer's foot.

"I think it was all a scam," my mother told me that day in her kitchen. "It fooled buyers into thinking they were getting a better fit through 'scientific' treatment. Fern didn't use the fluoroscopes much. It didn't take her long to see her husband was just a huckster, peddling anything he could. Including romance."

For which she yearned, poor Fern. Oh, how she pined for glamor: fashion-struck, desperate not to be related to the rest of her family. I imagine her now, a young girl on her own, staring hard into the fluoroscope box at a knot of curving bones. As if consulting a set of runes for clues to her future. "Whatever Ails You," Ray Tasuda had painted on rodeo signs. Fern must have seen those signs, growing up in Walters. She must have thought, *"Too much* ails me ever to be fixed. Cast the runes. Scatter the bones."

In the great American tradition, she lit out for the big city—Lawton, Oklahoma—and a life of sparkle and refinement. In time, that life would offer its *own* erotic bitterness, spiritual malaise, disappointments, and absurdities, but at least it would be different from anything she'd experience in Cotton County.

That day in my mother's kitchen, learning of Fern's early divorce, I considered my mother's choices, her stark contrast with Fern. Whether my mother was wiser than Fern, more hesitant, or simply lacking in opportunity, she never would have abandoned Deenie when Deenie had a child to raise. I knew this about my mother and took comfort in it.

She gave Natalie a call. Then we sat together in her kitchen, watching waves of red sand pummel the house.

− 7 −

The algorithmic universe is finite. That's why I'd come to Walters the day I ran into Bobby Hearon in the cemetery. I was practicing the fine art of research.

On the Internet you will not find the following letter, sent by Walters resident Ida Haskell to her state representative, the Honorable Tracy Daugherty, dated March 2, 1959: "If you join your fellow heathens in the House to allow the curse of strong drink to flood our streets, washing away the weak wills of this defenseless people, I pray in the name of God that you be smitten in a manner befitting. You will call the broken hearts of a thousand mothers down on your head."

Tracy may have been troubled momentarily, imagining a torrent of hearts, but his papers make clear he didn't hesitate to back Governor Edmondson's Prohibition repeal. In 1933, when the United States moved to allow the legal sale of liquor, Oklahoma's "Drys" — folks still supporting a ban — flexed enough political muscle to keep Prohibition secure in the state. Beer could be sold, but no hard stuff. "Oklahomans will vote dry as long as they can stagger to the polls," Will Rogers said.

Bootleggers flourished, some of them Tracy's good friends, freely dispensing business cards with their telephone numbers and price lists for pints and jugs. Private clubs charged one-time-only fees of less than a dollar to anyone seeking permission to drink in their bars; other clubs, like Some Other Place, hustled homemade hooch to minors. In public speeches as county clerk and as a candidate for the House of Representatives in the 1950s, Tracy insisted that tax dollars shouldn't be wasted on enforcing a useless and hypocritical system.

He had seen the "curse of strong drink" wreck the lives of his constituents — he'd arrested plenty of them while they flailed under the influence. He could sympathize with brokenhearted mothers. I like to think his support for repeal was based on recognizing and forgiving human frailties. I tend to idealize him, yes; but forgiveness *was* an aspect of his character.

In any case, he would have appreciated the governor's clever approach to the problem. "Let's enforce Prohibition. Strictly," Edmondson said. "I mean *really* enforce it — close the damn loopholes. If people can't get their illegal liquor, maybe they'll vote to have it regulated and sold over the counter." And that's what happened — backed enthusiastically by the Honorable Tracy Daugherty.

I found some of Tracy's Prohibition notes among the papers Zorah passed to me, but many of his public responses—like the transcripts of town hall meetings—remained stuffed into file drawers in a back room at the *Walters Herald* building, just up the block from Daugherty Hardware's old spot. It wasn't Prohibition I'd come to Walters to research. Tracy's stance on repeal was one of several incidental details I uncovered—including the fact that while running for the House, downplaying his socialist past and positioning himself as a mainstream Democrat, he still couldn't resist using as his rally song Sis Cunningham's "Strange Things Happenin'":

> Strange things happenin' in this land
> O the landhog boasts and brags
> While the tenant goes in rags
> Strange things happenin' in this land

I came closer to what I was seeking in the filing cabinets at the Cotton County Courthouse. Today, the American flag still flies above the courthouse lawn. Linoleum has replaced the old wooden floors. The wall radiator is gone. So is the Underwood typewriter.

An assistant to the current county clerk, a woman named Ruth Palmer, kindly allowed me to inspect documents from Tracy's time in office. "No one's touched those old folders in years," she said. "I think your grandfather would have been proud of the progress we've made. Do you know that just a few years ago, in 2003, every county clerk in every county in Oklahoma was a woman?"

It was during Tracy's tenure as Cotton County clerk, in his efforts to promote the rights of women—specifically, to enforce the Community Property Act—that he laid the groundwork for his House run. I'd long known this from his speeches and his public record. What was less clear was how much the Community Property Act had to tell me about who my grandfather was.

I'm digging a slant well here. Bear with me.

And yes, Bobby Hearon still waits for us clutching his white roses in the cemetery.

"I'd prefer we pass the act based on the notion of justice and respect for individual rights, but if it's tax savings and the desire to stop folks from running to Texas that gets us there, well, all right," Tracy said in a speech to the citizens of Walters in January 1939. He was talking about House Bill Number 565, making its way through the Seventeenth Oklahoma State Legislature. The bill proposed a more equitable property system for spouses. In 1939, women had enjoyed the vote in Oklahoma for nineteen years, but they still couldn't run for state offices. It wasn't until 1951 that they were allowed to serve on trial juries. Tracy would work hard to overcome these prejudices, but he recognized unfair property laws as a greater impediment to women's full citizenship. Too often in his work as deputy sheriff and now as county clerk, he had seen marriages dissolve around a husband's drunkenness or cheating. Each time it was the woman who wound up destitute. By default, the state awarded assets to men. Men had earned them, by toiling for the community's interests, said the courts; in contrast, a woman's housework benefitted only her family.

"In ancient cultures, when marauding tribes went to war, they were wise enough to recognize that when the smoke had cleared, domestic tranquility depended on letting the *wives* of the warriors divide the spoils of battle," Tracy said in another speech, one Fourth of July evening on the courthouse lawn. "I'm not asking the state of Oklahoma to go that far—only to recognize that the family is the bedrock of our civilization, and family happiness depends on the wife having the same rights as her husband."

Tracy stopped listing Zorah as an employee of Daugherty Hardware and named her co-owner.

"Is the wife *not* toiling for the community's interests while buying pork chops at the market to feed her working husband?" Tracy asked. "Is the husband advancing the community's interests when he plows his car into a pedestrian after spending all night with a bottle?"

At one county meeting, a farmer stood to challenge Tracy: "Is the wife an agent of the community if she comes to town to work with the Victory Girls and her husband disapproves of the Victory Girls, and in fact wants nothing whatsoever to *do* with the goddamn Victory Girls?"

Tracy answered, "Society has changed culturally, economically, and mechanically since the days when outside activities could only be handled by men. Involvement in *any* activity—physical control of an automobile, say—without legal responsibility is a dangerous situation, for society as well as for the individual."

House Bill Number 565 finally passed because well-to-do families recognized that pooling their property would give them a federal income tax break, and many Oklahomans were crossing the Red River into Texas, where community property laws had long appeared on the books.

In the county clerk's records, the sheer number of forms signed by couples electing to file for property equity beginning in 1940 shows how vigorously Tracy promoted the new act. The number of arrest notices in old issues of the *Herald,* throughout the 1930s, shows how many injustices he had witnessed stemming from failed marriages. It also shows that one marriage in particular obsessed him: that of Jack and Rachel Hearon.

My grandfather's active political career came to an end in 1964, around the time my political consciousness began to stir. Ostensibly, Tracy's defeat in his bid for reelection to the House in '64 came as the result of a three-judge federal court ruling. It said that Oklahoma's apportionment statutes violated the Equal Protection Clause of the Fourteenth Amendment, causing "invidious anti-urban discrimination." This was fancy language covering a power grab by the cities to dilute the rural vote, especially in Democratic Party primaries. Walters no longer had clout at the polls to put Tracy over the top in a race within a larger, newly drawn district. He refused to respond to his challenger that year, who'd dug into his "radical" past. The man accused Tracy of being a "red" and an ally of "Negro agitators."

The timing is far too neat, but I'm tempted to suggest there was a deeper reason for Tracy's public retreat in 1964. It was the year of the Beatles, months after the death of Camelot ("I look forward to working with you," JFK had written to Tracy). As a nation, we were on the verge of flaming cities, body bags in Vietnam, LSD, and campus riots. It is hard for me to imagine my grandfather—a man committed to fairness, but a man also disturbed by the Comanche family living across the street from him—negotiating, publicly, the shifting social shoals of the 1960s. I thought of him, achingly, the night I watched police officers on television clubbing protesters outside the Democratic Convention in Chicago. I pictured Tracy sitting in his living room, beneath Zorah's ticking clock, feeling his heart crack.

My father sat with me that night in front of our television set. I knew the screen's images were hardening his resolve to vote for Richard Nixon, the "law and order" candidate. "The poor people have too much money," he joked, by which I assumed he meant America was better when times were simpler, when everyone stayed in their place, refusing government handouts and demanding no "rights."

I was young and foolish, an idealist, attuned more to cultural than political changes, unconcerned with fine distinctions. Sex and the Silver Surfer: it was all the same to me, a sensual rush. I thought rock and roll was a viable manifesto, a revolutionary blueprint. *Of* the rockers, *for* the rockers, *by* the rockers. The Bill of Right-On.

It is easy now to become too self-critical or too nostalgic for one's innocence. But I note with interest this historical fact: in 1960, when nineteen-year-old Bob Dylan arrived in Greenwich Village to begin his singing career, one of the first people he asked to meet was Sis Cunningham. She lived in the Village with another Oklahoma ex-radical, a novelist named Gordon Friesen. The two of them were preparing to publish *Broadside*, a magazine of activist song lyrics.

The first issue featured a song by Sis entitled "Will You Work for Peace or Wait for War?" and a Dylan poem, "Talking John Birch," in the style of his hero, Woody Guthrie.

Art is renewal through immersion in the past.

Perhaps I am still innocent or too naïve . . . I hesitate to admit this, but it *is* central to who I became . . . in the 1980s, when Bob Dylan joined George Harrison and Roy Orbison in the Traveling Wilburys, along with Tom Petty and an Oklahoma drummer, Jim Keltner, it felt to me like an affirmation of the power of Okie rhythms, a secular musical tradition packing sacred strength, from slave blues to "This Land Is Your Land" to "Ooby Dooby" to "A Hard Rain's A-Gonna Fall" to "My Sweet Lord." The Voice of Rock and Roll . . . taking me right back to Cotton County, to the West Texas oil fields, to whatever that courthouse flag might once have meant, and might mean still.

I recall thinking, as I shuffled file folders in the late afternoon sunlight slanting through the windows of the Cotton County Courthouse, "I should stop, get out to the cemetery and see my parents' graves before it gets too dark." But that's exactly when some of the pieces began to fit—not in any clear pattern, not yet; more like a collection of driftwood.

Jack Hearon. Jack was at the core of this muck.

The hate he'd borne my grandfather from the robbery trial; the multiple arrests for domestic battery; the *Herald* attacks, accusing Tracy and the Tasudas of everything short of sedition. And now I'd discovered that when Rachel formally filed for divorce in the fall of 1942, the year Bob turned twenty-one, Tracy worked with Rachel's lawyer to see she got the house, the furniture, the car, though she and Jack had married well before the Community Property Act went into effect.

Tracy testified before a civil judge that from his "vantage point as a peace officer and now as county clerk," he could swear that Rachel had contributed more to the "community's interests" than Jack ever had. The judge ruled in her favor.

It's not clear where Bob was staying, but he appears not to have been living at home.

Chronologically (though I'd discovered this earlier in the day at the *Herald* building), the next item in the timeline was a crime notice. Three days before Thanksgiving in 1942, two men were brutally assaulted in an alley in downtown Walters. Both were critically injured. It was a confusing sequence of events made blurrier by the *Herald*'s sloppy reporting. It seemed likely that one man had assaulted the other, the paper said. After that, the attacker appeared to have been set upon by a third party.

The victims were Charley Tasuda and Jack Hearon.

The alley ran just behind the service entrance to Daugherty Hardware.

I said earlier I didn't think my grandfather had ever used his blackjack on anyone. I may have been wrong about that. I know he kept the weapon in a desk drawer inside the store until he retired. After that, he gave it to me, as a novelty to keep on a souvenir shelf.

If ever there was an occasion for him to use the club, it would have been after Jack Hearon clocked Charley Tasuda from behind in the alley by the store. The reason Charley was there I understood as soon as I read the report. Tracy once told me that Zorah saved extra turkey for the Tasuda family at Thanksgiving. Tracy passed the food on to Charley at the store.

As for Jack's presence in the alley that night: this was just after Rachel had been awarded community property as a result of Tracy's testimony. Drunk, Jack was waiting to jump my grandfather as he locked his doors.

Is any of this true? Certainly, it is only circumstantial.

In the remaining records I could find, I learned that Charley Tasuda and Jack Hearon had both died, apparently of natural causes, many years later. No doubt Jack carried his grudge against my grandfather all the way to his grave.

Two days after my courthouse visit, I was sitting in a waiting lounge at the Wichita Falls airport, preparing to fly back to Oregon.

(I had recently retired after three decades of teaching at Oregon State University.) I checked e-mail on my phone. While I still had a Wi-Fi connection, I Googled "Hearon and Tasuda, Walters, Oklahoma."

"Did you mean *Heamon and Tassoday*?"

I followed this curious prompt. It took me to the "precedential" court case I'd discovered years ago—the one in which the assistant county clerk had forged Tracy's name on a blank marriage license.

Scrolling down the page, I found numerous typos in the transcript. Digital scrambles. I hadn't noticed these before—"trail" instead of "trial"; "Waters, Oklahoma." In one blurry paragraph, the "appellee" became an "apple."

Heamon and Tassoday. Could it be? Were the appellee and the appellant in Cotton County, Oklahoma, on that late November morning actually *Hearon* and *Tasuda*? 1935. Bob *was* fourteen years old that year—the year my father worked as a film projectionist, the year he saw Bob and Mollie Tasuda holding hands at the picture show.

Bob had lived with the Tasuda family in their cottage that summer, after receiving a severe beating from his father.

Shortly afterward, Dad said, Bob and Mollie had a bad falling-out, and he never knew what it was about.

The father who'd annulled the marriage—if this *was* Jack Hearon, his objections to the union might've been less about the couple's youth than his disgust with Tracy and the Tasudas.

But why would Tracy enable an underage couple to marry? Apparently in secret? Spite? Contempt for Jack Hearon? That's not the Tracy I knew, or thought I knew. *Fear* of Jack? Could Mollie have been pregnant? Did Charley ask Tracy to do him this favor? Did Tracy figure that—crazy as it was—marriage to Mollie Tasuda was Bob Hearon's best shot at survival?

I suppose I will never know the answers to these questions. My father died before I'd discovered these possibilities and the narratives they may expose.

But I can imagine Walters at five o'clock in the morning, the last week of November 1935. Cockcrow. The distant bleating of sheep in the fields. Cassiopeia gleams in the northern sky. Leo lifts its mane in the east, Pegasus sets in the west. A waning moon brushes the Scorpion's long, curling neck, low on the southern horizon. A silent boy riding a bicycle circles dirt roads, snatching copies of the *Walters Herald* from a canvas bag strapped to his back. He tosses the rolled-up papers onto frosty lawns. Down an alley, past the hardware store and the Rexall's, a young couple stumble toward the court-house, where dawn's first rays brighten the empty flagpole. The boy is slightly drunk on Choctaw beer. The couple laugh delightedly, trying to stay quiet, the smoke of their breath like a canvas sketch—the shape of the house they dream of building together.

– 8 –

The year Bobby and I turned seventeen—1972—we saw each other in Walters. This was two years after his father had erupted on the golf course in Ruidoso, and it would be over forty years before we'd meet again. I was about to graduate from high school. Bobby had dropped out. I'd been accepted into SMU in the fall, to study literature.

My family was staying with Tracy and Zorah. Bobby and Natalie had come to visit her mother. Walters bored me. *Everything* bored me when I was seventeen years old except the music on the radio. I'd bought a small camera. I spent afternoons in the countryside out-side of Walters taking pictures of dilapidated churches. It pleased me to document the dying of the town.

Forced together by circumstance, but no chummier than we'd ever been, Bobby and I walked around Walters, looking for something to do. Near the old filling station across the highway from Deenie's house—the one that used to hold poker games late at night in its garage—we came across an abandoned two-story family home. Its windows were smashed, the doors slanting off their hinges.

We stepped inside, glass shards crunching beneath our tennis shoes. The rotting floorboards gave with our weight and threatened to collapse altogether. Kitchen hutches emptied of dishes sagged in a cobwebbed corner; a *National Geographic* map of Earth, torn in half, barely clung to the living room wall, which was pocked with rat holes. Flaking strips of wallpaper hung to the floor like a series of ripped tendons. Chunks of sheetrock loosened and fell as our movements shook the structure, making the windows tremble.

All morning, Bobby and I had endeavored not to talk. What was there to say? His father had died six months earlier of cirrhosis of the liver. At seventeen, I felt superior to the hypocritical niceties of society—a society that had anointed Richard Nixon, a crook, to be our leader—and I wasn't about to sully my principles by uttering lame condolences, especially when I didn't honestly mourn the man. Bobby wouldn't raise the subject of his grief—he'd never admit to what he saw as weakness. Given our situation, as stoic boys raised in the American Southwest, we followed our only option that morning: we tore the house apart.

Bobby sent his booted toe through one of the kitchen walls, causing nearly a third of it to crumble. We laughed. Chalky powder fouled the air. It rose toward the exposed wires of cracked ceiling fixtures. I picked up a broken piece of wainscoting and slashed the map, slicing off northern Scotland. A large square of the wall fell with it. Then we roared like little tornadoes through the rooms, smashing apart doorframes, breaking glass, splintering rotted wood, severing rusted pipes. I punched a hole in the wall; it gave easily and didn't hurt my hand. The dust made breathing hard. Suddenly, a loud croak froze our crazy motion: "Here, now! You boys! Stop that!"

The filling station attendant, a skinny old Kiowa man, had heard the pounding and hurried to the house to investigate. He stood now in the empty doorway, surveying falling plaster and wallpaper scraps floating like birds through the rooms. "I'll get the sheriff out here!"

Two days later, the old man would die of a heart attack by the gas pumps while hosing down his lot. I felt guilty about this, as, fleeing the ruins, I had thought, "I wish that old man would die!"

But that was minor guilt. My bigger crime was running, leaving Bobby alone to face our accuser. As soon as I heard the word "sheriff," I sprinted out through a gaping hole in one of the house's closets. I crouched behind a mesquite bush about fifty yards from Deenie's house. Horseflies circled my head. The smell of fear, stale and flat. I couldn't afford to get in trouble, I thought. I had too much to lose. My expensive private school education. My prospective career. Bobby—his father was dead, he'd dropped out of school. He was going nowhere, anyway. What did it matter if the sheriff nabbed him?

I must have seen Bobby again before we left Walters, but I don't remember a final meeting. My memory of that visit ends with the two of us facing arrest in the house we'd wrecked. The old man's threat was idle, just to scare us. Then he died. Bobby and I set off on separate paths in life. Many years would pass before I would admit to myself that I had carried into the next generation the class bias that had done so much harm to our families before us.

It is an irony I do not know how to assess: last year, on my return to Walters to look through Tracy's papers, I noticed that Tracy's home was essentially gone, Deenie's home was gone, but on the abandoned lot next to the filling station, there remains the skeletal frame of the house Bobby and I failed to dismantle.

– 9 –

"One January day, thirty years ago, the little town of Hanover, anchored on a windy Nebraska tableland, was trying not to be blown away": with that sentence from *O Pioneers!*, which I first read as an undergraduate at SMU, Willa Cather staked her claim on me and became my most cherished American writer. No one has more accurately, more elegiacally, described this continent's gouged and howling plains. Cather's wind has pressed on me all my life, sweeping down from the towering grasslands into Oklahoma and West Texas, scouring every sensation I have ever experienced.

Sometimes the wind brings with it added inclemency. Cather, lamenting the fact that as she aged, death seemed to rain down all around her, once wrote, "I have cared too much, about people and places—cared too hard. It made me, as a writer. But it will break me in the end." My family's death monsoon began in the 1970s and continues unabated. It has not been the cataclysm my father's brother witnessed at Normandy—slower, steadier, more expected, less historically important—but it has been just as terrifying and final, step by step, for individuals and the people they leave behind. Distant cousins, aunts and uncles, fall regularly with the seasons. For me, the first major storm was Deenie's decline, in a nursing home on the outskirts of Walters. I remember sitting by her bedside in the winter of 1977, holding her hand. It was no bigger than a fried chicken leg, and it bore a similar texture. She told me that "old oil field woman" had come in the middle of the night and stood just outside her window, laughing at her. "She's after Pop, just like she grabbed Jim all those years ago." It horrified me that at the end of her existence, her life came down to this: my mother's father's abandonment of the family. "Damn hellholes, oil fields!" Deenie said. In her worst delusions, she confused Pop with Jim. She berated him for his unfaithfulness as he was trying to feed her at night. It seemed to me a mercy for everyone concerned when Deenie finally slipped away one afternoon. Pop died silently in his bed just a week later. He had been a good man, a steady presence for Deenie, but essentially an unknowable cipher to the rest of the family, like Fern's husband Al, who died of a heart attack in his fifties, soon after Aunt Barbara succumbed to complications of her hysterectomy.

Tracy's last years were labored: "I guess most of you know I have a breathing problem." He'd developed emphysema after decades of smoking. "You never thought I'd run out of air. Not when I was standing on a street corner making a pitch for your votes or giving a sales talk. But that's my trouble. I guess I talked too much." He said all this for a cassette recording he asked me to take to the nursing home and play for his elderly friends there, including Laverne, the former all-night telephone operator. "I've often thought of you all. I wish it were possible for me to get out there and visit with each one of you."

In late May 1978, when I got a call from my mother saying Tracy had been hospitalized and "things look rough," I was finishing my first semester as a master's student in literature at SMU. "He's asked that you deliver the eulogy at his funeral," my mother said on the phone.

"Why?"

"You're his namesake. You're the family historian."

Right—carrying the family's burdens into the next generation, I thought, an uncharitable attitude based on the burden I felt most immediately at that moment: enormous grief.

Late in the day I took my last final exams, and then, after dark, I drove from Dallas to Walters in an old Oldsmobile my father had let me have when he bought a new car. I arrived around midnight. Zorah's house was dark. I didn't want to wake her or my parents, so I spent the rest of that night in the back yard by the goldfish pond, staring at the stars, imagining, soon, my grandfather's spirit mingling with the mists of the Milky Way.

Around dawn, when Zorah came out in her bathrobe to water her bluebonnets and found me asleep on the grass, she told me gently that Tracy had passed away at about ten o'clock the previous evening. In the leather booth around Zorah's breakfast table, I saw, for the first time, my father cry. I would see him weep a second time thirty-five years later, at my mother's bedside in Midland Memorial Hospital.

My mother insisted I go to the Hart-Wyatt Funeral Home to view Tracy's body—a morbid and grotesque suggestion, I thought, but she assured me it was the only way to accept what had happened, to achieve proper closure. A fellow called Bugs—I never knew his real name—managed the funeral home. He was tall and pale, born, it seemed, with dingy white hair and big buck teeth (hence the nickname, after the scurrilous bunny). He had a creepy crush on my mom. He'd give her long, wet kisses on the cheek whenever he greeted her, and his hands lingered on her back. From a very young age, I recall thinking, "You can't have her!" Even then, I knew I was addressing Death as well as its supercilious representative.

The funeral parlor looked like a knockoff from a bad Halloween carnival, a generic haunted house with black-painted walls, maroon carpets, candelabras on mantels and bookshelves (which appeared to conceal secret passageways), and overstuffed chairs whose arms would naturally grab you and strangle you if you sat. The place smelled of God knows what—a mixture of formaldehyde and mothballs, of congealed face powders, urinous cloth.

In his open coffin, Tracy looked like a marionette version of himself, an unreal puppet no longer twitching on vibrating strings. I kissed his cold forehead. Then I wiped my lips—I had a brief irrational fear of catching a death virus from his corpse.

Back at the house, Zorah brought me a ledger filled with Tracy's papers, along with a set of his old fountain pens. On the ledger's leather spine was printed "Record of Deaths: Cotton County"—the book was from his days as county clerk.

"This is just one of many files down in the basement. I want you to have them all. Nothing's organized . . . it may not be worth anything to anyone . . . but maybe someday something here will have meaning for you."

In the eulogy—my first written speech, my maiden attempt at the rhythmical art of language—I quoted from a scrap of notepaper on which Tracy had scrawled: "At home today I have two baby boys, little laughing fellows. They know nothing of the world's trouble. They only know that they are happy. The little fellows will be men someday. They will see inequality and injustice. They will find crime existing under the cloak of respectability and the protection of the law. They will face conditions which breed poverty and awful misery on the one hand and out of which grow opulence and unearned ease upon the other. When they find this, I want them to know two things. First, that their father was not responsible for these conditions and second that their father did all he could do to better and prevent such conditions."

After I'd delivered the speech in the dim blue chapel of Walters's First Methodist Church, a thin man approached me, shoulders hunched. His skin was rough and dark. He thanked me for my words. "Your grandfather would have been proud of you. He was a special man."

"I know," I said.

The fellow introduced himself: "Ray Tasuda."

Later, at the reception in Zorah's house, I heard him talking to my father. His sister, Mollie, had died of cancer the previous year. Dad told him about Bob Hearon. The men shook their heads. And then, spontaneously, without any signal between them, they both pretended to stuff a ball through a basket.

On the other side of the room, by a table stacked with hot apple pies, my mother deflected Bugs's busy hands, but obviously she enjoyed the flirting. Like my father in that instant, she seemed to me impossibly young. It was as though I'd stepped into the Cotton County of fifty years ago.

Within eight months, we'd all gather again in Walters for Zorah's memorial service. Lung cancer. Mercifully swift.

As I write (using one of Tracy's fountain pens), I am sixty-two years old. For the past decade, it has become apparent that every serious ailment my father suffered in his last years afflicts me as well, except in my case, the troubles—blocked arteries, gout, prostate cancer, skin cancer—occur twenty years earlier than they did for him. That "darned John Bircher," Dr. Wyvell, could probably give me an accurate estimate of my remaining time on earth, but on this point, it's just as well she's dead. I don't want to hear it.

It would be easy to mark the onset of a major disease as the beginning of my father's erosion, but I think that, more powerfully than the flaws in our genetics, my family saddles each successive generation with social faults hindering healthy individual progress. In this, we are no different from any other American family, I suspect.

As a young man in Walters, my father, through his dad's example and his innate decency, overcame class prejudice enough to befriend Bob Hearon and Ray Tasuda. It did not bother him to marry "oil field trash." But each generation carries its family's burdens.

When my sister first told me—she was fourteen years old—that she had experimented with LSD and that there was "no better feeling than being high," I thought immediately of the boy my father and I had seen from the Beetle walking barefoot in the snow. Instead I should have focused on Salon la Vida, the bodega out on Highway 20, the road to Walters, on Midland's "other side of the tracks." Debra's dalliances with drugs as a teenager—pills, pot, acid—would comprise a typical, not entirely unhealthy, expression of youthful curiosity. She would not slide into addiction or depravity, as our teachers warned us would happen with drugs. But her experiments also indicated something deeper, not unrelated to the period's unraveling social bonds, the changing mores my grandfather's life in politics could not have survived. In short, energized by the times, Debra did not—or did not *want* to—recognize any divisions between one side of the tracks and another. She dared to go wherever she wanted, and nobody was going to tell her that white girls shouldn't mess with dark-skinned boys, or that kids from privileged families shouldn't go slumming with "trash." The drugs were just a side effect—"intoxication" helped ease the cultural taboos.

Much of this part of Debra's life I missed, living miles away at college. When I did come home, at Christmas breaks, I'd hear my mother yell at my father, "Gene, you've got to do something with her before she goes off the rails entirely." My father answered, "It's just a phase, Annie. She'll outgrow it. Remember our nights together at Some Other Place?"

"What she's up to is much more dangerous than anything we ever did as kids."

"How?"

"It just *is*."

From the vantage point of sixty-two, I see that this argument was really about panties left forgotten in a car's front seat versus pistol shots behind a bowling alley, and the realization stirs in me an overwhelming tenderness for both of my parents, but at the time their bickering only irritated me. I couldn't wait to get out of the house, back to college and the solace of my studies in art, history, language. I didn't hide my impatience to leave. It prompted my father to say to me one night, "We're not much of a family anymore, are we?" Mom responded to me by shaking her finger in my face. "I thought *you*, of all people, would understand my point of view!" she said.

I gassed up the Olds and got the hell out of the oil patch.

In the long run, my father turned out to be right—Debra's "wild streak" (my mother's words) was more or less a phase, though it lasted longer than any of us thought it would, well into her twenties, and it took a toll on Dad.

By way of illustration, let me offer an experience Debra and I shared one Christmas. I was home from SMU for the holidays. Mom and Dad had gone to bed early. Debra wanted me to meet someone, she said. She said I should drive us to a place she knew on the south side of town, near Highway 20, where underage girls could get a drink. It wasn't Salon la Vida, but it was a joint just like it, located across the Southern Pacific tracks from the interstate, on a dirt street called Cotton Flat Road.

As I parked the car in the gravel lot, she told me she had a "Black boyfriend"—named Bobby (by coincidence)—and he was "waiting for us inside."

The bar's interior was murky blue. Stale-smelling. A black-and-white television plugged in above a blinking cigarette machine played a Bruce Lee video. Four or five guys in camo jackets slumped in a corner booth, spitting tobacco into Dixie cups. Two men in overalls and dusty Texaco caps prowled around a pool table. The tallest one, a slender Black man, called, "Deb-*ra!*"

She cocked her hip against the table. The man—at least ten years older than my sister—kissed her. I stood by a flashing jukebox. It pounded out a hip-hop tune.

"Name's Bobby," the man said to me. "How you doing, man? Debra's bro?"

"That's right. Tracy."

"You shoot stick?"

As a matter of fact, I did, courtesy of a poetry professor who moonlighted as a bartender in Dallas, and who'd taught me billiards after class each week.

"Okay, then. I'll rack 'em up," Bobby said.

Debra laughed and got a Lone Star. *You think you're better than we are. Bobby'll show you.*

Behind him, painted on a mirror on the wall, a redheaded woman in hot pants rode a jumbo beer bottle as if it were a bull. Next to her: a signup sheet for a Vietnam veterans' support group, a *Time* magazine picture of George H. W. Bush pinned to a dart board.

Bobby plucked a bottle of Johnson & Johnson's baby powder off the table. He sprinkled his fingers. "Okay, College Boy. Show me what you got."

The stick slipped in my hands. My break was poor. Three or four balls rolled from the pack, but most of them stayed where they were.

Debra chuckled. She *belonged* here, on the other side of the tracks. Just an old Okie. She wanted me to know.

Bobby ran three stripes off the table. "Watch it, College, watch it now!" He eyed his next shot. "So. Tell me. What's it like in the big, bad city?"

"Too many lights," I said. "I miss the sky out here. You know. Watching meteors and stuff."

"*Meteors*? What the hell? You a fireball, College? Ha!" He banked the twelve ball off a side cushion, just past the pocket. "Shit, Fireball! Here's your chance! Don't say I never gave you nothing!"

Rushing, I botched a simple setup. Debra joined Bobby's laughter. On the jukebox, she punched up "Play That Funky Music, White Boy." She danced by herself, by the bar. Bobby strutted back and forth in front of the mirror. "Gonna put you *away* now, College!"

His hotdogging cost him an easy bank shot.

The floor seemed to tilt beneath my feet. Warped boards, gritty, sticky, just like the sagging planks in the house Bobby Hearon and I tore apart. I chalked the tip of my stick. I remembered my teacher's advice about sizing up the table: *Think of it this way: it's just like narrative structure, he'd said, or a poem's opening stanza. Lines of incidence, one ball connected to the next.*

I stepped around Bobby and sank the yellow one ball. The two and the three.

Bobby stiffened, squinted his concern. Debra stared at me over her glass.

The jukebox went silent. I buried another ball and left myself a beautiful approach to the five. Powder. Chalk. I knew I should stop. Debra had quit dancing and slumped on a stool.

Using her beer bottle, she made wide, wet circles on the bar.

Give her some pleasure, I thought. Just once, she'd love to get the better of me. I could afford to let this one go.

But the final shot was too good to miss. You'd *have* to fake it to blow a gift like that. "*Damn*, College," Bobby said. He shoved his stick in the rack and sulked into the shadows of the parking lot outside. Victorious, I headed for the men's room, clapping powder from my hands. I didn't look at Debra.

No toilet paper, soap, or towels. Barely any water. I wiped the rest of the powder on my pants. Taped to the wall above the sink, to cover a hole in the wood, a *National Geographic* shot of a bear.

In the car on the way back to our parents' house, Debra and I didn't talk at first. A freight train caught us at Cotton Flat Road. Bells rang, lights flashed.

"Debra—," I said.

"Forget it," she said. It would be some time before we could cross the tracks. "Merry Christmas, okay? Merry fucking Christmas."

"Stop it," I told her. "Just stop it."

"And a Happy—"

"I'm *sorry*, all right?" I reached over and took one of her hands. She tried to pull away. The train shook the car. I kept her still until she quit fighting me. For a long while, once the tracks were clear, we didn't move. We sat there holding hands.

The little town on the tableland . . . in the 1970s, it was trying hard not to be blown away.

My father never met Debra's boyfriend, but several months after the pool match, "I'd forgotten I'd left a bunch of Polaroids on the desk in my room," she told me on the phone. I was back at SMU. "Pictures of me and Bobby in bed. We'd been goofing around one day, holding the camera above our heads and taking silly shots of ourselves. Well, when Dad saw them, he nearly had a stroke. He never said a word to me about any of this. I learned it all from Mom. You know how he is. Always indirect. But he was so upset, he agreed to see a shrink for a while. Took sedatives to sleep at night. And that gave Bobby the excuse he needed. Instead of being straight about not wanting to stay with me, he could point to Dad and tell me, 'Your old man's a bigot. No way I could ever be part of your family.' And that was it."

And that was long before doctors put a stent in my father's heart, before he underwent radiation treatments for prostate cancer and declared to me quietly one day, "My time is getting short, son. I've seen too many winters."

– 10 –

On Christmas Eve 2012, my mother gave me a desk calendar featuring articles from the satirical newspaper the *Onion:* fake horoscopes, parodic profiles of world leaders, twisted commentary on cultural trends and pathologies. Every day during the first four months of 2013, I tore pages off the calendar, keeping track of the dates, laughing at the jokes. A few weeks ago, for the first time in several months, I happened to notice the calendar on my kitchen shelf. It had stopped, which meant *I* had stopped, on Wednesday, May 8.

The *Onion*'s May 8 headline read: "Journey of Self-Discovery Leads Man to Realization He Doesn't Care."

The article began, "Three months after setting off down a long spiritual path to find himself, 38-year-old Corey Larson arrived at the conclusion Tuesday that he does not care. Larson said of his soul-searching journey, 'Fuck it. Fuck it all.' [He] briefly considered writing a self-help book to make the journey easier for others, but decided that he also didn't give two shits about whether other people arrived at the same conclusion he did."

As a language lover, I appreciated what it was that made the humor work in this piece. For me, it wasn't the clever concept. Instead, it was a simple detail. The man's spiritual non- awakening occurred on a "Tuesday."

My experiences grappling with family history had convinced me that simple details (trial testimonies, lists of common property) always tell us the story. Or part of it, anyway.

I lost track of 2013 on a Wednesday. Five weeks later, on a Sunday afternoon, the day my *Onion* horoscope read "You're starting to think that maybe the funny nose and glasses won't actually be enough to hide you when Jesus returns in all his glory," my mother died. That I had abandoned the calendar, her gift, five weeks earlier tells me in hindsight: May 8 was the day I accepted after months of denial that my mother *was* going to die, and my depression was such that time, the future, anticipating anything, didn't matter. "Fuck it, fuck it all," I thought and still sometimes think.

But that word, "sometimes," makes me pause even as I write it. It's like a coordinating conjunction, a continuation, in the middle of a sentence. If researching the past has taught me anything at all, it's that we are time's creatures, *in* and *of* its muddy flood. We tell stories in time, and as long as its movement *hasn't* stopped for us, not today (as long as Zorah's clock still ticks, even if it is only in my imagination now), we make narrative links, however tenuous.

Narratives begin in the family womb. My mother's gift of the calendar and its sudden cessation helped me experience what had been, up to then, abstract: the knowledge, as any capable drummer will tell you, that time's passage—its pressure and its management—is one of the essential aspects of our life's stories.

Within a month of my mother's death, I helped my eighty-seven-year-old father put the house he had shared with her on the market (he'd moved into an assisted living facility) and pack up sixty-four years' worth of accumulated property for an estate sale. While examining closets and cupboards, I discovered my mother's 2013 calendar, Scotch-taped inside a kitchen cabinet stuffed with prescription pills, emergency telephone numbers, and old Kleenex tissues still smelling of her, imprinted with her lipstick. The first three months of the calendar were marked, in her precise handwriting, with cramped notices of social engagements, upcoming doctor appointments, reminders of the housekeeper's schedule. Her time was full. The trickle of the foreseeable began to run out in mid-March, by which date, in actuality, she'd fail. A blank spot occupied June 16, the day she'd die. The calendar noted that on June 21, the day we buried her in the Walters Cemetery, "Summer begins."

To the writer in me, the historian, nearly dormant with grief, my mother's plans, followed by mocking blank squares, exposed time's limitations: while essential, time is not ample enough for *story*. And I confess: I was looking for a story that day, a continuation. Something other than "Fuck it."

Staring at the calendar, at the labels on the half-empty bottles of pills (*Two per day for thirty-three days, refill expires in August*), I realized time is merely a story's through-line — a guide perhaps to nowhere, certainly not to the beating heart of the matter.

Here's a brief excerpt from the journal I kept while helping my father pack up his house. It's raw and unedited, the kind of stuff the world doesn't give two shits about. "We sat in my sister's old bedroom, my father on the bed, me on a stack of boxes. When he was ready, I pulled other taped boxes from a closet, the word 'Office' scrawled across them in black Marks-A-Lot. My mother's handwriting. I pulled off the tape and opened the flaps. One by one, with my foot, I pushed the boxes gently toward my father so he could see what was inside. He bent, groaning a little. 'This has no earthly value,' he said, holding up, one after another, the thin mementoes of his life: a plaque honoring five years of service with the Sinclair Oil and Gas Company, a ten-year pin, twenty, a photograph of his retirement party, my mother, smiling, toasting him with a flute of champagne. A small, blank canvas on which he'd done a preliminary sketch for a painting he'd never begun. 'No value at all,' he said. 'Just take it away.' 'You're sure?' I asked. He replied, 'No earthly reason to keep it.' No. Aside from me hoarding Tracy's papers, my mother had been the one to save and document, to chronicle our lives. She had been our witness.

"I hauled the plaques and pictures to the dumpster in the alley until I stuffed the bin and had to stumble to other dumpsters several yards away — over a dozen trips, tears in my eyes, my mother's name on my lips, not in gratitude for cherishing our lives' humble transitions, but in shame at my undoing of her efforts."

I'm not moved to analyze the journal in any way except to say that whatever fragile structure it has, written on the fly, is, I think, grammatical. The grammar of correct usage, nouns and verbs and syntax, certainly. Through the years, I've learned a *little* of the music of language. But it's more than that: it's my *family's* grammar, the way we talk to each other, the way we sit together, our bodies' dialogue—my foot pushing the boxes at my father "gently," as if I had no agency in the matter, as if the box were moving on its own, *I have nothing to do with this erasure of our past, Dad, please don't make me do this*, what we understand without speaking and what we fail to understand, my father's drone, "No earthly value." It's not just the nuts and thorns of this phrase that are so familiar to me, so ingrained in the family stories I've been tracing here. It's the grammar of my father's being-in-the-world, his movements, the speed of his metabolism, all of which I share, along with those of my mother, in my DNA. It's his melancholy squint at life—certainly part of my family's deep structure. I know that now. I know it better when I write, trying to mimic the movements of our bodies and minds, my family's cadences, the syntax of our talk, its comic or tragic tones, the qualified dodges, like little parenthetical dances, of negotiating family spaces, rooms, landscapes, houses.

Our personal music.

Self-discovery? Who gives a shit? Really.

I believe now (with Willa Cather as my witness) that the stories of our lives rest in simple details, arranged in the fluidity of time, fixed by family grammar.

On the day she died, my mother, like Deenie before her, moved in and out of lucidity. She thought she'd been admitted to the hospital to give birth, first to me, then to my sister. These were the experiences pressed into the folds of her body like seals into wax, even as her mind was letting go of the self. "Are the babies in the room?" she asked.

A little later she said, "I'm trying to figure it out." And then: "This wasn't supposed to happen to me."

Are the babies in the room? I'm trying to figure it out. This wasn't supposed to happen to me.

The story of an old Okie, of one small swirl spreading from the center of Cotton County. The story of my mother.

– 11 –

My father didn't die from the shock of discovering a stack of racy Polaroids featuring my sister. He died nearly twenty years later, in Midland Memorial Hospital, where my sister and I had been born, where my mother had died. He succumbed to what the coroner called "sepsis"—which I took to mean his body's reaction to the germs he had picked up in the hospital once he was admitted for stomach pains, the cause of which doctors never found.

"We could run some more tests," a physician told him one day.

"What for?" he said, exasperated, flailing his skinny arms. His arms were black-and-blue from the nurses' rough poking whenever they inserted IVs. I stood helplessly by his bed, convinced that no one in this hospital had any idea what they were doing. The truth was, Midland was experiencing one of its periodic oil booms. Fracking and recent petroleum technologies had opened up whole new possibilities of discovery in the Permian Basin. Blue-collar workers were flocking to West Texas, overwhelming its medical system. The night Debra and I had taken our father to the emergency room for his stomach pains, we'd seen the ER treated as a pediatric clinic by desperate low-income families, new arrivals in town, many of whom could not speak English and probably had no health insurance. Midland was one of the richest communities in the nation; because of that, its social services were strained to the point of failure. Amidst sniffles, soiled diapers, and the constant wailing of babies whose parents' hopes and options were few, Dad had to wait three hours to be examined that night. Already, I feared—with justification—he'd never leave the hospital.

He refused further tests. "Take me off the antibiotics," he told his physician. "Just keep me out of pain."

This was depression talking, I thought. He had not been diagnosed with any terminal condition. But to my surprise, the doctor agreed. He called in hospice workers, who said they would "keep him comfortable" in the hospital instead of at home. They would work in tandem with the hospital's regular nursing staff.

"Are you sure this is what you want to do?" I asked my father.

He gave me the same impatient look he'd shown when I'd flown in from Oregon a few days earlier, after receiving a phone message from Debra that he was ill. "What are *you* doing here?" he'd said, upset that he'd caused me "trouble."

Now, in the hospital, he said, "Yes, this is what I want to do. What earthly reason do I have to prolong anything?" I knew what he was saying: *Without your mother, what do I have to live for?*

You have me! I wanted to shout at him. You have Debra!

But he didn't. For thirty years I'd lived in Oregon, teaching writing and American literature at Oregon State University. I had my own life. Debra still lived in Midland, but—no longer "wild"—she was married with a boy in high school. She was too busy to spend as much time with Dad as she used to.

So he turned to morphine—and it sent him off his head. Far from reducing his pain, it made his body spasm. His teeth chattered. He thought he was flying in an airplane over the ocean. Then he'd grab my shirt and scream at me, *"Do* something! Kill me!" I leaned over him, took him in my arms. I raised and lowered his torso whenever he groaned, as though we were riding huge breakers together. "Up now!" I'd say. "Okay, easy. We're going back down." This *did* seem to soothe him. Later, Debra said, "It was like watching a woman giving birth, going through labor pains."

At night he'd moan, "I'm dying. I'm dying."

"I know, Dad," I said.

Hospice did not communicate well with the hospital staff. Every eight hours, when a fresh nurse came on duty, I had to explain we weren't using this or that medication. Most of the nurses I'd see only once. In Midland's thriving economy, staff turnover was high. I'd call the hospice number and no one would arrive. Dad's pain did not abate. He'd grip the back of my neck. "Kill me now. Why can't I die? Do something!"

Cherish me, murder me.

Once, in the middle of the night, a nurse named Comfort, a Nigerian woman with minimal English, just stared at me when I said my father needed to use the bedpan. "What am I supposed to do with it?" she said. So I showed her, doing her job for her. She did not return the following night.

Why had the physicians agreed to rush my father into hospice care (such as it was)? He was old: that's what their cavalier attitudes said to me. He was an unnecessary strain on the system. Time for him to go. The doctors brushed aside my questions. Life in the glorious Texas boom.

Finally, a hospice nurse (no-nonsense, like Dr. Wyvell) increased the morphine to thirty milligrams every four hours, and my father slipped into a coma. If he still felt pain, he couldn't express it. That very afternoon, J. C. arrived in town. He'd insisted on flying from Oklahoma City. His youngest daughter, Barbara (the spitting image of her late mother), brought him into the room in a wheelchair, to which his oxygen tank was strapped. He grabbed his brother's hand. "Gene!" he barked. "Gene, don't you give up on me now! Gene, can you hear me?" My father didn't stir.

J. C.'s mouth twitched. His features stiffened. As he fought tears, I remembered my Aunt Barbara's belief that he might have glimpsed the Holy Spirit in the cathedrals of wartime France.

That night, in his hotel room by the airport, he, young Barbara, Debra, and I split a bottle of Jack Daniel's. I toasted him and thanked him for coming—given his age and condition, his visit did, in fact, strike me as a holy gesture.

The room my father died in was on the hospital's sixth floor. From its window I could see the town in its spectacular barrenness, its flatness and aridity. I could see the squared-off housing lots, the streets running parallel and perpendicular, the railroad tracks, and the power lines. I could see the schools and stores—Hank's Superette (shuttered now), where my father had driven me in his Beetle so I could buy a comic book after viewing the "facts of life." I could see my family's history, the neighborhoods we'd lived in. Pumpjacks and derricks. The scene resembled a map on my father's office wall those many years ago, a map bursting into color and movement.

On the night of the Fourth of July, while my father labored for air, I sat by the window watching fireworks flare above the land. Near dawn—the sky still smoky with bottle rockets—Dad emitted a little "ha," struggled with a couple of shallow inhales, and stopped moving. For weeks, my body's metabolism had been keyed to the erratic rhythms of his heart and lungs. I knew he was gone.

Debra and I paid to have his body driven from Midland to Walters, past Salon la Vida and the Light Bub Place in Big Spring, so we could bury him next to our mother, Deenie, and Fern in Cotton County.

The Hart-Wyatt Funeral Home in Walters was run now by a pleasant young man named Philip. Bugs had died years before (and it pleased me to learn he was buried in another county, clear across the state, far from my mother). Philip told us that since our father had served in the navy, he was entitled to a military funeral, complete with a flag-draped casket and a pair of buglers blowing "Taps."

In a back room at Hart-Wyatt's, in low candlelight, my father lay in his open coffin. His face was sunken, his cheeks hollowed, as though all his concentration had turned inward. Almost everyone he'd grown up with who might have come to pay their respects was dead, but late in the day I recognized Ray Tasuda hobbling up the parlor's front steps, so hunched it pained him to raise his eyes from the ground. "Ray," I said. "So good to see you. Thank you for coming."

He nodded, too choked up to speak.

I took his arm and escorted him to the back room, our feet sinking into the soft maroon carpets. Ray stood above my father, lips trembling. Then, gently, with his open palm he pounded my father's chest as if exhorting him to wake up. "Good man," he said. "Good journey."

Besides family—J. C. and his daughter Barbara, a smattering of other cousins—Ray was the only other person at the burial. The cemetery was beautiful that day, bluebonnets blooming in golden light. I said hello to Tracy and Zorah—mildly startled at the sight of my name etched into their dark granite stone—and laid a rose on my mother's grave.

Debra had asked me to say a eulogy, but I could only manage "He was the most decent man I have ever known."

As Philip had promised, an American flag draped the coffin. Two men in uniform played "Taps." Together, with silent, solemn precision, they folded the flag into a perfect triangle.

Then they turned to J. C., sitting graveside in his wheelchair, saluted, and presented the flag to him. He had not known that we had arranged this ritual, or that I had told Philip he was a combat veteran. He wept uncontrollably. After the service, Ray Tasuda, moving with obvious pain in his joints, knelt to hug J. C. "Ah, you stinking ol' Indian, goddammit, Ray, how I love ya," J. C. said, patting Ray's back.

— 12 —

From the roof of the Cotton County Courthouse, looking out past the flagpole toward the west, you can see the lots on which my grandparents' houses stood; the bare patch where Tracy's dog, Blackie, lies buried; the filling station, still operating just across the highway from Deenie's old yard; the Hart-Wyatt Funeral Home; the rodeo arena; the unused railroad depot; Sultan Park; the Electric Co-op's grain elevators. You can see the road to Lawton, where my parents drank and danced at Some Other Place (long gone). Since last year, what once formed downtown Walters is a blackened sea of ash—one weekend in July, an early morning fire took out the Cotton Bowl, the movie house my father burned to the ground (rebuilt, now wrecked again), and a couple of small businesses (a nail salon and a karate training center) across the street from the shell that housed Daugherty Hardware. A pair of pumpjacks, the size of sewing thimbles from the courthouse roof, pinpoint the golf course and the cemetery.

Graciously, Ruth Palmer, the county clerk's assistant, escorted me up top once I'd finished reading Tracy's papers. She appreciated my interest in the county's records. "We don't get many researchers," she said. "Especially researchers with a personal history in town. Our rooftop has the best view of the area. I think you'll like it."

I followed her up a back staircase through the attic and onto the roof. A church bell rang across town. *Tink-tink.* It was late afternoon. Most of the sky was blue, but in a bright quadrant where the sun perched low, a splash of light like a thin yellow tarp appeared to spread round Earth's slender curve. Near the western horizon, a blue, shimmering line, pumpjacks moved up and down, pulling my eye, and I saw, from miles away, tombstones, like black pepper flakes, dotting the green smudge of the graveyard.

I thanked Ruth Palmer for her kindness to me, for showing me this splendid panorama of my childhood acres, and then I hurried to my rental car, hoping to beat sundown to the cemetery so I could visit my parents' graves.

And that's how I came to be standing with Bobby Hearon on a small bluff where he'd just laid three white roses by his mother's headstone.

"Long time," he said to me. "Long, *long* time."

"Yes. Walters hasn't changed much. What's left of it."

He shook his head. "Sad business, that downtown fire."

"You remember Butterball?"

"Sure."

"Whatever happened to him?"

Bobby shrugged.

We sat on a marble bench by a mausoleum whose family name had long since worn away. Bobby told me he'd moved to Oklahoma in 2008. "I's wildcatting in West Texas and Mom was in a rest home there, but when she really started to fail, she wanted to come back here. Turns out, all this time, she's owned a few acres in Geronimo"—a small community on the road to Lawton. "Been in her family forever," Bobby said. Natalie had died in the nursing home where Deenie had suffered visions of the oil field woman. "She was always frail—that early breast cancer took so much out of her, but amazingly, she lived a long life," Bobby said. He neglected to mention the toll his *father* had taken on his mother, and I understood that one of our talk rules would be scant attention to the past. Bobby had built a small ranch on Natalie's land, he said. He was married. He had a son who'd served in Iraq and Afghanistan. He and his wife raised cattle and sheep. They donated hay to the Cotton County food bank every year so it could be sold to purchase canned goods. They volunteered for the local fire brigade.

He'd got the call last July when a *Walters Herald* paperboy making his morning deliveries noticed smoke in a weedy lot between the bowling alley and the nail salon next to the movie house. "A bunch of Kiowa teenagers had been squatting in that lot," Bobby said. "Intoxicated. Homeless. No jobs." He said they'd been doing crystal meth. It was the new scourge here in the Heartland, much worse than pot or alcohol had ever been. It was big business in places like Walters, ghost towns in the making, where oil and cotton had been largely depleted and many farms foreclosed.

Trash. The whole county—hell, the whole state of Oklahoma, to many Americans. Bobby didn't need to say it. "The reddest [i.e., the red-*neckiest*] state in the country," pundits called it on radio and TV. It was Exhibit A in Hillary Clinton's "basket of deplorables"— her 2016 campaign reference to "ignorant" conservative voters. A far cry from Great-Grandpa Andy's socialist haven. "Texas? Oklahoma?" so many of my Northwest friends have blurted over the years when I've told them where I was raised. "God, I'm sorry! It must have been awful to have been brought up in such a . . ."

Backwater. Hellhole. That's what they barely keep themselves from saying. Am I exaggerating? Only slightly.

That day in the Walters Cemetery, Bobby and I wisely avoided politics, made no spoken judgments of each other's appearance or choices in life. We agreed that time had seemed to get away from us, and neither of us could believe our parents were gone.

Darkness and the slight chill of summer dusk were beginning to swirl among the stones. Our moment together was coming to a close. There was no question that he would not invite me back to his place and that I would not suggest we get supper together somewhere in town. I regretted all that had gone unsaid between us, but it was clear that the time for saying had passed. We remained strangely important to each other—I sensed this was true of him as it was for me—but we did not belong in each other's present.

"So," I said, half-rising, trying to bring our conversation to a fitting end. "What happens to kids like that? Those Kiowa teenagers who set the town on fire? I can just imagine, if my grandfather was still the deputy sheriff—"

"We took them in," Bobby said. "Court wanted to throw them in the slammer, but we offered to let them help us work the ranch. Sort of a community service deal. And good for us, of course. I made an outbuilding, kind of a bunkhouse, for them to sleep in, and they're still mowing the back pastures. They're learning responsibility. Off the drugs, far as I can tell. Yeah. They're doing all right."

I shook his hand. "You're a good man, Bobby," I said.

He shrugged. "Take care y'self."

"You, too."

He started down the bluff, a stiff old man twisted by years of labor. I thought I heard him sniffle. My eyes burned. I headed toward the western fence where my parents lay. Since my father's funeral, a war veteran had been buried in a nearby plot. His family had raised a small steel pole by his grave marker, and the Stars and Stripes fluttered in the breeze.

Fireflies flitted around the headstones. "Mom, Dad," I said. I knelt and pressed my palms to the granite. It was still warm from the sun. "I wanted to come see you because I don't know when I'll ever get back here again."

A few days ago, I received by registered mail from a lawyer in Tulsa representing Citizen Energy LLC a notice that the company had applied for "pooling relief" involving two square miles of land to which I owned the mineral rights. ("Comes the Applicant, and prays that the drilling and spacing units be ordered," said the reverent notice.) The land was located north of Walters, in Dewey County, Oklahoma (Section 8, Township 17 North, Range 16 West). Citizen Energy LLC wished to "commence operations," drilling an oil and gas well. According to the notice, Debra and I owned these rights as living representatives of the Estate of Zorah Daugherty. Citizen Energy LLC was seeking to pool our interests with those of numerous other small owners so it could send a pipe horizontally under several parcels of property, without having to barter with dozens of families. A court hearing was scheduled two months hence in Tulsa.

Savvy friends in Oregon assured me it was a foregone conclusion that the court would grant Citizen Energy LLC its pooling relief. The company was obliged to notify me, but this meant very little. I didn't own enough to help or hinder the outfit, nor to benefit significantly if it did find oil and gas. Oklahoma had recently passed a law permitting horizontal wells to be drilled up to two miles long in non-shale rock layers. Counties in western Oklahoma were booming. Citizen Energy LLC, a self-proclaimed "leader in horizontal concepts," was fracking up a storm and making its investors rich. (Possibly, it was also causing multiple earthquakes in Dewey County, according to the newspapers.) As a two-bit mineral rights owner, I was more or less a legal impediment to the company's plans. Its lawyers had dispatched me by sending me this notice.

Why or when Zorah had bought these rights, I had no idea. Perhaps she had wanted to invest some of her upholstery earnings. Maybe my father had told her, years ago, that Dewey County would be a good long-term prospect. I will never know.

But I felt briefly, irrationally giddy, learning that I owned a little piece of Oklahoma. It wasn't enough to do anything with; I would never even see it . . . but it made me think of Bobby, his decision to move back to his family's land. It made me think of Debra saying once, "I can't believe what a good little housewife I've become. I confess, sometimes I miss my part of town." She meant "the other side of the tracks." "My life there didn't work out so good, but you know, sometimes I long for the old me."

The old me. Yes. The old me missed the bulky filing cabinets I'd sold to make more room in my study. I went to an office supply store and replaced them. I decided to ignore the Internet and resume my newspaper clipping. I had discovered that efficiency didn't matter to me as much as my former rhythms, the beat I moved to that helped my mind grasp certain mental music. I sat at my study desk, beneath my father's painting of the Artful Dodger, beneath a vintage concert poster—Woody Guthrie and Sis Cunningham—and a framed cover from *Song Hits* magazine. It offered "exclusively, the lyrics to Roy Orbison's 'Pretty Woman.'"

I clipped pieces about the Cherokee Nation in Oklahoma, how its "carefully tended heritage, traditions and memories, handed down through generations, are at risk, with so many families now being ruptured by drugs"; how the Cherokees had sued the "pharmacy chains" for flouting "federal drug-monitoring laws and allow[ing] prescription opioids to pour into Cherokee territory at some of the highest rates in the nation."

I clipped a piece from the *Texas Observer* called "Big Spring vs. Big Oil," which said a "fracking bonanza" had "overtaken parts of the Permian Basin," severely depleting the Ogallala Aquifer on which West Texas ranchers relied for cooking, drinking, laundering, and keeping their animals healthy. On the "human timescale," said the *Observer*, "the Ogallala will never recover."

This was the music I pursued: the metabolic strains and stresses of my region. Whenever I caught the groove, my mind danced; it moved under and above the ground I had walked all my life, imaginatively seeking, sometimes finding meaningful connections.

It was meaningful that my grandfather had once defended a Kiowa family against trouble from Jack Hearon, and that many years later Jack's grandson had rescued a troubled group of Kiowa kids. A lovely regional ballad.

But beneath the music I strained to hear, I caught another sound: my body's metabolics, thumping and clunking, burdened by my father's ailments. Joints, prostate, heart. My childhood asthma revived whenever the pollen counts in Oregon's grassy valleys grew too high. One morning I stood in my study trying not to despair as I considered hundreds of news clippings spilling randomly out of my cabinet drawers. It was likely that in a few years, my body's failings would overtake me before I had a chance to compose whatever I hoped to make of all this—some vast overture celebrating my family, my ancestors, my land.

Cotton County.

I realized I had probably already written my truest account of these things, and I had delivered it as a eulogy in the Walters Cemetery.

As I stood by my parents' graves at dusk, once Bobby had left me alone with the flag's whispers and the creaking of the nearby pump-jacks, I remembered the second time I'd seen my father cry. We were sitting with my mother in the hospital. She was sleeping in the bed. Her emphysema was worsening by the hour (like Tracy, she had been a smoker all her life). My father was trying to be strong for her, answering, "Everything'll be okay" whenever she asked, "What are we going to do?" But now he slumped in his chair, exhausted. Then he groaned. "Dad, what's the matter?" I asked. He leaned forward, rubbed his right ankle, and I saw it was swollen and blue, as big as an icepack. I knew he suffered from gout, but this looked worse than that. I called a nurse into the room. She said, "We'll get him down to emergency and have them take a look. It may be he's having circulatory problems." My mother was still asleep. The nurse assured me she'd look after her so I could accompany Dad to the ER. As we waited for an orderly to arrive with a wheelchair, Dad bowed his head and wept. This was the moment he'd feared. Maybe he'd feared it all his life, ever since he was a kid in Walters and first set eyes on my mother's soft, round face. She was leaving him, and he was powerless to stop her despite the promises he had made to her. He was failing, too. The steady movements of his mother's clock and the clock he had built, Gene Krupa's locked-in grooves—they couldn't help him now. Control of time was beyond him. His blood wasn't flowing. And his wife no longer had the energy to chase each breath.

A young man with a wheelchair knocked on the open door. I rose and touched my father's shoulder. "Dad," I said. "You ready?"

As we left the room, I turned to glance at my mother. She opened her eyes. "What are we going to do?" she said.

"It'll be okay," I said.

Her final slide had begun the day of Fern's funeral. Fern lived to be a hundred and two, dying finally of "general wore-out," said a doctor, in an assisted living facility on the south side of Lawton. The facility sat next to an Army-Navy Surplus Store, where one day, when I was twelve, I asked my mother to buy me a military jacket with stripes on the shoulders so I could look like the Beatles on the *Sgt. Pepper* album cover.

To her last breath, Fern was determined to be a fashion model. She wore bright Japanese kimonos over silk pajamas in her bed, got her wiry hair done every morning by a personal stylist brought to the home just for her. She had been born oil field trash, but by God, she was going to quit this vale of tears a proper woman. In the end, she wound up back in Walters, lying next to her mother—an indignity so fierce, Debra and I joked privately, that in her rage she swore she would take our mother with her. In reality, my mother caught a chill at Fern's graveside. It developed into pneumonia.

I was the "professor," the public speaker in the family, following Tracy. I was expected to deliver a eulogy at my mother's funeral, but I couldn't do it. As I sat in a rickety plastic folding chair in the grass, facing the coffin, my throat tightened. My eyes blurred. My sister sat beside me. I fumbled for her arm. She understood.

It was her finest moment. She rose with great dignity and—unused to speaking in front of formal gatherings—said in a firm, steady voice, "My mother was just a simple girl from Cotton County, Oklahoma. She only ever knew how to do things straightforwardly, with absolute sincerity, dedication, and honesty, and that's what made her special. I can't express how much I loved her." Whatever troubles she had caused our mother in her "wild" years, she more than made up for them that day.

Six months earlier, when Fern died, Mom had asked if I would say a few words at the service. "You do such a nice job when you speak," she said. "It would mean a lot to me."

"Of course," I said.

I think I knew it the instant she asked: my valediction would be my way of speaking to my parents past death. They wouldn't be able to hear me at their own burials. Fern's funeral was a practice run.

They thought so, too. On the morning of the service, my father circled Deenie's grave. Next to it, Fern's coffin rested on a metal contraption erected above a hole in the ground, waiting to be lowered. He bounced once or twice in the grass, his heels sinking half an inch into the earth. "I guess they'll put me right here," he said. I didn't know what to say to that. My mother took his arm. "Look, Gene," she said. She pointed to the small lake in the middle of the lot, the gentle bluff. "When we're finally at rest together, we'll have a lovely view, won't we?" He held her hand and she leaned into his shoulder.

They sat in folding chairs with the rest of the family, facing Fern's casket. I stood by the grave. I began with Willa Cather: "'The light air about me told me that the world ended here: only the ground and sun and sky were left, and if one went a little farther there would be only sun and sky, and one would float off into them, like the tawny hawks which sailed over our heads making slow shadows on the grass.' Like Cather's narrator," I said, "we have lived our lives on the 'gentle swell of unbroken prairie,' and it has made us the steadfast people we are." I said a few words in praise of Fern, and then I gazed directly at my mother and father. "And so we say, with gratitude and love, 'Well done, this life you have lived.'" My mother sniffled—crying, I thought, but now I think manifesting the first sign of the chill that would take her from us in another few months.

Now here I was again in the cemetery, talking to my dead parents and telling them I didn't know when I'd ever get back to Oklahoma. Dusk purpled the west; a cardinal lifted from the limbs of an oak over by the lake. People in stories I'd heard all my life lay scattered at my feet: Tracy and Zorah, Deenie and Pop, Bud and Bill, cousin Philip (his lost glass eye tucked deep into black sediment), Jack and Bob Hearon, Natalie, the Tasudas.

The stories were only stories now, a sad, fading music.

After we'd buried my father, Debra had told me, "We're orphans now."

"Not technically," I said.

"*Don't* get technical with me. We're orphans."

"Okay, we're orphans," I said.

I sat in the grass, facing my parents' names. The pumpjacks moaned behind me. The first evening stars appeared. I searched among them—I really *did* search, thinking that if I saw a meteor, it would be a spiritual sign. My parents were watching me from above. I didn't really believe this. I'd never become the good Catholic Aunt Barbara thought I would be; my temperament, my early studies of astronomy, my skeptical bent of mind excluded religion as a form of comfort. But I entertained the thought because all I had left were stories.

Stories throughout history, ancient art and myths, had extolled the underworld, not just as a place of terror (filled with unimaginable monsters, like fifty-foot frogs!), but also as a realm where a seeker could find wisdom and commune with the dead. This option was lost to me, too. If I drilled into the underworld, I'd find only minerals, shale, aquifers, oil and gas. My parents' yellowed bones.

The ground and the sky were no help. The past was no help. From now on, grief would define this place for me, and everything that had ever occurred in it.

But the moment I thought this, the moment I felt the truth of it seep into my body, I felt another truth: you don't mourn trash, you mourn what matters to you. And what matters, *matters*.

It was the best I could come up with.

I stood and brushed the grass from my pants. A breeze excited the flag above me. I gazed across the graveyard, mourning everyone, across the bluff and the lake, mourning the grass and the water, mourning the soil. I gazed down the road, out past the cemetery gate, across the dark prairie, as the lights came on in Cotton County.

The Unearthly Archives

—September 1, 2018, to April 18, 2019

So far as we can see . . . some record of the life on earth is laid up in some unearthly archives, and . . . under some circumstances this record is accessible to the minds of the living.

—*Saturday Review*

The question of immortality is of its nature not a scholarly question. It is a question welling up from the interior which the subject must put to itself as it becomes conscious of itself.

—Søren Kierkegaard, *Concluding Unscientific Postscript*

PART ONE
James's Ghosts

– 1 –

In my junior year of college at SMU in 1975, in a seminar I took on the writings of William and Henry James, I wrote my final paper on William's *The Will to Believe*. He argued that on matters resistant to intellectual analysis, our passionate, emotional natures are forced to decide. He said our beliefs manifest the paths we take. I don't remember whether I agreed with James—and anyway, who was I to question his thinking? The professor gave me an A on the paper but offered no comments on the points I raised. His only remark, scrawled at the bottom of the last page, was, "You write better than you think."

I wasn't sure if he meant by this that my writing skills were finer than I thought they were or if he was warning me that the quality of my thoughts didn't match my ability to compose a sentence. I suspected the latter, but I didn't ask him. The semester had ended, and I didn't see him again.

At the time, the seminar's most valuable lesson for me lay outside the classroom. Lugging heavy, important-looking books around campus occasionally attracted the attention of an interesting girl. I continued my acquaintance with the James family, clutching their books in the campus lunchroom, in coffeehouses, and around the dorm.

In my senior year, the volume that drew the most comment perched beneath my arm was not *Society the Redeemed Form of Man*, *The Varieties of Religious Experience*, or *The Turn of the Screw*. It was Julian Jaynes's *The Origin of Consciousness in the Breakdown of the Bicameral Mind*. "Oh, you're reading *that*, are you?" a comely

Tri-Delt exclaimed to me one day outside a noisy classroom. "How fascinating!"

Unfortunately, her brief awareness of me amounted to nothing, just as little came of Jaynes's book, which has now been largely dismissed by scientists. I forget how I'd heard about it. Jaynes was a psychologist who argued that what we call consciousness emerged in human beings about three thousand years ago, when a series of global disasters—among them, tumultuous wars and the volcanic eruption of Thera on the Greek island of Santorini—forced the sudden integration of the brain's two hemispheres, so individuals would be better suited for survival. Prior to that time, Jaynes said, the brain was "bicameral," loosely joined, its left and right hemispheres and their various functions operating at cross-purposes. The inner voice we hear, the voice we sometimes call the self, emanating from the murky right hemisphere, struck the more alert areas of our ancestors' brains as a detached presence—the speech of a god. As proof of this, Jaynes cited the *Iliad* (circa 769–710 B.C.). In Homer's account of the Trojan War, the characters, lacking inner lives, are manipulated like cheap pawns by the gods. For instance, the great warrior Achilles wonders whether or not he should kill Agamemnon, but he does not act until ordered to do so by the goddess Athena. Jaynes points out that Achilles's hesitations are described as physiological reactions rather than mental deliberations—the fighter's gut churns. Finally he hears Athena's voice, a hallucination swimming up from his right brain, according to Jaynes. Only then does he perform his soldierly duty.

With the subsequent development in world literatures of characters' rich inner lives, wrestling with moral conundrums, we see the full, cooperative functioning of the brain's many facets, and the appearance of a sense of self, or consciousness.

None of my teachers had assigned me to read Jaynes's book. Somehow, I came to it on my own, and somehow, even without the philosophical or scientific background to unpack Jaynes's ideas, I doubted the argument's thrust.

I lived off campus in those days, in a small apartment near a noisy North Texas freeway. At night, the rumbles of produce trucks, the hissing of brakes, broke my concentration when I tried to read in bed. If I couldn't regain my focus, I'd set the book aside, grab a pair of drumsticks, and perform mindless paradiddles on my practice pad (playing an actual drum would have gotten me evicted for disturbing the neighbors). Sometimes on mild afternoons, I'd sit in the tiny courtyard outside my apartment, beneath the black oak tree in which honeybees swarmed in the spring, marching through Jaynes's long paragraphs.

It took me a while to understand why the book nagged at me, but finally I concluded that the flaw in Jaynes's map of consciousness lay in his misconception of literary history. When Homer described Achilles's doubts about killing Agamemnon as gut-wrenching, wasn't that just a metaphor for mental agitation rather than a literal distinction between mind and body functions? Metaphor was clearly part of Homer's literary arsenal. Later, when fictional characters fully assumed complex inner lives, especially in the period between the eighteenth and twentieth centuries, wasn't that a sign of growing artistic sophistication through long familiarity with the medium? Novelists refined third-person limited point of view the way painters gradually perfected pictorial perspective.

The bees in my little yard, working together in a manner that would have pleased William James's father, a fierce proponent of collective action, moved in efficient circles in the budding oak limbs, a solid, melded unit. It's strange how vividly I remember those bees. I recall being both aware and unaware of their flight patterns while I read. Their buzzing lulled me, a musical drone beneath the voice in my head, enhancing my contemplative mood—the experience was as soothing as practicing paradiddles. I wondered why. A fusing of self and world? I see now how mired I was in the weeds of my obsessions.

Despite my disappointments with Jaynes, he *had* articulated the problem I'd been chasing ever since reading *The Will to Believe:* the difficulty of using the self to search for the self. In a witticism worthy of Mark Twain, Jaynes said the challenge was like using a flashlight to look for darkness.

My seminar teacher's comment — "You write better than you think" — stayed with me, and I began to consider what and how I'd learned through the years, how my writing had changed as I matured. I could trace my developing consciousness, my personal sense of self, through my youthful scratchings.

Before I moved to Dallas to study at SMU, I loved to write stories. Essays and fiction. I had few models for my ambitions. My hometown, Midland, Texas, a large windbreak in the middle of a tumbleweed desert, was not an especially bookish place. My first concentrated writing took the form of a daily diary. I started it in my early teens. Now when I reread its entries, I cringe at the boy exposed there: his shallow inner life makes the characters in the *Iliad* seem positively baroque. The range of concerns is shockingly narrow: expressions of longing for a girl with whom I was obsessed at the time, lists of rock and roll songs whose drum parts I was trying to learn, and complaints of exhaustion after staying up all night to watch the stars. Along with drumming, astronomy was my major pursuit back then. There was little beauty in the terrain of the petroleum-rich Permian Basin, spiked in every direction with steaming refinery spires, so my eye was naturally drawn to the sky.

Narcissism colors each passage in the diary. The self was my subject, but I had no self to speak of.

A developmental turn is apparent when, after several repetitive entries, the diary gives way to an observation journal recording, complete with hand drawings, glimpses of Jupiter and three of its moons. I'd aimed my 2.4-inch Sears-Roebuck refracting telescope just past the power line crossing my parents' back yard ("At approx. 12:30 A.M. CST — 6:30 UT — 4th moon became visible. It appeared from behind Jupiter's disc. Planet's bands invisible due to moonlight"). I noted the Martian polar caps — attempting to sketch ice in the notebook gave me no end of trouble—and two comets gracing West Texas's night skies in the spring of 1970, Tago-Saro-Kosaka ("Position in the sky: directly southwest, approx. 1 h, 20 m, 5 degrees. Magnitude: approx. 4") and Comet Bennett ("Speed rapid, passing just north of Pegasus").

Unconsciously, my focus had shifted from expressing my thin, bare self to enriching it by taking in more of my surroundings. By the end of that year, I had secured my first publication, in *Sky and Telescope* magazine—an enhanced reproduction of one of my night-sky drawings. It was accompanied by a description on the magazine's "Amateur Page" of the August 1970 Perseid meteor shower: "On August 12th at 8:23 Universal time, T. Daugherty and three others at Midland, Texas, saw a magnitude –10 Perseid that exploded 10 degrees above the northern horizon, leaving a white train that persisted for 1½ minutes. At 9:59 UT, these amateurs saw a second bolide, nearly as bright."

Years would pass before my second publication—again, improbably, in a science journal, the *Annals of Allergy*. When I got to SMU in the fall of 1973, I enrolled in a poetry-writing course. By happenstance, one of my classmates, a sweet elderly gentleman who was auditing the course, had been my childhood lung specialist. I suffered from severe asthma as a kid. Twice a year, my parents drove me to Dallas for treatments with this man. These days, he was bearded and bald—resembling the busts of Virgil I saw in art history books. In class, when we recognized our connection, he convinced me to write a poem about an asthmatic's experience of the world, my terror of breathlessness. A short time later, in a journal "devoted to the interests of the practicing allergist," this notice appeared: "The following poem was read recently by the young poet, Tracy Daugherty, in an advanced poetry workshop at Southern Methodist University and was sent . . . with a note from Dr. Salmon R. Halpern of Dallas, Texas, who remembered Tracy when he was a patient of his at five years of age. Dr. Halpern wrote: 'In my forty years of practice I have never seen or heard of a poem about asthma written by an asthmatic . . . This poem beautifully describes the feelings of an asthmatic child.'"

The poem was not particularly distinguished, and I won't reprint it here. What interests me about it now is the extra layering of self it represents over and above my earlier writings.

The diary was pure indulgence; the observation journal was a form of detached witness; the poem was self-awareness in search of its links to shared human experience. Consciousness becoming conscious of itself.

But the question remained—for *all* of us, even Julian Jaynes, after so many centuries of written history: what *was* consciousness?

Recently, the question gained new urgency for me, prompting these memories of my early writing and my college readings on the subject. Despite my first appearances in print, I am not and never have been a scientist, so my approach to researching the question has been highly personal and idiosyncratic.

After a pair of medical scares in my forties and fifties (double bypass heart surgery and surgery to remove prostate cancer), I began living each day with a keener-than-ever awareness of mortality. And then, as I was about to turn sixty, the "massacre" of aging commenced, to paraphrase the novelist Philip Roth. Within two years, both of my parents died, and so did my beloved mother-in-law. Three of my favorite old teachers left us. Concurrently, nearly half a dozen dear friends were diagnosed with various maladies. One by one, in a stunningly short time, these precious folks passed unexpectedly from life.

It is a cliché to say I was left reeling by wave after wave of grief, but engulfed by so much sorrow, the mind goes limp. Weeping, it is almost impossible, and probably obscene, in any case, to reach for richer expression.

I retired early from the position I'd held for nearly thirty years as a teacher of writing and literature at Oregon State University.

I believed I could no longer serve my students well in light of the "wreck" I'd become, "reduced from a state of firm, vigorous, joyful manhood to one of almost helpless infancy," as Henry James Sr. had written, citing an emotional collapse he'd experienced.

Following my parents' deaths, while preparing to sell their house and disperse their goods, I rediscovered, in my mother's bedroom closet, my copies of *Sky and Telescope* and the *Annals of Allergy*. I found my old diary and my observation journals. My mother had saved them all. It struck me, sitting inside that cluttered space: until now, my memories had heft because they weren't my memories alone. In my observation journal, in a sketch I'd made of Comet Bennett, I'd included a dark square in the left corner at the bottom of the page: "The dark square represents the roof of our house." Now, only I was left to remember that house, the brief instant in time when I stood in my family's back yard watching the sparkling visitor while my mother and father slept peacefully beneath the dark square.

The immense weight of what a person loses when she dies had never been clearer to me. Another old cliché: watching an individual perish is like watching a library burn to the ground. When physical life departs, it drags along with it—to oblivion?—the mind's intangible rhythms, records, impressions, arguably life's most essential elements. And the living, whose minds embraced those elements along with the now-dead, feel a sudden loss of gravity, as if the intangibles (*my mother's memory of me preparing my telescope for a night of comet watching*) were as physical as the flexing of a muscle.

The world's literatures, from Shakespeare's sonnets to Walt Whitman's celebratory songs, attest to the paradox: much of the urgency of sexual pleasure lies in grief. The body's knowledge that bliss is fleeting heightens the bittersweet beauty of the moment. Precious sadness. Early in our marriage, I was surprised when my wife, Marjorie, a fellow writer and lover of literature, sometimes cried after intimacy, grieving the loss of our bond in advance. The inevitable passing away of one lover, leaving the other behind, the loss to body and mind, was unbearable to her. It became especially so in our period of mourning our parents and friends.

The mourning didn't end. Not for me. People I knew who'd lost loved ones assured me, "I feel their presence every day. Their spirits are still with me." No. For me, these absences were screaming voids, ripping wider every day. I'd been raised in the Methodist church, raised to believe in life after death, but church teachings couldn't survive the chill of *nothing*. In the past, I'd asked Margie, who is Jewish, what she believed. She said the afterlife had never been a topic of concern, at least not in her family. For her, Judaism was a history of homelessness in the world and—from that perspective—of offering empathy to others, performing good works on earth. Eternity would take care of itself.

Following my surgeries, I firmly believed I'd enter eternity first, long before Margie passed away. And that was good, I thought. She had a healthier response to grief than I did. Grief paralyzed me. Margie continued to push forward, eyeing the pleasures still available to her, seeking fresh and joyous experiences.

Her mother, a skilled amateur organist, had always hoped that Margie would develop her innate musical ability. Her ear was a miracle. Play her a phrase on a Wurlitzer, and immediately she'd enter the melody's structure, playing it back to you and following it out wherever it could go. After her mother died, Margie took up Celtic guitar playing with a passion, in part to cope with her grief, but also as a way of honoring her mother's wish. She practiced every day, took lessons several times a week, and joined weekly sessions of Irish and Scottish music, featuring fiddlers, flute players, and bouzouki men, in private homes and pubs around our town. (She'd fallen in love with Scotland after several trips there over the years, starting when she was twelve years old, traveling with her parents, extending to college, and then later to frequent getaways with me.)

I'd long urged her to discover the thrill of playing music with others, based on my experiences performing in raggedy garage bands over the years. "There aren't many pleasures in life as great as those moments when a group of musicians really click together, when their bodies and whatever they're hearing in their heads lock into unison," I'd told her. But I'd not been able to rekindle this pleasure since the recent spate of deaths.

Hoping to help, Margie bought me a bodhran, an Irish handheld frame drum, and asked me to accompany her on jigs and reels. ("It's your heritage!" she said. O'Dochertaigh was in fact my family's Gaelic name, before our seventeenth-century ancestors immigrated to the New World from Donegal, Ireland.) Sometimes I did play tunes with her. But mostly I went to local sessions just to watch her perform with others, blissfully transported by the music. Occasionally, her beaming face gave me vicarious comfort in spite of myself.

In the summer of 2018, she enrolled in a music camp called Fiddle Tunes, to be held in Port Townsend, Washington. There, for seven days, she'd be able to take guitar lessons and jam with musicians from all over the country. I went with her, slipping my tipper—the stick—into my back pocket and slinging the bodhran across my shoulder, hoping to join in some jams, improve my skill with the instrument, and maybe shed some of my grief in the excitement of communing with others.

We left on an unusually chilly late June morning. Ice crystals—a rime of frost—coated the windshield of our car. Myth-minded, and burdened by so much grieving, Margie chose to see clearing the glass as an act of *breaking free*.

Port Townsend, a deep-harbor port nestled into the northeastern tip of the Olympic Peninsula at the roiling crosscurrents of Admiralty Inlet and the Strait of San Juan de Fuca, boasts one of the oldest and best-preserved downtown districts on the West Coast. A building boom in the 1880s, sparked by shipments of lumber culled from the peninsula's forests, came to an abrupt halt in 1890 when the railroad linking Port Townsend to Portland, Oregon, went bankrupt. Because the economic crash was so sudden and no new industries popped up to fix it, most of the Victorian-era buildings remained in place downtown, neglected and forgotten until renovated for tourism. As a result, Port Townsend lays claim to a rich trove of ghost stories. Local contractors entertain pub patrons with tales of poltergeists stealing tools during upgrades of old Queen Anne mansions on the harbor front — "The spirits don't like change," they say. The Palace Hotel downtown, built in 1889, is allegedly a center of paranormal activity. A large painted portrait of the "Lady in Blue" hangs atop a staircase inside — a mysterious woman said to have been a madam in a brothel operating in the hotel as late as the 1930s. Her spirit now haunts the corridors.

Fiddle Tunes convened in an old military installation turned into a public park. It's called Fort Worden. Originally constructed between 1898 and 1920, it was established on Admiralty Inlet to defend Puget Sound in the event of an attack on the American mainland. Its gun batteries were removed in World War I to be used in the fighting in Europe. Today, its old balloon hangar has been converted into a performance space. The former officers' quarters serve as meeting rooms, lecture halls, and a tavern. The large two-story wooden structures where soldiers once slept have become dormitories for students attending various educational programs throughout the year. A military graveyard on the grounds, as well as a complex of dank concrete bunkers, provides fertile soil for ghost tales. Apparently, misty blue apparitions of maimed and moaning men have been sighted by many visitors to the park.

Port Townsend struck me as a hub of grief, delicately lovely and fragile, sweetly melancholy. What else were these spook tales but elegiac expressions of longing for the past?

As it turned out, Margie and I had a private ghost to contend with. We rented an old cottage for the week, overlooking a marina just east of downtown, at a spot called Port Hudson. Built in 1936, it once housed boat pilots who, in the years before seacoasts were accurately charted, would board ships entering the local waters and guide them safely through Puget Sound. These days, the cottage is privately owned and rented to tourists.

Margie and I had a friend, a poet and a writer, who a few years earlier had rented the Pilot's House and composed much of the first draft of a novel in a small bedroom there. She was one of the dear ones who had recently died.

We arrived in Port Townsend late one afternoon, beneath a daylight moon, and unloaded our luggage and Margie's guitar from the car. The path from the front gate to the house's door was lined with crushed oyster shells. The porch overlooked sailboats rocking gently in the marina, just a few steps away. A spindly young deer, unafraid of us, approached an apple tree growing wild on the south side of the cottage. The deer stretched its neck into the limbs, searching for fruit and unleashing a small swirl of bees. Inside the house, old sea charts and drawings of Popeye the Sailor Man covered the walls. Wooden shelves displayed old sextants, compasses, pairs of binoculars. I set our bags in the bedroom where our friend had written her novel. A soft white hand-sewn quilt lay across the bed in which she'd worked late into cold, watery nights. I closed my eyes and concentrated, wondering if I might feel her presence, some breath, some residue of her time there. Nothing.

Right away we discovered that the music camp was as hierarchal as the rows of spirits seated in Dante's Empyrean. There were pure saints, lesser souls, and those who had barely slipped into heaven.

In the last few years, ever since my surgeries, I'd carried with me wherever I traveled a copy of Dante's *Divine Comedy*, and I had it with me in Port Townsend. I was constantly rereading it, studying it, teasing out its references for my own pleasure. I'd always loved its astronomical descriptions, ever since I'd encountered the poem in college. I admired the fact that, alone among the world's literatures (including the Bible, the Koran, and the Upanishads, if you got right down to it), it was epic poetry based not on military matters, but solidly on the spiritual. And I suppose that, after my illnesses, I liked using the verses to meditate on . . . not the afterlife, exactly, but *last things* (though I didn't quite admit this to myself).

At Fiddle Tunes, the pure saints were, of course, the fiddlers. Generally, in Irish and Scottish music, the fiddle not only carries a song's melody, it sets the rhythm as well. When pipers aren't present, the fiddle is all—in fiddlers' minds, in any case. Other instruments—flutes, accordions, guitars—are secondary, but they have their place, as long as the instrumentalists know their roles. Margie, still learning, still developing her chops on guitar, was happy to be a backup player, and the fiddlers welcomed her into the jams.

At music camp, drummers were not saints. They didn't even rise to the level of sorry beggars saved by grace. They were freaks. Instantly, it was apparent to me that most of the players, especially the fiddlers, hated the bodhran—disdained its very concept. The bodhran, though old and often used in the fields (perhaps as a chaff-sorting device as well as a drum), was not a common instrument in Irish songs as they have come to us. Its dynamic range was limited; its contributions were superfluous, given the innately rhythmic nature of most Celtic melodies. Moreover, it was clear that the experienced players had encountered, in the past, raucous drummers who hadn't bothered to learn the traditions: they smacked the thing like head-banging rockers.

All my life I'd endured drummer jokes: "Drummers are people who like to hang out with musicians!" "What do you call a drummer without a girlfriend? Homeless!"

But the viciousness reserved for bodhran players shocked me. "Damn noisemakers: all they do is whack the goat" (goatskin heads distinguished most fine drums). "What's the best way to play a bodhran? With a penknife."

(I remembered a pub Margie and I had visited once in Edinburgh. Sandy Bells. In one of its windows a bodhran was lodged, a thick red line painted across its head: "No Drums!")

The dark looks I got whenever I approached a jam circle carrying the drum on my back warned me to keep it firmly packed away inside its black cloth case. Margie tried to encourage me, but I wasn't going to press my luck with these strangers. I'd stand behind the circle, melting into the shadows, watching her join in. Or I'd walk around the grounds of Fort Worden, looking for the first evening stars. Moonlight whitened the dormitory windows. The reflections could have been flitting spirits, watching us from the topmost floors.

Sometimes I'd return to the cottage early while Margie was still playing. One night I fell asleep in a rocking chair on the wooden porch, lulled by the creak of the sailboats' riggings. I dreamed that I was sitting in the dark somewhere and I was swaying, as if I'd boarded one of the boats, but I didn't know where I was, and I couldn't see anything. I felt a chill and then a gradual warming. The smell of sage or something like it rose on mild air currents. And then one of my buddies who'd recently died, a fellow named Ehud, was sitting next to me. We said hello. I asked him how he was. He shrugged. Silence. Not unpleasant. We sat together "as nobody talking with nobody," in the words of Henry James. (In his story "The Great Good Place," two strangers who feel as if they're brothers find themselves mysteriously transported to an indistinct dream-place— a vast sea of consciousness.)

I said, "I don't know if this is real."

Ehud smiled. "It's real," he said.

I woke with a start in the rocking chair. In that groggy interval between sleep and full alertness, I felt certain he hadn't come to me, but I had traveled instead—gone some uncharted distance to wherever he was.

I stood and walked a little, down a cobblestone path into the historic downtown district, just behind the cottage. The shops were closed. I could imagine trolley cars clattering along the streets. The old nineteenth-century brick walls, some still featuring faded ads

painted on their sides—pictures of soda bottles and bottles of elix-
irs—transported me into an indeterminate time. I felt unbalanced,
and not just because the road was dark and uneven: stumbling,
uncertain, as if I didn't quite belong in the world.

This detached sensation, resembling the onset of fever, persisted
the following morning. It deepened, like a mild case of vertigo,
and intensified once Margie and I arrived back at Fort Worden for
the day. My bodhran, tucked in its black case across my shoulder,
served as a shield of invisibility. The moment the fiddlers saw it,
they glanced quickly away from me, as though they hadn't noticed
me or as if I wasn't really there. I stood at the back of a room in
the late morning, undetected, as Margie took a guitar lesson with a
dozen other players. In the evening I stood aside, unnoticed, as a jam
circle formed in an open field and Margie, clearly worrying about
me, took a spot in the middle of the group. I gave her an encouraging smile. Soon, buoyed by the music, she was beaming, strumming
rapidly, calling upon her muscle memory.

The pleasure she was getting, *clicking* with other musicians,
warmed me. My vertigo blurred—again, not unpleasantly—into
what I can only describe as a stark awareness of *Margie without me.*

If, as I suspected, I'd enter eternity first; if, in my dream the night
before, I'd met my pal (despite continuing doubts about an afterlife,
apparently I'd developed William James's "will to believe"), perhaps now I was being offered a glimpse of the future.

Margie without me. It wasn't so bad, I thought.

This is what she would do. These were the people with whom
she would surround herself. They would sustain her. She'd be
okay. Music would be her solace and her blessing. It would lift her
through her grief.

And maybe . . . maybe this is what *I* would do: stand silently,
invisibly, to the side, watching her face flush with joy.

Relief pulsed through me, a swift, rhythmic wave like the hop-
skip of a jig. My wife's lovely hand stroked the strings of her gui-

tar. I settled back on the grass in the night's moonlit shadows. Stars bobbed in thinning clouds. I was practicing to be a ghost.

— 2 —

Mornings at the cottage were always pleasant and quiet. I'd lie comfortably in bed next to Margie before I'd come fully awake, hearing the soft approach of the deer just outside our window, the drone of the bees. Down the short hallway, in the other bedroom where our late friend had worked on her novel, pops and creaks sounded occasionally, but that was only the sunlight, slanting through lace curtains, warming the honey-brown wood of the bedframe and the wood in the walls, loosening the pent-up aches and groans of the old house.

I'd take a cup of coffee to the rocker on the porch where I'd dreamed of Ehud. He was a writer and a former colleague at Oregon State University. In late December 1988, he and I had begun a conversation. He was looking for a job, and I was a member of the school's hiring committee. The committee had settled into a New Orleans hotel suite at an academic conference to interview job candidates. By the third day, the hiring team was a little punchy, having heard and said the same things over and over. Ehud arrived for his appointment and knocked on the door. I answered it. In those days he was a robust fellow: big shoulders, long black hair, a full beard. A confident stance, a little cocky. Later I learned he liked to joke that he was a gay young swain. And he was.

We shook hands, and I told him, honestly, that I had just read and loved his first book, a short story collection. He told me that after three days of interviews, he could say, honestly, that I was the first person he'd met who'd actually read his book. He came into the room, and from that point on, I don't remember anything about the formal interview except the (mistaken) impression that everyone else had left the room. Ehud and I sat face to face, locked in an intense discussion. We talked about his writing, then about writing in general. We imagined building a graduate program together. Wouldn't that be amazing, we said. We began a conversation that day, and for just shy of the next thirty years, we didn't stop.

As the decades passed, our talk, rooted always in our mutual love of literature and language, expanded to include our hopes and terrors, our thoughts about teaching, our love for our wives. He became the brother I never had. We shared many buoyant occasions—Ehud loved a good time—but even the lightest conversation with him was fierce, often profound, an excavation to the heart of whatever was going on in his life and whatever was happening in mine. I never came away from a talk with Ehud without thinking I had learned something essential about what it means to be engaged with others on the planet.

I realize now that part of what we explored together was that tricky old puzzle, the nature of consciousness. He loved nothing more than direct and meaningful communication, but he also felt that, due to people's individual complexities, their interiority, their different backgrounds and upbringings, direct and meaningful communication was virtually impossible. We were all frozen inside our heads.

This contradiction—the desire to *really* talk and the crushing difficulty of it—formed a graceful tension in him, and it made every face-to-face encounter with him quietly moving. He wasn't going to let the challenges of communicating—especially with those he loved—stop him from trying.

Ehud was raised Jewish. Along with Margie, he instructed me in the relentless textual questioning at the center of so much Jewish learning, the sifting of language's many layers. The various drafts of his stories were records of the most essential human striving to strip away everything extraneous, everything that blocks our ability to speak to one another usefully.

Inevitable in any prolonged conversation between two friends is the work of confronting mortality. In 1999, when I had my heart surgery, Margie and Ehud stayed with me. With Ehud sitting on my bed and holding my hand one afternoon, I was finally able to cry and talk about my confusion and fear.

And then he was diagnosed with leukemia. Ever the questioner, he refused to countenance the easy, familiar phrases, "battling cancer," "bravely fighting the odds." To him, this was sloppy language; it didn't reflect his daily experience. His illness was not external to him. It was not a foreign invader. It was part of his body, causing changes as natural in their progression as *anyone's* aging process, the whitening of his beard, the thinning of his shoulders. This did not mean he would passively accept his circumstances. He insisted on observing himself with rigor, not only to understand impending death, but to communicate to the rest of us this baffling aspect of our shared humanity.

One time he told me he felt he was in the palm of a giant hand, and the fingers were slowly closing. Over time, he felt all of the emotions any of us would feel, *will* feel, in that condition—fear, anger, weariness—but above all, I think he felt fascination.

Our talk continued in various locales up and down Oregon's Willamette Valley, often now in hospital rooms and doctors' offices. One of his favorite spots was a grungy little bar in Portland, around the corner from the Benson Hotel downtown. The Tugboat. It was like the cabin of a trawler wrenching apart at night in a sea storm, but Ehud loved it. Every time we went there, one of us brought a copy of *The Complete Poems of Emily Dickinson*, a big book that nevertheless felt light. While the rest of the bar crowd was shouting or listening to music or watching sports on television, we'd sit in a dim corner reading Emily aloud, parsing her syntax, studying her imagery, trying to figure out how the hell she conveyed what she did. It was a high-level seminar; we were still teaching each other after all those years. We'd pause on Emily's description of a hummingbird in flight: "A route of evanescence." *A route of evanescence.* Isn't that amazing, we'd say. Isn't that amazing?

Until he no longer had the mental or physical strength, Ehud worked on a novel based on his family's history. He called it *The Land and the Days.*

The last time I saw him alive, he was hooked to machines in an ICU. Margie and I walked into the room. I took Ehud's hand, as I had grasped it in New Orleans so many years ago. He was weak, but he made a little joke: he said he was sorry he was no longer the gay young swain he'd once been. Soon it became hard for him to breathe. The nurses placed an oxygen mask on his face. He had to communicate with us—fittingly enough—by writing, using a little erase board. The last thing he wrote to me was "We'll talk again." I remember thinking I hope so, brother. I hope so.

Back at Fort Worden for the day, Margie headed off to a guitar lesson. I did my ghost-drift among the old buildings and along the blue inlet. The bank was thick with white dust from crumbled old oyster shells. "We tarried by the seashore, like those / who think about the way [to salvation] and in their hearts go on— / while still their bodies linger," Dante wrote in the second canto of *Purgatorio,* puzzling over the split between body and soul. I had reread that canto just that morning, over coffee. It seemed appropriate to the setting. In it, Dante, guided by the spirit of his poet-mentor Virgil, begins his climb up the purgatorial mountain, where dead souls must finish their penance before entering paradise. Near the shore at the foot of the mountain, he encounters a spirit who sings a beautiful love song. Dante knows he shouldn't tarry to listen—love and music are earthly concerns to be shunned in pursuit of heaven—but he is enchanted by both the memory of physical love and the loveliness of the melody. Who could let them go, if given a choice? Not even Dante. He has to be prompted to move by a scolding angel-guardian.

I stood for a while by the water, gazing at a lighthouse in the inlet, listening to the distant strains of fiddles and flutes floating among the trees. The setting reminded me: William James had once been a skilled amateur painter, with a delicate sensitivity to light. "The broad sky and sea are whanging with the mellow light . . . [it] is shrieking," he'd written of a scene he was trying to capture on canvas. As a young man, he'd taken art lessons from a New England painter whose studio overlooked a Jewish burying ground.

Ehud had refused a traditional Jewish funeral—as an adult, he'd rebelled against his father's Orthodox teachings, losing all patience with religious rituals. Still, bowing to custom, he *did* ask to be buried in a simple pine box in a raw hole in the ground in a sweet, mostly neglected cemetery just outside of town. I thought this was partly his way of forcing his mourners to face reality. But on the morning of the funeral, a gray day with a single streak of sunlight piercing a cloud, a magnificent golden cougar stood at the edge of the graveyard, patiently watching Ehud's family and friends gather round the coffin. His widow told us that a cougar had appeared behind their yard on one of Ehud's last nights at home, and they'd watched it together, reverently. She was convinced that the animal in the meadow, standing still just beyond the graves, was Ehud's spirit, come to bless us.

In the early afternoon, I followed Margie into a big, drafty room with dirty windows and rippled oak floors, scuffed into splinters. Band Lab was about to begin. The idea was this: a teacher would take a group of beginning and intermediate players and whip them into shape for a public performance by the end of the week—three or four tunes. Dozens of fiddlers had gathered in the room, along with several guitarists and other instrumentalists. The teacher's name was Win Horan. Classically trained at the New England Conservatory, she had made her name as an exceptional Celtic fiddler, touring the world with a band called Solas. She was charming, funny, and energetic, bouncing on the balls of her feet as she bowed her instrument, reaching to adjust the cloth headband tightened round her wild, springy hair. What she *wasn't* was an experienced teacher.

She frittered away the first hour chattering about her touring schedule, about constantly losing her car keys, about craving extra cups of coffee. Whispers drifted through the room: how was this group *ever* going to be ready in just a few days?

After that first hour, sitting around with nothing to do, I knelt by Margie's chair, wished her luck for the day, and told her I was heading back to the cottage. "You okay?" she asked. I squeezed her arm.

Across the grounds, I walked unnoticed among groups of chatting fiddlers. As I approached the fort's entrance, heading for the road to Port Hudson, I glanced up at a dormitory window. Hummingbirds fluttered among dark green honeysuckle vines climbing the wooden walls. A ray of reflected sunlight wisped across the glass, a skittery, ephemeral presence.

On my way to the cottage, I detoured through the historic downtown along a pitted cobbled road—delving into the past: a quaint stone water fountain, tall leaded windows, ornamented oak arches flanking ancient doorways. Did these objects retain fading energies in the fibers of their wood or in swirls of sandy blue glass, traces of touches from the fingers of the dead, warmth from decades-old sunlight?

Ehud remained powerfully on my mind. I thought once more of that Henry James story "The Great Good Place": two men talking in what seems to be an "absence of everything"—"there [is] nothing now to time."

"The thing [is] to find [the truth]!" one man says to the other.

"Ah, [isn't] it?" the second fellow answers. "And when I think . . . of all the people who haven't and who never will!"

"Every man must arrive by himself . . . We're brothers here for the time, as in a great monastery . . . but we must have first got here as we can . . ."

"Ah, don't speak as if we were dead!"

The first talker pauses. He confesses, "I shan't mind death if it's like this."

And then, together, they watch "the sweet wide picture darken into tepid night."

More than the fiddlers, grief had prompted my withdrawal from Fiddle Tunes. I knew this. My sadness was like a large barnacle crusting the hull of a boat. I missed my buddy's smile. My parents' voices. For months, I'd tried to console myself: "Okay, if you can't accept the church's view of life after death, if you don't believe you'll be reunited in heaven with those you've lost, then how about this: the atoms in decaying bodies enrich their surroundings and create new life. *In some form* everyone persists, reabsorbed into a giant mother-sea of existence."

Cold comfort.

It was the *personal* I missed. A wry wink. The brush of a finger. (The problem of attachment, Buddhists would say. Well, yes. I cherished my attachments. Sorry.)

On a street corner, from a shop window full of black-and-white photographs of literary figures, the French novelist Colette, one of my favorite writers because of her frank celebration of bodily pleasures, smiled seductively at me from underneath a feathered hat. She sat in a curtained parlor, on a small divan fluffed with velvet pillows. Her head tilted toward an open space beside her: a hearty invitation.

I walked into the shop. Used and rare books. The smell and weight of bound paper, dust, and ink: among the reasons I'd become a writer, having first smelled old paper in my grandfather's ledgers, binding the speeches and family stories he'd composed. Someday I hoped to be memorialized like this.

I moved past the travel section in the foyer: an atlas of the world's remotest islands; *The Big Book of Glaciers.* Sepia photographs of giant slabs of ice. Immediately, in the center stacks, two bright volumes caught my eye. Virgil, Dante's beloved teacher—high on a shelf above me was a translation of his *Georgics.* I stretched to reach it. The book's paper cover felt exquisite in my hand. Parchment-like. I'd never read the *Georgics:* "What makes the crops rejoice, beneath what star / To plough, and when to wed the vines to elms, / The care of cattle, how to rear a flock, / How much experience thrifty bees require: / Of these . . . I . . . sing," the poem began.

My other great find that afternoon was a slender volume titled *Human Immortality*. It was the text of a speech William James had delivered at Harvard in 1898 (the year my grandfather was born). I couldn't now remember, from my college seminar on the James family, what William, raised by a man who talked to angels, had to tell us about the afterlife.

A glass of red wine. The wooden rocker on the porch. The bees and the deer's shy approach. The sun setting in folds of purple clouds above a schooner's blue cloth sail. I paused to appreciate these brief pleasures as I sat with James's meditation on eternity.

At first he seemed to straddle the *duality* problem. What people called the mind (or the self or the soul) needed the brain—James flatly accepted this. The mind did not exist apart from the body's scaffolding: "What the laboratories and hospitals have lately been teaching us is not only that thought in general is one of the brain's functions, but that the various special forms of thinking are functions of special portions of the brain." So, then, "how can we believe in life hereafter when Science has . . . prov[ed], beyond possibility of escape, that our inner life is a function of that famous material, the so-called 'gray matter' . . . How can the function possibly persist after its organ has undergone decay?"

But then James complicated the issue: "Even though our soul's life . . . may be in literal strictness the function of a brain that perishes, yet it is not at all impossible . . . that the life may still continue when the brain itself is dead." How so?

By distinguishing among various "functions," he said. If we think of the soul as a function of the brain the way steam is a product of a teakettle, then the soul cannot survive the brain's loss. But if we imagine other arrangements—a crossbow releasing an arrow, a prism permitting light to refract, air transmitting sound through an organ pipe—we understand "function" differently, not as an engendering source but rather as a conduit: in the case of brain and soul, a conduit allowing something preexisting and unique to enter the physical world.

"Suppose . . . that the whole universe of material things—the furniture of earth and choir of heaven—should turn out to be a mere surface-veil of phenomena, hiding and keeping back the world of genuine realities," James wrote. "Such a supposition is foreign neither to common sense nor to philosophy."

Even so, in such a scenario, wouldn't the soul, losing its portal into the world, spiral back into that amorphous mother-sea of matter, no longer the animating spirit of a special individual but simply part of the common universal *stuff*? Not necessarily, James said. Just as "air now comes through my glottis determined and limited in its force . . . by the peculiarities of those vocal chords [*sic*] which . . . shape it into my personal voice, even so the genuine matter of reality, the life of souls . . . , will break through our several brains into this world in all sorts of restricted forms." Similarly, the soul released from the dying brain will carry the specific imprint of the individual whose body now lies abandoned—like wax shaped by a golden seal. Personal immortality, then, is not out of the question.

Outlandish? Perhaps. But then James challenged his readers: is it easier to believe that consciousness forms anew with each gestating brain than to entertain the possibility that consciousness may be a permanent field—resembling electricity—transmitted, individually and uniquely, through fresh brain cells?

The wind shifted slightly over the water—a salty, briny smell—and I heard, from far away, a slow fiddle air drifting lazily from the fort.

Margie would play late into the night. I walked back to town. Late diners filled the streets, bundled in sweaters against the evening's growing chill. Two men, apparently homeless, dug through public trashcans looking for food, but even they seemed to be enjoying the summer night. Amid frightening coughing fits, they cackled and slapped each other's backs.

On an open dock overlooking the harbor, a young woman wearing a long satin dress gripped the arm of her companion and laughed lightly, a bright chiming sound—Colette charming one of her lovers.

On a brick wall, a poster advertised a local production of *A Midsummer Night's Dream*. A stray line from the play traipsed through my head: "I have had a dream, past the wit of man to say what dream it was!"

For over an hour I wandered through town, humming a slow air, enjoying the crisp evening. At one point, randomly, I turned down a narrow alley. Power lines crossed the alley, above the roofs of low wooden buildings. The modern cables seemed out of place in this historic district. In Midland, a massive power line swayed above my parents' house. Often it obstructed my night-sky rambles with the telescope. Even then, in the early 1960s, before many of us worried about environmental dangers, my family joked that the crackling currents would give us cancer. Later, when scientists affirmed that power lines *did* damage human cells, I wondered if my asthma had been affected by the cables—or if my heart had been weakened by years of exposure to a constant electric field. At the time of my bypass, I grew so concerned about this, I read a good deal about electricity's relationship to the body.

As it turned out, electricity had implications for the possibility of the *soul*, as well. Or so said many observers.

Scads of serious researchers cited instances of electromagnetic fields affecting cardiac function. The heart muscle itself emitted an electric field, as did the central nervous system. Most neuroscientists said the brain's electromagnetic impulses were "relevant to consciousness," and one man even went so far as to claim that consciousness was "identical with certain spatio- temporal patterns in the electromagnetic field"—a sentence so startling to me that I memorized it on the spot and have never lost it.

A philosopher named Karl Popper formulated a "mental force field hypothesis," arguing that human minds—and thus, perhaps, our souls—share the following properties with electromagnetic fields: they are "located," "incorporeal," "capable of acting on bodies," "dependent on body," and "capable of being influenced by bodies."

The effects of calm and fear on the human heart were easy to chart; less provable were the claims of some researchers that groups of people coming together, radiating positive energy, could alter the earth's electric field, maybe even changing behavior, causing crime rates to drop significantly. Such examples might provide evidence of the existence of an actual human spirit.

In any case—electricity aside—William James was clearly right, I thought: we all had powerful wills to believe in unseen forces, gently sheltering our lives.

But were these forces aware of *us*?

Later, back at the cottage, from the rocker on the porch as I waited for Margie to return from camp, I became aware of a musty odor rising from the side of the house, near the apple tree. I walked through the gate and, in the moonlight, saw a dead opossum. I didn't want to touch it, but it seemed wrong to leave it lying in the open, inviting scavengers—though that's what would have happened in the wild, without a human presence. I was bringing conscience and even a mild sense of mourning to a situation otherwise emotionally and morally neutral.

Standing beneath the blue half-moon, covering my nose, I recalled a talk I'd attended years ago by a colleague of mine at Oregon State, a biologist who'd asked the question, "Do animals grieve like humans?" Yes, in the case of gorillas and elephants, he reported. He wondered why. Did they think that performing sadness would convince their companions to stop being dead?

I thought I remembered him saying adult chimpanzees rarely exhibited sympathy when an elder crawled into the forest to die.

Apparently, honeybees lacked death receptors. They couldn't smell death, so it didn't concern them—unless a rodent got trapped inside a hive, in which case the bees, unable to lift its body out, would embalm it in tree resin.

With my right foot, I rolled the opossum into a ditch by the side of the road in back of the house and covered it with a little dirt. Do I need to say it? In the morning it wasn't there.

That night in bed, I pulled Margie close. Her hand throbbed from all the reels she'd played: "Raivlin," "Spinnaker," "Bulgarian Red." I slept a dreamless sleep.

$-3-$

Some mornings, at the kitchen table in the cottage, Margie worked on a talk she was scheduled to deliver two weeks after music camp. Every summer she taught for ten days at Pacific Lutheran University in Tacoma, Washington. PLU offered a Master of Fine Arts degree in writing through a program called the Rainier Writing Workshop. During the summer residencies, faculty members met with students, read manuscripts, and gave craft talks. This year Margie had decided to speak about the ancient Jewish practice of midrash and its applications for contemporary literature.

"In its original form, the process [of midrash] might have gone something like this," she wrote:

> A midrashist, reading along in the Torah, would find himself caught on a word or phrase, or other moment in the text—a sticky spot if you will—that seemed to invite questioning. Picture an extremely alert close-reader of a complex modern novel. She's not just reading for plot. She's listening for small resonances and repetitions that signal buried riches of possible meanings in the language itself . . . From these signals, the midrashist would

locate a *gap*, an entrance point, and dive down, metaphorically speaking, expanding the brief episode from within, giving voice to submerged characters and complexities brimming beneath the unforthcoming surface of a biblical episode.

As an example, she offered the story of Abraham, Isaac, and Sarah. In the book of Genesis, we follow the saga of Abraham, ordered by God to sacrifice his son, Isaac. At the last minute, his hand is stayed by a merciful angel. But where is Isaac's mother while this fretful drama unfolds on Mount Moriah? She goes unmentioned. Following the scene on the mountain, we read "And Sarah died." Why did she die? How? As in Homer, Old Testament characters are presented to us with little detail. Here, the *drasher* finds a gap worth exploring.

Doesn't the proximity of Sarah's death to her husband's near-murder of their son suggest an immediate link: shock, grief, horror?

Sitting at the table one morning pondering Sarah's fate, Margie poured me a cup of coffee. I gave her a good morning kiss and watched the deer outside the window step toward the apple tree. "How did you sleep?" Margie paused. "More Ehud dreams?"

"No." In fact, after a couple of dreamless nights, I'd had a not-so-subtle nightmare early in the morning. All about my father. He and I were standing in a cemetery, surrounded by freshly prepared open graves. My father kept inspecting the holes, bending down near the crumbling edges to feel the dirt and pluck the yellow grass. I kept saying, "Dad! What are you doing? Be careful! Don't get too close!"

I woke, remembering his final days in the hospital—how, missing my mother, feeling no need to go on, he rejected his medications and asked simply to be kept out of pain. I should have tried harder to dissuade him from this plan of action. I would never forget the way he'd grab the back of my neck, pull me toward his bed, and whisper, "Kill me."

That morning in the cottage, thinking of Dad in the context of Margie's midrash exercise brought to my mind William James's relationship with *his* father: James struggled to take seriously the old man's claims of communing with angels. He interpreted his father's emotional collapse as an expression of suppressed guilt: as a child, Henry Sr. had rebelled against his family's religious orthodoxy. Like Achilles, he believed he'd received a visitation, a direct warning from God to reorder his life, but he may have been duped by an out-of-whack brain.

William, too, invited careful interpretation: as it happened, his immortality argument followed years of traumatic grieving. *Need*, more than *conviction*, seemed to inspire his writing.

When his father died in 1882, soon after his mother's death, William confessed to his wife that he'd begun to consider "the tremendousness of the idea of immortality. *If only he could be joined to mother.* One grows dizzy at the thought."

When his child, Herman, died of pneumonia in 1885, William reflected, "It *must* be now that he is reserved for some still better chance" in a world beyond earth. And when his sister Alice lay ailing with cancer in 1891, he wrote to her, "When that which is *you* passes out of the body, I am sure that there will be an explosion of liberated force and life till then eclipsed."

After Alice died, William selected a passage from Dante to be inscribed on her urn: "After long exile and martyrdom comes this peace." *Exile* and *martyrdom* described William, as well—the terrible effects of his depression in his long years of mourning.

Win Horan had rapidly become a better teacher in Band Lab. She responded positively to deadline pressure. Each day, she drilled her students with cheerful discipline. Still, it was a large ensemble, composed of various skill levels, and time was short. The group had chosen to perform a traditional waltz, "The Black Velvet Band" (in honor of Win's head wraps), and two jigs, "The Connaughtman's Rambles" and "Out on the Ocean." Always, the transition from 3/4 time to the first up-tempo piece caused trouble, a chaos of squeaks and blats as if from a freeway collision.

Inadvertently adding to the group's fits and starts was my dear wife. She'd become enamored of an unusual guitar tuning, DADGAD, because of its "rich tonality," she said, "its drop-D bass line and opportunities for playing up the neck. It opens up more chord possibilities." The problem was, the sound clashed with guitars tuned the standard way, and a pair of older musicians didn't know what she was up to.

She wouldn't be deterred. From across the room, she heard another DADGAD player. Margie moved her chair and introduced herself—"Karen," the woman responded happily—and in no time, the two of them, along with a couple of other folks who liked what they heard, a bouzouki man named Bill and Carla, a fiddler friend of Karen's, had commandeered the rhythm section. The standard players slunk away in silence.

After two hours, I grew weary of my ghost dance. I decided to take a walk. When I slipped out the door, Margie, hunched over her capo; Karen, in a floppy straw hat; Bill, switching strings; and Carla, pounding her fiddle, sat laughing in a warm, sunny corner: the cool kids.

It was a windy afternoon. Crisp salt air drifted off the inlet, a sour tang tamping down the odor of freshly mown grass over by the military cemetery. I ducked out of the breeze inside one of the concrete bunkers, a dark, chilly hole beneath a mound of dirt. Stale. Humid. I don't know why I carried my drum—I wasn't going to join any jams—but I'd gotten used to its weight on my shoulder, along with my book bag, lumpy with *Human Immortality*.

I pulled the drum from its case and tapped out a series of eighth notes. They echoed like gun cracks beneath the bunker's sharp overhang. I reeled off a slip jig. The amplified sound could have carried across a battlefield. Next I played a martial beat—an ancient warrior leading a regiment through a bloody meadow. "It's your heritage!" I remembered Margie saying when she'd presented me with the drum. True enough—O'Dochertaigh meant "Destroyer" in the Old Country.

Maybe I was one of my clannish ancestors, reincarnated. Not just the DNA. The spirit, the soul.

The bunker's dampness tightened my lungs. I scrambled out of the hole, settled on the mound above it, and turned again to poor William James.

Shortly after his son Herman's death, his mother-in-law, wracked with grief, desperate for solace, consulted a Boston medium named Leonora Piper. Convinced of the woman's honesty and integrity, she talked William into attending Mrs. Piper's séances. Over several months, in spite of his natural skepticism, he came to feel she was genuinely "in possession of a power as yet unexplained." She "was strong [in her knowledge of] the events in our nursery, and gave striking advice . . . about the way to deal with certain 'tantrums' of our second child, 'little Billy-boy,' as she called him, reproducing his nursery name. She told how the crib creaked at night, how a certain rocking-chair creaked mysteriously, how my wife had heard footsteps on the stairs . . . Insignificant as these things sound when read, the accumulation of a large number of them has an irresistible effect." To the end of his life, James would not commit to an absolute belief in dead spirits, but he regularly risked his professional reputation by conducting interviews with people who claimed to have encountered ghosts. He continued to attend séances. He professed his bafflement over Mrs. Piper, whom he trusted despite nagging uncertainties about her performances.

In the spirit of midrash, we might interpret his regard for her as indicating his need to believe he'd reunite someday with his folks. "Our immediate family is a part of ourselves," he wrote once. "When they die, a part of our very selves is gone."

On May 21, 1906, James sat with Mrs. Piper and spoke to a friend of his who had died the year before. "Did you get my messages?" the spirit said to him through the medium. "I am so delighted to see you to-day that words fail me."

"Well . . . take your time and don't be nervous," James said.

Later he reported that the spirit revealed facts about their friendship that no one else, certainly not Mrs. Piper, could have known. At one point during the session, he asked his friend to recall a particularly important talk they'd had. The spirit demurred, saying, "I want you to understand one thing, that in the act of communicating it is like trying to give a conversation over the telephone, that the things that you want to say the most slip from you, but when you have ceased to talk they all come back to you. You can understand that." James did not argue with him.

He wasn't sure he believed in ghosts, but he was willing to forgive them.

What sadness looks like in the brain.

I wasn't sure where this sentence came from at first. It seemed to ride the cool salt air. Then I realized it had risen in an echo from a nearby bunker. Apparently, someone else sitting out of the wind was listening to an audio book or a podcast. Seagulls flew across the inlet. I strained to hear. I caught just enough of the recorded voice to gather a few scattered facts: the amygdala, the brain's most primitive part, was the section producing strong emotions, I heard. The hippocampus was the seat of memory. In research tests, both of these areas lighted up when brain-wired subjects reported feelings of sadness. Melancholy appeared to be the result of an intense conversation between memory and emotion.

Late in the afternoon, I walked my sad brain to Taps, Fort Worden's bustling tavern. I sat in a quiet corner with William and a tall glass of wine. Scraps of fiddle tunes drifted through the trees on the patio.

What were the implications—and the parameters—of James's views of immortality? First, he believed that purely materialist theories of consciousness were inadequate: scientists could explain brain functions, but the results of those functions, particularly the *sense of self*, remained elusive. What was it? Where was it located?

If, say, the amygdala and the hippocampus were the self's musculature, the self still stood apart from them. An end product is not necessarily the same as the process that forms it. Steam is not the flame that boils the water, nor is it the water . . . not any longer.

"To explain a cognitive function, we need only specify a mechanism that can perform the function," the philosopher David Chalmers would write many years later, echoing James. But *why is the performance of these functions accompanied by experience?*"

James speculated that consciousness was a "field," composed of many other fields: neutrons, electrons, protons, atoms; bacteria, cells and molecules, parasitic microbes; these phenomena combine to form lungs, hearts, muscles, brains; they exist within larger fields of oxygen, hydrogen, nutrients, water; in turn, these are enfolded within the earth's electromagnetic field, which is tucked inside the solar field, the galactic realm, the universe with its regions of unexplained dark matter, and so much more, always eluding us . . .

Throughout human history, consciousness has also manufactured social fields, cultural fields, environmental fields. These shape the self, as well . . . the self is "all shades and no boundaries," James wrote, and then, sounding like the Dante of *Paradiso*, he added that the universe consists of "centres of reference and action . . . these centres disperse each other's rays." They flow in and out of the self, informing it, churning it into "a mass of . . . sensation, in a cloud of memories, emotions, concepts, etc. Yet these ingredients, which have to be named separately, are not separate." Fundamentally, consciousness is a "much-at-once, in the unity of which the sensations, memories, concepts, impulses, etc., coalesce and are dissolved. The present field [of awareness] . . . came continuously out of its predecessor and will melt into its successor continuously again, . . . giving the character of a gradually changing *present* to the experience, while the memories . . . place whatever is present in a temporal perspective more or less vast."

In sum, James saw consciousness as an evolutionary process retaining some fixed identity, as in the transformation of sperm/egg into embryo into fetus into infant into adult human being.

For this self to be immortal, it could not be limited to the physical fields on which it depended while occupying an individual human body. Its links to fields beyond the body, from electromagnetism to as yet undiscovered forces, would keep it alive after it had shed its physical residue.

Still, according to James, like a creature emerging from a withered cocoon, it would carry an imprint of its former existence.

He admitted that neither the self nor its immortality could be proved, but he insisted that our *felt* awareness of self, as well as the range of human behaviors inexplicable in describing the mechanics of atoms, cells, synapses, plants, other animals, and so on, worked strongly in their favor.

Since James's day, what David Chalmers calls "the hard problem of consciousness" has bedeviled thinkers. "There is nothing that we know more intimately than conscious experience, but there is nothing that is harder to explain," he says.

Attempts to address the problem have ranged from the philosopher David Dennett's outright denial of it to the "neurobiological theory" proposed by Francis Crick and Christof Koch. In their lab, in the 1960s, they isolated electric oscillations within the cerebral cortex (pulsing between 35 and 75 hertz). They suggested that these oscillations were the basis of consciousness, binding the visual and olfactory systems.

Still, Chalmers asks, "Why should physical processing give rise to a rich inner life at all? It seems objectively unreasonable that it should, and yet it does." This "inner life" is the missing substance in much AI research, some of whose practitioners conceive of the brain as hardware running the mind's software. At an extreme—as in the writings of Ray Kurzweil—predictions abound of information-processing machines into which we will download ourselves in the near future, ensuring a mechanical immortality.

Antonio Damasio, a contemporary neuroscientist, offers a more nuanced outlook. "Conscious minds result from the smoothly articulated operations of several, often many, brain sites," he writes. "The key brain structures in charge of implementing the requisite functional steps include specific sectors of the upper brain stem, a set of nuclei in a region known as the thalamus, and specific but widespread regions of the cerebral cortex. The ultimate conscious product occurs *from* those numerous brain sites at the same time and not in one site in particular."

What unifies brain and body, giving rise to conscious experience, he says, is homeostasis, an organism's attempt to achieve a balanced or neutral state, fit for survival—a self-regulating process. It's like developing an internal thermostat. We share this striving with Earth's simplest life forms, even bacteria.

In Damasio's view, emotions, largely a product of the central nervous system, are the mental expression of homeostasis, giving human beings a leg up in the survival game: the ability to deliberately map the body's needs (unlike mindless bacteria). Emotions allow us to assign *value* (pleasure, pain) to biological operations, ensuring behaviors in the direction of survival.

"Unless the process behind what became pain was *experienced*, it would have been a mere body state . . . in the clockwork of our organisms," Damasio writes. "To be experienced, the patterns of operations related to pain or pleasure had to be turned into feeling, which is the same as saying that they had to acquire a *mental* face, . . . that the mental face had to be owned by the organism in which it occurred, thereby becoming *subjective*, in brief, *conscious*."

On matters of the self, Damasio always engaged me, but it was James I found most moving. His personal longings—and his grief— were palpable just beneath the surface of his essays. Inevitably, I absorbed other thinkers through James's anguished prism.

When Damasio discussed homeostasis in plants—how they "grow in the direction of the terrain where the homeostatically required molecules are likely to be"—I couldn't help but think, in a somber Jamesian mood, *Even tulips long for immortality.*

"Blue orbs," someone said.

The wind had died. I'd moved to an outside table at the tavern where young families were gathering for dinner along with some of the musicians drifting down the path from Fiddle Tunes. Near me, in a big group huddled over baskets of steaming fries, one man was telling his friends he'd recently watched a cheesy ghost-hunter show on one of the cable television networks. They'd done a segment on Fort Worden: a photographer using a special camera had taken shots at night on the lawn in front of the tavern. Though he had seen nothing, he'd felt an unusual chill in the air. When he developed the pictures, the prints were speckled with "blue orbs," he said, floating in front of the tavern's front steps. He surmised they were spirits of dead soldiers.

The group laughed and fake-screamed, upsetting a pair of children sitting on a nearby verandah. Their young parents hugged them and shushed them, shot the group hostile looks.

Margie has always believed that if we'd met earlier in life, we would have produced a passel of kids. Apparently, by the time we got to know each other, our bodies were too exhausted to do the job, though we tried. Sometimes she refers to our "ghost children." I wondered now if one version of immortality was the past that might have been—unspent, it might still exist somewhere, in an alternate realm. *In potentia.*

Evidently, such thoughts engaged the physicist Stephen Hawking at the end of his life. He had recently died—on Einstein's birthday, four months earlier. Sitting beneath the trees at Taps, watching for blue orbs, I remembered an NPR report on his passing.

As a young researcher pondering time and eternity, Hawking had agreed with Einstein's theory that what we called black holes—

collapsed stars—were so dense that any "information" pulled by gravity into the stars' cores would be lost forever. "Information" was a physics term meaning various states of matter giving rise to different effects, but it could refer to anything governed by physical laws, including light and human beings.

In the 1970s, Hawking had explored the idea that black holes could "leak"—perhaps random jets of matter streamed from their hearts, he said. Eventually, black holes would explode and disappear. In spite of this, he agreed with Einstein: the stars' densities consumed any information they snagged. If you were sucked into one, then dribbled back out, all the information that made you—gender, hair and eye color, political preferences—well, it'd be gone.

Reincarnation, perhaps; personal immortality, no.

"It's the past that tells us who we are," Hawking wrote. "Without it, we lose our identity." (*I was my father's son. My father is dead. I am no longer my father's son.*)

Following Hawking's death, colleagues discovered that his final research paper concerned the possibility of escaping black holes. Based on mathematical equations, he speculated that light playing on the surfaces of dead stars might be manipulated by objects approaching their demise—an object could encode its information in the undulating light before being tugged inside the maelstrom.

Eventually, on the surface of the star, "the information will be re-emitted when the black hole evaporates," Hawking wrote.

Immortality!

Colleagues thought this the fanciful wish of a man reluctant to die. Like William James, Stephen Hawking had a powerful will to believe.

When *his* time came, James wanted very much to go. After a series of hiking trips around the country, including long walks through Washington and Oregon, he was saddled with chronic chest pains. Thereafter, he lived with the knowledge that he possessed a weakened heart. He agonized over whether or not to retire early from Harvard. Finally, he had no choice—he'd grown so "tired."

Human Immortality was written after an especially painful heart episode in 1898. Angina had made it difficult for him to breathe. That same year, William's brother Henry published his masterful ghost tale *The Turn of the Screw*, based on William's investigations into paranormal activities. The story's ghosts may be real or they may be phantoms of the imagination—the reader never knows. Henry had perfectly captured his brother's ambivalence.

Increasingly feeble toward the end, William enjoyed leisurely dinners with friends, including Mark Twain, who was debilitated now by his own many griefs, and curious, like William, about life beyond death. "Poor man," William said of him. "[He] is only good for monologue, in his old age . . . but he's a dear little genius all the same."

William took pleasure again in sketching and drawing. As a young man studying painting techniques, he had been most impressed with Delacroix's famous portrait *Dante and Virgil in Hell* (1882), hanging now in the Louvre. In the painting, Virgil, in a flowing white robe, hovers protectively over Dante, who all but trembles on the canvas before us. The men are standing in a boat crossing the black River Styx, surrounded by naked, writhing bodies of the damned. The sky, full of pitch and fire, roils around them. William loved the drama, the bold colors, the browns, the reds, the blues, but most of all he loved the moment: the clash of hope and fear on the edge of uncertainty.

That was where he found himself as his heart wound down. On August 26, 1910, he passed away in his wife's arms: "No pain at the last and no consciousness . . . He had worn himself out," she wrote. "He wanted to go and departed swiftly as he always has when he made up his mind to move on."

Afterward, she believed he was still "safe and living" somewhere, "loving and working, never to be wholly gone from us." The objects he had touched in the house, in his study, still resonated with his raw, pulsing energy.

Strenuously grieving, brother Henry ignored his deep-seated doubts. He scheduled evening appointments with a series of Boston mediums, hoping for contact with William's spirit. He admitted he experienced only "the grim refusal of the dead."

PART TWO
Virgil's Bees

– 4 –

Colette's splendid memoir, *Break of Day*, begins with a middle-aged Colette, alone in the Midi, in a house that might be her "last," mourning her mother. She remembers a letter "one of [her] husbands" received from her mother the year before her mother died, explaining why she would not come for a visit: "my pink cactus is probably going to flower. It's a very rare plant . . . and I'm told that in our climate it flowers only once every four years. Now, I am already a very old woman, and if I went away when my pink cactus is about to flower, I am certain I shouldn't see it flower again."

Colette observes that her tired face in the morning mirror is assuming her mother's likeness. She imagines the maternal spirit dropping by: "I wonder whether . . . she would recognise me for her daughter, in spite of the resemblance of our features. She might if she came back at break of day and found me up and alert in a sleeping world, awake as she used to be, and I often am, before everyone. Before almost everyone, O my chaste, serene ghost!"

I had reread *Break of Day* for the third or fourth time just before traveling to Washington—books, my constant companions—and its elegiac tone may have been a reason for my receptiveness to what appeared to be visitations while staying in the cottage. Some of my most powerful dreams that summer came to me early in the mornings, in a state of not-quite-sleep, below the lid of consciousness, lulled by the lisping slap of waves beyond our door. More than once, I found myself sitting with Ehud. And one morning, while some gully in my brain registered the deer's delicate steps beyond the bedroom window, stirring up the bees, my mind revisited my father. He and I were standing in the middle of a street somewhere, facing one another, each with a pistol in our hand (in reality, guns were never part of our lives). "Kill me," a voice whispered—from *outside* the dream, it seemed. Then my father said that bad things were happening inside the house across the street, and he was going to march over there and settle matters. I didn't know what "bad things" meant, but I pleaded with him not to go. It was dangerous, I said. He ignored me and headed for the house. Briefly, I pointed my pistol at his back, as if I'd stop him that way. Then, reluctantly, I followed him through the front door. Immediately, in the darkened hallways, I perceived lumbering figures stalking my father, surrounding him, raising heavy weapons. I fired at them. One by one they fell, until my father and I stood in a circle of gun smoke and carnage. (O'Dochertaigh—"The Destroyer.") I lowered my pistol and gazed at him imploringly. Tears stung my face. "See what you made me do," I said.

Nothing subtle there. My brain liked to bludgeon me while I slept. I'd killed to protect my dad, though in life I'd failed to finish him off as he had ordered me to do. Guilt and confusion.

"You're suffering from PTSD," Margie was convinced. In the last ten days of his life, I'd rarely left his hospital room. My breathing keyed to his increasingly shallow breaths, his slowing metabolism. I lived his dying rhythm.

Each morning, from his sixth-floor room overlooking the city of Midland, I re-experienced my family's history laid out in the streets below: the neighborhoods of my childhood games, my first drum lessons, my first lunar eclipse party, my first kiss, the route I took when I left home for college; the houses where my parents' (dead) friends lived; all the places we'd laughed and wept together . . . under storm clouds, apple trees, power lines. Early in the morning of July 5, 2015, as traces of firework smoke smudged the air, my father drew his last breath in his hospital bed. I'd felt the end coming just seconds before, walked over and lifted him into my arms.

I confess I'd hoped for some grand revelation at the moment of his death: an experience of his soul leaving his body, a rippling glow lighting a corner of the room. No. I walked out and drove numbly to Denny's for a breakfast I was probably lucky not to be able to taste.

Now, trying to shake off the dream-slaughter, I padded through the cottage to the kitchen, made some coffee, watched the deer through the dirty windowpanes. Then I went to drink my cup in the room where our late friend had written her novel. Sunlight flittered through white lace curtains, warming the bed quilt, brightening Popeye's squinting face—he was printed on a slick poster tacked to the wall.

As a kid, before I could write sentences, before sketching comets, I tried to fix the world on the page—to grasp it with all my might— by drawing it. I was pretty good, and Popeye was one of my masterpieces. I could make a fine likeness of him, and I did so everywhere, including on my mother's cherrywood desk. With a nail I'd found in my father's toolkit in the garage one day, I etched the intrepid sailor into the desktop, infuriating my mom. In my defense, I'd been utterly bored that morning. My mother, concerned about my breathing, had forbidden me to play outside. I expressed my displeasure through the power of art.

Years later, after I'd grown, long after she'd repaired the desktop, she said she was sorry she'd erased my handiwork. "I should have held on to it—that drawing was a precious record of your childhood." Oh, Mother, I spoke to her now: we didn't know it, but we'd both lose so much more in the fullness of time. I'd given everything away after she and my father died—every part of her, except my memory of her ghost.

Strange how we're haunted, I thought. And by whom. I smoothed the quilt. In that small bedroom where my friend had drafted her book, *she* should have been the one to trouble me. But I felt not a dust mote of her presence. In my life, she had always been a happy figure. She reminded me of Colette—not physically. But temperamentally.

Voracious. Hedonistic. Ferocious in her love of words and domestic animals. Perhaps since I associated only high- spiritedness with her, no ambivalence, no guilt, none of the complexities of deepest intimacy, my mind was at peace with her. I could let her rest. Or: she left me alone.

Before Margie and I lost our folks, if someone had asked me who would grieve the most, I would have said Margie. She was intensely close to her mom, called her almost every day. She rarely thought about her absence. I believed she was unprepared for the future; no doubt she'd fall apart. Me—I worried frequently about my parents' frailties: *getting ready.*

Perhaps, on reflection, it's no surprise that the level of my grief matched the depth of my fretting. Similarly, Margie. Foresight and planning? Forget it. We are who we are.

"This wasn't supposed to happen to me," my mother said on her deathbed. "Kill me," my father whispered.

(Dante: "I would not have thought / Death had undone so many.")

Almost gleefully, as we gathered by her bed, Margie's mom told her family the story of the first time she'd gotten drunk as a young woman. Then, still chuckling, she swallowed a handful of pills— going out as she had lived, precisely on her terms.

An easier death to deal with? Perhaps. It's not that Margie didn't grieve. She missed her mother every day. But our rhythms were remarkably different. I needed to slow down. She needed to speed up. We'd responded, each in our way—metabolically, in spirit?—to the sting of mourning.

As we made our way to Fort Worden that day, I carried Virgil in my book bag. I left my drum in the cottage. Invisibility no longer required it. My apartness had been firmly established.

Band practice remained dispiriting. Win reserved herself for rehearsing the fiddlers. This left Margie, Karen, Carla, and Bill to work out the backing. The big public performance was only days away. Somehow, melody and rhythm would need to mesh. Like body and soul. *When* and *how* was not yet clear.

At Taps, Margie and I ate lunch with Karen. Lovely twins, the women—black leggings, long cotton skirts printed with floral patterns, flowing blouses, guitars strapped across their backs. Karen told us she'd been widowed a few years earlier. She didn't dwell on details. It was her husband's voice she missed, she said. He'd been a fine singer: the most moving voice she'd ever known. As with Margie, her immersion in music in the past several months had sprung from her need to be active, to move forward creatively. She'd just met a new man. A musician. They had a long-distance relationship, and they were trying it out, to see if it would work. One problem, she confessed: she couldn't stand the tinny sound of voices on the phone. "It's like they're speaking from beyond the fucking grave," she said. "Spooky. Like a séance."

Naturally, her talk reminded me of the most plaintive voice I'd ever heard, cracking with pain and confusion: my father, late one night in his hospital room.

I'd fallen asleep in a window seat in the dark. I woke to his stirring. That night, for some reason, in spite of the fact that he'd made up his mind to die, the immensity of what he'd chosen, of what he faced, frightened him. "I'm dying," he said, stunned. "I'm dying."

Don't try to keep him. He needs to know it's okay for him to go, nurses told me days later as he lay in a coma.

Afterward, when it was all over, I wondered if that despairing cry I'd heard was the self, the part that cherished the body, telling some other thread of its being, *It's all right for you to leave. You've done your work here on earth. Now seek your immortality.* Or was the end just the end?

In my father's hospital room, gazing out across my childhood desert, it was hard not to dwell on my first presentiment of dying. I was twelve years old. With friends from a local astronomy club, I was lying in the dark, on the ground in a West Texas watermelon patch, watching meteors. Suddenly, a wide-body pickup truck, hauling two spotlights in its bed, roared across the field: night hunters chasing jackrabbits. They'd snap on the lights, flushing the frightened creatures—bounding as swiftly as beating hearts in the brush—and reel off rifle rounds, blasting mesquite in every direction. Thorns peppered my face. Bullets *pinged* at my feet. I didn't know whether to sit up and announce my presence (and risk getting shot) or lie there hoping the truck wouldn't mash me. Finally one of my friends yelled, "There's people out here! Hold your fire!"

In the damp dirt, I imagined—as in myths—my body rotting in the field while my soul rose into the stars, tracing a lovely pattern among the constellations.

After lunch with the girls, I took myself to the inlet, in the shadow of the lighthouse, to read.

Already, in my head, moved by memory, by the visits from Ehud and my grief-imposed exile, I'd begun to write this book. I imagined not only the book's contents, but the contents' *embodiment:* the pages' creamy texture, the smell of ink. I wanted the record I left to feel as pleasant in the hand as Virgil.

The *Georgics'* pages were old, light, easily torn. It occurred to me that an author in print exists without a body. In the words of a book we encounter pure mind.

Virgil's spirit remained long after Virgil the man passed away. The man lived from 70 to 19 B.C. He was born in Mantua, in Italy's marshy Po Valley, a farming region plagued by mosquitoes. He achieved fame early. As a result, he never lacked political patronage—which forced him to honor, in his writing, military adventurism. Apparently, toward the end of his life, he regretted how graphically he'd glorified violence in the *Aeneid*, his epic on the founding of Rome, and he died remorsefully, calling for his work to be burned.

To me, sitting by the water with the *Georgics* in my lap (the book comfy, warm, snug), Virgil was *song:*

[Farmers,] we need to watch the stars, Arcturus' phase,
The Kids', the bright Snake, just as sailors do
[When] homeward bound, . . .
Or [when they] brave the jaws of . . . oyster straits.
When Libra brings in balance day and night,
Bisects our world in halves of light and shade,
Then work your oxen, sow your barley, men,
To the very verge of stubborn rainswept winter.

Obviously, Dante had learned from Virgil to praise the splendor of the stars, and to track the seasons by their shining. And it was in Dante's *Comedy* that I had first encountered Virgil. Are you "living man or shade," Dante asks him, a figure "seem[ing] nearly to fade / As though from long silence," when the poets meet in the Dark Wood. In the middle of his life, Dante is wandering lost, surrounded by mysterious beasts (I flashed on the cougar appearing in Ehud's yard, the cougar at the graveside). Virgil has come to guide the younger poet through the afterlife—a father figure whom Dante will, of course, murder, narratively speaking, before the *Comedy* ends.

"No living man, though once I was," Virgil informs his poet-son.

In the *Georgics*, Virgil celebrates the past, before mechanization overtook farming (in 32 B.C.!). He extols the glories of earth and the tiller's mission. He praises human labor, placing it in humble perspective beneath the cosmos's canopy.

In spite of the verses' pastoral pleasures, each of the first three sections of the *Georgics* ends with litanies of human madness leading to slaughter and war, or of rampant disease eradicating animals and insects ("The hides were useless, and the flesh so foul / That fire and water could not salvage it; / None could shear the fleece, nor touch the web. / If someone tried to wear the loathsome cloth, / He burned and blistered, rank repulsive sweat / Poured off his fetid limbs; and, soon enough, / His stricken body felt the sacred fire").

It was as if Virgil, patiently describing the cycles of the seasons, needed to believe in continuity, in perpetual birth and regrowth. But he feared darker realities: "The world is like a chariot run wild / That rounds the course unchecked and, gaining speed, / Sweeps the helpless driver on to his doom."

This wasn't supposed to happen to me.

Late in the afternoon, I walked along the water's edge, gripping my book, meditating on Virgil's expressions of hopelessness. He was like my mother in her last days refusing even to pretend to appreciate the flowering plants we hoped would brighten her room. I understood her gloom. Following my prostate surgery, I'd been confined to bed for a week, roped to a catheter. I learned how quickly enforced helplessness can spawn a loss of hope.

One night my right ankle swelled to the size of a grapefruit. The surgeon had warned me that blood clotting could be a side effect of bed rest. A clot could cut loose, travel swift as a bullet to the heart, and that would be that.

Margie and I phoned the number of the doctor on call. "Yeah, well, just keep an eye on it," said the arrogant young man. "Let us know if anything changes."

Right, I thought. I'll do that—and afterward I'll *haunt* you from beyond the fucking grave! One minute, I'm talking to an idiot. The next instant, it's the void.

All night I lay awake counting the seconds, certain that each one was my final moment of awareness. What would that *be* like? Here, and then—*blank*.

The next morning—the miracle of the body—my ankle had returned to normal.

Years before her decline, hoping to outwit her fate, my mother had purchased insurance policies. They were intended to protect her financially, so when her health failed, she wouldn't be forced to stay in a hospital or physical rehab facility. She could count on quality home care. But the policies were outdated; the economy—and the culture—had changed to such a degree, the guarantees were worthless. Death was not going to be the nicely organized, well-prepared-for experience she'd expected.

She'd die of emphysema, but the fatal turn began with a bowel obstruction—nurses' aides didn't believe her when she complained of abdominal cramping. Her charts said she'd been regular for days. The aides trusted the charts instead of the agonized woman in front of them.

Ehud confessed to me once that the worst moments of his long illness involved the loss of bowel control. And Margie's mom timed the taking of her pills to her calculation of when she'd no longer be able to clean herself in the bathroom. The end of life seemed inexorably tied to shitting.

Antonio Damasio says "the enteric nervous system, [which] . . . regulates the gastrointestinal tract," is, in fact, "the second brain." It is the "key to processing energy sources." (In the *Iliad*, maybe Achilles's mental agitation really *was* "gut-wrenching.") Rather than a mother-sea of consciousness, perhaps the human sphincter is the most powerful force in the universe: intestinal fortitude. Could digestion, not divinity, be the movement propelling our fates?

When the body is reduced to its basic functions, knotted to bedpans and catheters, transcendence becomes a mocking rumor whispered in a fog.

At Fiddle Tunes, on the night of July 4, the cool kids got together after band practice to watch the fireworks over the inlet. Margie, Karen, Bill, and Carla bought two six-packs of beer and set some lawn chairs in the bed of Bill's pickup, parked near the dorms. We sat beneath an old building's darkened windows (moonlight etching movements on the glass) watching fountains of red, sparkles of gold, shimmer, hissing, into black water.

Even in *this* happy group, hierarchies had formed. Carla was a novice fiddler. Insecure, she deferred to her companions, even in silly conversations having nothing to do with music. Karen let nothing stop her. Whenever she missed a chord, she kept going, laughing and smiling. Her exuberance, more than her skills, made her the natural leader. Bill liked to be the expert; he wasn't an obnoxious man, but he *was* insistent. At one point Margie told him, "Yes, yes, I appreciate your tuning tips, Bill, but I can't absorb another lesson at the moment, so please *stop talking!*"

Swayed by my reading, I experienced the group's dynamics as a model of the "redeemed form of man": each individual had his or her frailties and musical gaps, but as a collective, like a working hive, they strove toward harmony.

An ashen smell rose from the water's choppy skin. I opened a beer. A Roman candle burst above the lighthouse.

Watching the sky-lights flicker, I imagined Virgil strolling along the shore. Just that morning, I'd read Dante's loving appreciation of him. Virgil was like a man carrying a flickering lantern so those behind him could be saved, Dante said. In his sadness (forever consigned to limbo), Virgil was forced to enter an impenetrable, unknowable darkness.

Sitting in the bed of Bill's pickup, I jotted a note about Virgil. I thought it might be useful for the book I was composing in my head. "*Melancholy,*" I wrote. "A mix of memory and emotion; the seat of the brain *and* the mind?"

On a dark autumn evening four months after music camp, in my local bookstore back in Oregon, I read from some of my work. Ehud's mother-in-law came to listen. Afterward, near the front counter, she pulled Margie aside and said, "Sometimes as he stood behind the podium tonight, Tracy turned his head and tightened his jaw the way Ehud used to do. He looked just *like* Ehud. It gave me chills. It was like a ghost was in the room."

One of our favorite things to do together, my ghost and I, before he became a ghost, was to attend the annual Portland International

Film Festival. He was a damnably difficult person to plan with: he was so enthusiastic about *everything*. Weeks in advance, he'd go online, download the festival's schedule, and pepper me with options: "On Saturday, we could squeeze in the Icelandic detective drama between the German documentary and the Danish comedy, but if we did that, we might not have time to eat and hear live music afterward. What do you think?"

I didn't care what we did. I tagged along for his fine company. In our first year at the festival, we must have seen six movies in one day, followed by a set of live jazz in the evening. His hunger for sensory immersion nearly crippled me. Certainly, he would have given that old sensualist Colette a run for her money.

In time, he admitted our pace was exhausting him, too, and it might be best to taper off a little.

In the years of his worsening illness, he slowed considerably. Instead of walking from one theater to the next, we took cabs. He leaned on my arm for support. I remember thinking, again and again, "This could be the last movie we see together. I wish it were better."

One night we stood alone on a sidewalk, shivering in a bitterly cold breeze, outside a theater since razed. We'd seen a disappointing farce. He looked ghostly, as I'm sure I did beneath the marquee's blinking yellow light. Our cab was late. The city felt deserted. Now I am the only person on earth storing this lonely image in his head: Ehud and I isolated together, hunched in front of a place no longer a place.

"Why are you . . . mistrustful? Do you / not believe I am with you?" Virgil asks Dante early in *Purgatorio*, when Dante, disoriented by his surroundings, fails to see his companion's shadow on the ground. He fears he's been abandoned.

But, of course, before *Purgatorio* ends, Virgil *will* leave Dante: his question sounds an early note of grief in the poem.

In fact, as soon as he poses the question, Virgil recalls his grave back on earth: "It is already evening where the body / is buried in which I made a shadow."

The first time I visited Ehud's grave, a few months after his funeral, I remembered another passage from Dante, this one from *Purgatorio* VIII, one of the *Comedy*'s most beautiful:

It was the hour when a sailor's thoughts,
the first day out, turn homeward, and his heart
yearns for the loved ones he has left behind,
the hour when the novice pilgrim aches
with love: the far-off tolling of a bell
now seems to him to mourn the dying day—

It was a serene spot, Ehud's grave, with a view of the blue Cascades, vivid snowy peaks on the earth's crest. The grave was unmarked. I rolled a loose tree stump over by the scorched yellow grass, the mound of dirt hardening in the shape of an inverted oyster shell. I sat. As in my father's hospital room the morning he died, I longed for a sign of Ehud's continuing presence, some signal from beyond.

No cougar came to watch me. No voice whispered in the trees.

Why are you mistrustful? Because I am the embodiment of grief—a state of paralysis Virgil grasped all too well.

Dante is a different story. Dante is the Redeemed Man. At the gates of hell, despair nearly freezes him. Medusa threatens to turn him into stone, locking him in his hopelessness. But he manages to shake off his anomie, escape, and emerge stronger than ever from perdition.

On the shores of Mount Purgatory, Virgil washes the infernal grime from Dante's face, among gentle reeds resurrected the moment they are plucked from the ground. Dante has found his place.

Virgil . . . Virgil cannot share it with him. He can only carry the lantern so those coming after him will find their way. He is forever barred from paradise—that joyous collective—because he lived before Christ. Virtuous as he was, he had no faith. Thus, he holds no hope. As evening closes around him, Virgil bows his head. The *Comedy*'s message is clear: the grieving are not redeemed.

– 5 –

Often in Taps, in the early evenings while I waited for Margie to finish band practice, I'd pick up a stray newspaper. The headlines—mostly about the erosion of America's democratic principles—made me crave not immortality but rather its opposite.

"How sweet it would be to find oneself no longer [a] man," Henry James Sr. wrote in *Society the Redeemed Form of Man*. His son's short story "The Great Good Place" was a variation on this fantasy, a dreamlike immersion into an all-encompassing nothingness, a warm bath of absolute zero. The story's main character wishes for obliteration after reading "newspapers too many—what could any creature want of so much news?—and each [item] with its hand on the neck of the other," like Dante's damned, "so that the row of their bodiless heads was like a series of decapitations."

Indeed—especially as the digital world rapidly replaced newspapers, muddying our very notions of information, with nationalism, anti-Semitism, and white supremacy on the rise again in our country, and endless wars abroad. Virgil's doubts about humanity and its fate, so vividly expressed in the *Georgics*, seemed to be reaching a climax in our time. But perhaps every generation has felt that.

My fleeting desire to be "no longer" was not, I thought, a death wish or a cry for help (though I've always believed that no one who has not considered suicide has learned to cherish life). It was, rather, an urge to remain conscious without the torments of ego, susceptible to hungers, ambitions, and the smallest social quake. An expression of ghost mode. An angelic state.

"For the third year in a row, America's life-expectancy rates have dropped," I read in the Seattle paper, sitting one night at a table in Taps. The statistics reflected increasing numbers of middle-aged suicides and a growing opioid epidemic. One doctor quoted in the article wondered if America's political turmoil, ever more divisive, was creating massive despair, and if despair should be listed as a public health risk.

A bit later that same evening in the bar, I imagined invisibles drifting all around us, among the tables and bottles and chairs. I'd ordered my second glass of wine. In every corner, I'd overheard sixtyish fiddlers, mostly women, sharing their experiences of surviving their spouses' deaths. It seemed a large number of them had turned to music late in life, to assuage their grief, to repair the wrecks they'd become.

Silently, I raised my glass to the husbands, the ones undone by death. Nodding politely to the women, I walked to the window overlooking an open field and a row of dorms beyond it. I squinted into the twilight, scanning the field for bobbing blue orbs. None appeared.

When Dante goes stumbling, lost, in the Dark Wood, Beatrice, his soulmate and savior, enlists Virgil to make first contact with him, on the path to redemption. She can't entreat Dante directly—she knows he is not yet capable of heeding an angel. It takes a fellow poet to reach him.

Book IV of the *Georgics* provides a powerful argument for Virgil as history's greatest poet. No wonder Dante followed him. The verses are astonishing and insane. They begin gently enough, informing farmers how best to raise their bees:

> Plant laurels all around, and fragrant thyme;
> Set out a crop of pungent savory,
> And violet beds to drink the trickling spring.
>   The hives you stitch from hollow bark, or weave
> From pliant osier, need a narrow door:
> For winter thickens honey with its cold
> While summer liquefies and makes it run—

The bees dread both extremes, and sensibly
They smear the chinks with wax, fill crevices
With juice of flowers, and keep in store a glue
That binds more fast than Eastern pitch or bird-lime.
And often, if we may believe the tale,
They burrow underground to make their homes,
And will be found deep inside porous stones
Or in the hollow shell of rotten trees.

Collectively, Virgil's bees form a "perfect, model state" — a redemptive society: "Their children are common property; they share, / As partners, the city's dwelling, and live their lives / Under majestic laws . . . / They work in summer, planning for the cold, / And store their gatherings in a common place."

If humanity followed the bees' example, even partially, the world would no longer resemble a runaway chariot. The creatures are so brilliant, Virgil writes, "some [people] draw the implication . . . / That bees possess divine intelligence / And drink of heaven's aether." For them, "death is nowhere, [their] immortal souls / Soar aloft to join the starry throng."

A day or so after I'd picked up the *Georgics*, I returned to the bookstore in historic Port Townsend (nodding warmly to Colette as she lolled languorously in the window). There I found a companion volume, a rarity, *The Beasts, Birds, and Bees of Virgil: A Naturalist's Handbook to the Georgics* by Thomas Fletcher Royds, first published in Oxford in 1918.

"The fourth *Georgic* is farthest of all from the truth as science, but perhaps [it is] the most beautiful," Royds wrote. "Little as he knew about the inside of a hive, Virgil loved his bees, and through them . . . saw 'Universal Nature moved by Universal Mind.'" He saw an image of the soul.

On certain matters, Royds conceded, Virgil *did* hit the mark: bees do need moisture, and beekeepers, in their gardens, leave saucers of water for the busy workers hauling pollen back to the others; green woodpeckers and blue tits are fierce bee hunters—in frosty weather they tap mercilessly at hives; the wind generated from bees' wings can reach gale force, relatively speaking—enough to snuff a candle flame.

Entirely apart from Virgil, Royds offered his readers obscure bee lore: blue is bees' favorite color; musicians, working with scientists to test bees' hearing, have, in the past, attempted to entice queens with tuning forks and violins (the results were sadly incomplete); bees must not dream, as apparently they do not slumber, "the sound of a 'sleeping' hive [resembling] the angry roar of the sea."

The collective mind of a hive is a stunning field of consciousness, containing "the sum and total of all bee experience since the world of bees began."

Isolate a bee, and it will die of "loneliness."

Why are you mistrustful? Do you not believe I am with you?

A report in a newspaper left in Taps one night said that a South African bassist plagued by memory loss had been asked by his doctors to strum an acoustic guitar while surgeons removed a tumor from his brain. The procedure was known as an "awake craniotomy." "It can be very difficult to tell the difference between the tumor and normal brain tissue," said one of the surgeons. "Once you're near a critical area, you can pick it up early, because [the guitarist] will tell you" by playing an errant, buzzing note.

This was not the first time a musician had been asked to perform during brain surgery. In 2014, said the paper, a tenor from the Dutch National Opera sang Schubert's "Gute Nacht" while doctors dug a hole in his skull.

In the fourth *Georgic*, Virgil dwells on the world's many threats to the hive-life of the "Universal Mind." Brutally, he lists numerous ways bees can perish.

Still, a few of them managed to escape and fly into the *Divine Comedy*.

In *Purgatorio* XVIII, we witness Virgil explaining love to Dante, drawing heavily on the teachings of St. Thomas Aquinas. Virgil posits love in the soul, which is "at once / distinct from matter and united with it," imbuing each "substantial form" on earth with a "specific virtue" unique to it. Our virtues are "in" us, Virgil says, "as the need to make honey / is in the bee."

And in *Paradiso* XXXI, in the "luminous white rose" of heaven, Dante describes angels as "a swarm of bees that in one instant plunge / deep into blossoms and, the very next, go back / to where their toil is turned to sweetness," in the presence of God.

Honey: a promise of immortality.

"I thought I'd live forever," Margie said. She was referring to raw oysters. "Once, at a party when I was a teenager, I ate two dozen of them with lemon and horseradish, and I'd never felt so alive!"

We were sitting at dinner one evening in a seafood restaurant in the oldest part of Port Townsend. It was midweek at the music camp. As we talked, she flexed her right hand—weary from hours of practice. I'd been reading about bees all day. She'd ordered half a dozen oysters, sweet Kumamotos and the larger ones culled from Willapa Bay, and she was contemplating asking the waiter for a second round.

Years ago, before we knew each other well, we'd flirted over oysters at a university get- together. She'd been grilling piles of them on an open flame in her back yard. While our colleagues gathered on the patio, discussing poetry, politics, and various modes of realism, I watched Margie flip the rocky shells on the grill and spill oyster juice down her thin green shirt. The juice was clear and thick. She saw me see her; we buzzed with vivid awareness of the moment.

"I'm worried," she told me now in the restaurant. Gingerly, she set a cuplike shell on the tray (she protects her fingers fiercely these days). She feared her hand would not be loose or fast enough to sound good in performance. Apparently, Win had picked a jaunty pace for the tunes.

"More oysters. That's your answer," I said.

"I'm serious."

"You'll be fine."

"You're one to talk." She said she wished I'd return to camp with her after dinner, bring my drum, and join a late-night jam. "If you just ignore the looks you get, edge your way into the circle, you'll do great. As soon as they hear you play, they'll know you're not obnoxious or intrusive. You're polite and you've got good taste. You know the rhythms—"

I confessed it wasn't just the fiddlers that bothered me. I had no confidence on the bodhran. I'd not taken a proper lesson. Probably I wasn't grasping the drum right, or using the tipper efficiently. My wrist wasn't as supple as it needed to be—the moves were completely different than in rock drumming—so I compensated by tapping my fingers *inside* the drum (the bodhran was open on one side).

I felt sure a special chamber in hell was reserved for abusers of the drum.

"Anyway, you understand," I said. "You just told me you're worried about performing."

"Yeah, but even so, I have to trust it will all work out. You'll never get better unless you try," she advised me. Absolutely true. "*You're* the one who encouraged *me* to play with others."

Nevertheless, I couldn't bring myself to return to camp that night. My head was full of bees. Perhaps perversely, I'd come to enjoy my invisibility.

Margie ordered more Kumamotos. She insisted I take an extra—or two.

I sat for an hour or so on the patio at Taps, under the stars, reading Virgil in reflected light through the bar's windows. Fiddle scraps floated through the pines. I walked inside to get a nightcap. On a wooden bench, next to a scattered Seattle newspaper and an open *Field and Stream*, someone had left a wrinkled old copy of the *New York Times Magazine*: "Can a Delicate Little Creature of the Sea Unlock the Secret of Immortality?"

I laughed, startling the bored bartender. How do such things happen? Strangely often, it seems, through wild coincidence, the world appears to feed our obsessions.

Do we *will* things to come to us when we need them? Can we do so with no awareness of it? Writers would kill for that power—defying credibility, snapping the bonds of narrative! (Or is there something about the *state* of creativity—obsession leading to heightened consciousness, a keen awareness of the connectivity of *everything*?)

According to the magazine, in Rapallo, a town on the Italian Riviera where Nietzsche once wrote "Everything goes, everything comes back; eternally rolls the wheel of being," researchers had discovered a type of jellyfish capable of reversing its aging process. At any point in its development, the creature could return to its earliest stage of life, as a polyp, "thus escaping death and achieving potential immortality." It did so by converting one sort of cell into another, motivated by "environmental stress or physical assault." The more the world deteriorated, the longer this guy decided to stick around. Go figure.

Jellyfish were proliferating across the seas by "'hitchhiking' on cargo ships that use seawater for ballast," the reporter, Nathaniel Rich, wrote. "It is possible to imagine a distant future in which most other species of life are extinct but the ocean will consist overwhelmingly of immortal jellyfish, a great gelatin consciousness everlasting."

One man engaged in culturing the creatures expressed his hope that "we will evolve and become immortal ourselves." Rich described this man as neglectful of all areas of his life except his lab studies. He survived on takeout food each night. For well over a decade, he had been conducting his painstaking research. "So young" at the start, he sighed. "So old now."

The bees in the apple tree were still and silent this time of night, but I approached with care, scrabbling in my pocket for the key to the cottage. I remembered the gist of a passage I'd read that morning in Royds—the poet Samuel Butler's sage advice: "thou must not be unchaste and uncleanly [in the presence of bees]; for impurity and sluttiness . . . they utterly abhor: thou must not come among them smelling of sweat, or having a stinking breath, caused either through eating of leeks, onion, garlick, and the like . . . thou must not be given to surfeiting or drunkenness; thou must not come puffing and blowing unto them . . . In a word, thou must be . . . sober, quiet, and familiar, so will they love thee, and know thee from all other."

The fourth *Georgic* concludes with a bizarre resurrection ritual involving bees.

"Bees sustain vicissitudes / Like ours, their bodies languish in disease," Virgil tells us. But "for the man whose swarm fails all at once," there is a "method" of "breeding"—of bringing the bees back to life—"from slaughtered bullocks' putrid blood."

Here's the trick, Virgil says: First, near the moribund hive, build a "narrow site" with a "narrow arching roof"; limit its light; next, "find a two-year calf with sprouting horns," gag its nose and mouth, and "beat and pulverize / The carcass, . . . keep[ing] the skin intact." Enclose the carcass inside the narrow space; spread "sticks / And sprays of thyme and new-cut cinnamon beneath [its festering] flanks." Leave it there until early the following spring.

"Within the corpse / The fluids heat, the soft bones tepefy," Virgil writes. Suddenly, "creatures fashioned wonderfully [will] appear; / First void of limbs, but soon awhir with wings / They swarm; then more and more they try the thin air, / Until they at last break through, like rain poured down / From summer clouds."

How did this stunning ritual evolve? Virgil explains by launching into an elaborate tale, unique to him in Western literature. He tells the story of Aristaeus, a shepherd boy who's lost his swarm. Eventually, he learns his bees were cursed by Orpheus as he was "rag[ing] . . . with grief" for Eurydice.

In the spirit of midrash, Virgil has parsed the myth of the lovers broken by death. He supplies the missing reason for Eurydice's banishment to hell: she was running from Aristaeus's advances, Virgil writes, and she "failed to see / The monstrous serpent lurking on the shore."

Virgil says Orpheus refused to forgive Aristaeus for pursuing his wife, causing her death. In vengeance, he killed the shepherd's swarm. Then he took to the hills, "a nightingale concealed in the poplar's shade," offering a "tragic song" of grief "to the frozen stars." Eventually, the Dryads, insulted by his inattention, his "unwavering faith" to Eurydice's memory, tore his body apart.

Aristaeus's mother, the goddess Cyrene, advised him to flatter the Dryads, and to "sacrifice / A calf to reconcile Eurydice." Through these means, he'd break Orpheus's curse, and learn to breed his bees from the "rotten flesh" of a steer.

Virgil was hardly alone in extending old stories. As the hero of a myth about music, Orpheus has always fascinated Margie.

Knowing this, an anthology editor asked her a few years ago to compose a *modern* myth. The book featured living writers' takes on timeless themes. As her subjects, Margie chose two of her favorite things: Orpheus and the oyster. Endlessly inventive, responding to the music in her head, she decided to link the oyster's watery origins to Orpheus's grief.

In her euphoric telling, Eurydice vanishes one day in a briny estuary, a place of "deceptive calm," surrounded by alert blue herons. Searching for her, Orpheus floats on his back in the water. He perceives a melody in the taste of the brine on his tongue, "a melody of blue autumns, of ancient beds where a story so old nobody knew it anymore still played its melancholy song of waiting, of the hope for reunion and return."

Orpheus rides the water's swells: "Musician that he was, he understood that a lift must necessarily lead to a fall." And then he sinks. In a greeny-black realm, he spies Eurydice, her eyes "gone silver" as if reflecting candle flames. She wears a strange ruffled collar, like the lip of a rocky shell.

When Orpheus loses her, his "damp" heart floods with a weird new music. The strains of grief, brine on the tongue. And so "it's no accident that there is always music playing when you approach an oyster—if you dare approach at all," Margie writes. The taste, like the song, is "so tender it seems wrong." You feel "a shudder of longing, and then an unaccountable desire to close your eyes."

Longing, loss, saltiness, sweetness . . . none of this can "stop you from hurting yourself," taking a knife and "trying to pry . . . open [an oyster] at a party," Margie's story concludes.

To this day, I have not asked her what she was thinking when she committed that line to print, but I can't read it without recalling her back-yard gathering, watching the oyster juice dribble down her shirt front, thick and slow as motor oil, seeing her catch my gaze . . . then, thrumming desire. Desire and *hurt:* like her Orpheus, Margie is a gifted musician. Always, she anticipates the lift's natural fall, the major's minor, the joy's unmissable grief.

One night near the end of the week, Margie and the cool kids stayed at camp to play for a contra dance in an upper room in one of the fort's old buildings. Strings of starry lights wove among the rafters, blinking like fireflies. Through the windows at the room's far end, the night was black as pitch. I stayed for a while, delighted by Margie's bliss. She wore a bright red blouse and a red scarf (in honor of Win's head bands), and her deep-bass DADGAD anchored the flying fiddlers.

After midnight—the dance was just then kicking into gear—I got sleepy and returned to Port Hudson. In the moonlight, I walked beside the marina. The ships' folded sails looked like great white birds, heads tucked into snowy breast feathers. The boats rocked in the water's light chop. Slurping, sucking, oystery sounds.

What ancient forms of consciousness were rooting around now in the water's black depths?

I remembered one of the first books I'd loved as a boy, a boating adventure, Joshua Slocum's *Sailing Alone around the World*. As I recalled, he'd made his solo voyage across the planet in what I now knew was the year William James wrote *Human Immortality*.

Somewhere in the Azores, Slocum was seized by debilitating cramps and couldn't steer the boat. Suddenly, a gentle spirit appeared on the deck, took the wheel, and admonished him for mixing cheese with plums. Slocum passed out. When he woke, the waters were calm. The phantom was gone. The boat was still on course.

His book made him famous. In December 1900, he was asked to speak at a dinner honoring Mark Twain. For the rest of his life, he refused to disavow his ghost tale. The spirit, he said, was either the pilot of the *Pinta* or his father.

In 1909, Slocum followed whatever he'd seen into the void. He disappeared at sea and was never heard from again.

Not long after completing her Orpheus myth, Margie wrote and published three short stories about a modern married couple. The couple is loving, deeply content. But there's trouble. In all three stories, something mysterious, a sad, irresistible force, tugs at the husband. In one case, it's a distant woman who may or may not exist; in another, it's a mythic white cat; in the third, it's the sea.

I didn't need a midrash exercise to understand that, beneath her amazing artistry, Margie was expressing worries about my health; circling and circling again the anxiety she'd felt, ever since the first juicy oyster, that she'd lose me.

Margie without me.

The musical lift and fall.

We were, both of us, hearing the melody clearly while at Fiddle Tunes, in a summer, a year, when—I can honestly say—we'd never been closer, bonded more tightly than ever by our grief.

"I just want us to be a little couple again," my mother pleaded quietly with my father in her hospital room the night before she died.

Waiting with my mother in the hospital, hearing her breath fade, I remembered I'd seen it before in women just like her: that hopeless longing to be young.

In Dallas, while in college, to earn a little money, I'd worked in a bookstore in a high-end neighborhood. The owner insisted we call him "Captain." He'd sit in his office smoking a long-stemmed pipe, cocking a sweaty sailor's cap on his head. I swear he looked like Popeye. His clientele consisted entirely of wealthy matrons, recently widowed, each of whom spent hundreds of dollars a month on astrology books.

Inwardly, I laughed at those women. If someone had told me then that one afternoon many years later I'd be standing in a bookstore in Port Townsend, Washington, studying titles in the "Spirituality/Self-Help" section, I'd have scoffed. I had more sympathy now for those tottering ladies needing reassurance that the past was not lost and the future remained possible.

In Port Townsend that day, one title in particular caught my eye: *The Physics of Immortality* by Frank J. Tipler, a Tulane professor. I sat on the grungy red carpet in the aisle, pulling back the stiff, dusty cover. "Physics will permit the resurrection to eternal life of everyone who has lived, is living, and will live," Tipler wrote. "If any reader has lost a loved one, or is afraid of death, modern physics says: 'Be comforted, you and they shall live again.'"

It occurred to me many months later: when my mother, on her deathbed, told my father she wanted them to be a "little couple" again, she was dreaming happily of a time before I was born.

Tipler's view of eternal life depended on mechanized space vehicles equipped with antimatter engines that could travel to nearby star systems at approximately nine-tenths the speed of light. These vehicles were necessary because "Earth [was] doomed," and humanity's survival depended on getting away from the solar system.

From there, our descendants could colonize far-flung planets or, failing habitable worlds, build orbiting space stations. It would take about six hundred thousand years to populate the Milky Way, Tipler wrote. Then we'd head to Andromeda—three million years. By the time ten billion billion years had passed, humanity would have seized control of the universe.

With a series of strategically placed explosions, we would force the cosmos to contract in certain places and store vast energy reservoirs in others. At the Big Crunch—the collapse of *everything*—enough energy would have been amassed in the universe, under our control, to perfectly replicate every creature that had ever lived. All information generated in the course of time would exist in that energy.

Tipler predicted that the universe would shrink to a final singularity of infinite density and infinite temperature, the End-Point, in which all creatures, great and small, with their memories intact, all their *potential* selves, would be brought back to life.

On my desk in my study at home, I've framed an old photograph of my parents in their early twenties, standing in small-town Oklahoma, holding hands. Fireflies sparkle above them. At the end of her life, in her grief, that split second when the camera shutter clicked was my mother's ideal of the golden eternal moment.

The will to believe.

Tipler dedicated *The Physics of Immortality* to his wife's Jewish grandparents, who were tortured and shot to death in Poland in 1940, and who "died in the hope of the Universal Resurrection." He said he became convinced that "death is not inevitable" after visiting a Nazi detention camp and seeing that "nothing is uglier than extermination."

– 6 –

"So, technically, you were dead, right?" a colleague asked me a few weeks after my heart surgery in 1999. I suppose that was one way to look at it.

The surgery lasted four hours. The surgeons split my breastbone, then hooked me to a machine that breathed and pumped blood for me while they stopped my heart. My heart was packed in ice, like an oyster, cooled to a temperature of about twenty-eight degrees. Afterward, the doctors warmed it up and shocked it back into rhythm. Rock and roll.

They rerouted my left mammary artery and harvested a saphenous vein from my right leg, suturing it to the aorta to bypass the blockages. This type of surgery had only been performed since 1962. During my recovery period, on a web page entitled "Pioneers of Heart Surgery," I learned that "for most of history, the human heart has been regarded as a forbidden organ too delicate to tamper with." Dwight Harken, a young U.S. Army surgeon in World War II, was among the first to try emergency heart procedures. "All of his first subjects died," his profile stated.

In the years since my operation, I've driven many times past the hospital in Corvallis and thought, "That's where I died." What happened to my "self" during those four hours when my heart lay on ice? ("According to current medical knowledge it is impossible to experience consciousness when the heart has stopped beating," the cardiologist Pim van Lommel has written.)

I remember being wheeled into the chilly operating room. I remember waking, terrified, from the anesthetic: plastic tubes clogged my throat, and I couldn't breathe—my primal fear realized. In between, where was I? What was I?

Had I died, in effect, long before my parents did? Do chronology and continuity have *any* meaning at all?

Since the early 1970s, largely as a result of technical advances in cardiology, reports of near-death experiences have become commonplace in the popular media: the famous white tunnel with a big bright light shining at the end. Almost universally, patients emerging from life-threatening crises have insisted that death is not final—it is a state of heightened consciousness, separate from the body (whose cells have replaced themselves several times over, in any case; could it be that cell death is not physical death any more than bodily death is spiritual death?).

For years, doctors have fiercely debated these reports. Some argue that the white tunnel is a hallucination resulting from a natural substance called ketamine, released by the brain during moments of oxygen deprivation. Others disagree. Out-of-body travel has been described in minute detail by perfectly healthy people.

Curiously, near-death experiences often precipitate extreme light sensitivity, as well as surges in odd electrical phenomena. Van Lommel cites one cardiac patient who recalled, after flatlining briefly, "every piece of equipment I touched, such as lamps, dishwasher, kettle, the light in the cooker hood, it broke. I gave off energy everywhere."

Worldwide, hospitals have collected voluminous accounts of patients aware of the rooms they were in after their hearts stopped, when respiration and all measurable brain activity had ceased. "Consciousness may be nonlocal," van Lommel concludes from such accounts. It may be that "all matter has phenomenal properties" receptive to physically unknowable fields and that "consciousness has a primary presence in the universe."

From that standpoint, he entertains the possibility that the link between consciousness and matter resembles the process by which solar energy (photons) is converted into chemical energy in plants — a connection between "electronic and molecular oscillating states."

To illustrate, he cites medical studies of "biological luminescence." "Living cells emit coherent light," he writes. This light "appears to be involved in intracellular communication," suggesting that "electromagnetic and other coherent fields are responsible for directing biological functions such as cell growth, cell differentiation, and cell division." Similarly, "the electromagnetic fields of the brain [could be] . . . the effect rather than the cause of consciousness."

We know from electrocardiograms that the heart's sparks can be measured in any part of the body: they are found in each of the body's cells, van Lommel says. The heart's rhythm creates a self-organizing field, establishing "reception . . . for certain aspects of our consciousness." It is a process exactly like bee swarms coordinating at a distance. The queen, "probably on the basis of her DNA function," sets "all of the colony's activities by creating and maintaining a collective consciousness."

"The red surface of an apple does not *look* like a matrix of molecules reflecting photons at certain critical wavelengths, but that is what it is," says Paul Churchland, a contemporary philosopher. Unlike van Lommel, he rejects any notion of self beyond brain matter. "The sound of a flute does not *sound* like a sinusoidal compression wave train in the atmosphere, but that is what it is . . . If one's pains and hopes and beliefs do not *introspectively* seem like electrochemical states in a neural network, that may be only because our faculty of introspection, like our other senses, is not sufficiently penetrating to reveal such hidden details."

Undoubtedly true. But it is also true that physical causes of pain are not identical to the *experience* of pain. Nor is it the case that watching ocean waves is the same as being overwhelmed by a feeling of awe at the sight of those waves. Molecular movement does not automatically trigger emotion, any more than a printed word on a page — "grief," say — generates the meaning associated with that word. We can describe the word on the page, from the history of the alphabet down to the chemicals in the ink composing the word, but it does not begin to touch the actual wellsprings of human grief.

Again and again, classical physicists have told us that in any given system, energy cannot be created or destroyed. It simply changes form—losses in one area signal gains in another. Traditionally, anti-dualists, philosophers such as Paul Churchland, have cited energy conservation as an argument against the existence of the human soul. Where does its energy come from? Where does that energy go when the body dies?

By contrast, more recent researchers—Stephen Hawking et al.—conversant with Einstein and quantum mechanics, have determined that measurements of kinetic energy are much thornier than previously supposed. Consistently, the principle of energy conservation breaks down.

Further, quantum mechanics suggests that light is both a particle and a wave, and that electrons can never be accurately measured (existing in some states, *not* existing in others—like Dante's angels). In effect, *determinative values* may be a meaningless concept.

If we accept this premise, and follow it to an extreme, then neurons arranged in certain patterns could generate a *soul* inside the brain without being determinative. To grasp this possibility, imagine a magnet. If we place the atoms in a bar of iron just so, we generate a magnetic field. But the field is not the bar; the field holds its own properties, its own powers apart from the bar.

Destroy the magnet, erase the field? Not necessarily. Einstein's theories of gravity predict that an intense magnetic field can survive the loss of its source.

And yet . . . and yet I confess: none of these dizzying speculations will ever stop me from mourning my *self*—the four-hour gap in its history—the day my heart lay on ice.

"I'm not sure this is real."

"It's real."

For the third or fourth time in a dream, I sat with Ehud in darkness, swaying—on a boat? On the mother-sea? And for the third or fourth time in a dream, Ehud assured me it wasn't a dream.

He looked older. Could he still be aging?

"Is there an afterlife?" I asked.

"Yes. Yes, Tracy, there is."

I woke in the cottage, my slow brain operating at very low voltage, aching to believe him. It was the day of the big performance. Carla, unsure of her fiddling, had opted out. She'd packed up and left camp early, telling no one goodbye. Mostly on their own, Margie, Karen, and Bill had worked up their rhythm parts. In rehearsal—at least to my ear—the melody makers weren't listening. There were too many of them, with a vast range of experience. "The whole point is just to have fun," Win said wisely—too late for poor Carla to believe it.

Margie still worried about the speed of her hand, but in general I'd seen her confidence grow. She'd worked hard, and I knew she'd be exhilarated by the thrill of performing.

While the band made its final run-through, I took one last stroll through town. The homeless men I'd seen days before were sitting on a harbor wall, sharing the treasures of their trash with a flock of seagulls: sandwich scraps, potato chips. Pedestrians' ghostly reflections in storefront glass seemed perfectly in keeping with Port Townsend's sepia mood. I said goodbye to Colette in the bookstore window. She smiled at me as seductively as ever. Her vitality in the photograph made it hard for me to believe in her death. "Death should never be something public," she had remarked shortly before being granted the first state funeral ever staged for a woman in France. "No one must see me after I've died."

According to an old biography I'd read years ago, Colette had spent her last days in bed, elderly, suffering heart failure, whispering to unseen presences. Perhaps her dead mother. Her body, once the source of so much pleasure, was now a painful burden. At the very end of her life, packs of swallows swarmed the garden outside her bedroom window, chasing bees. She swept her arm toward the rustle of wings and cried with the delight of a child—as if she saw what others could not—"*Regarde!*"

Onstage, in the small auditorium at Fort Worden, Win placed the rhythm players right up front, in full view of the audience, so they wouldn't be bothered by distracting echoes bouncing off the back brick wall. From my seat in the very last row, I saw how much the exposure rattled Margie. She smiled uncertainly.

And then one of the older guitar players, one of the standard-tuners who'd quit Band Lab after the DADGAD takeover, walked onstage and took a chair next to her. He hadn't been practicing with the group. Once the music began, it was clear his tuning remained out of step with the others. The fiddles wobbled, off pace.

But then, like a great sea liner steadying itself on erratic waves, the group found a seam, a spot of calm. It drove forward, forging a groove. Melody locked into rhythm. Harmonies soared. After the waltz, before the segue into "The Connaughtman's Rambles," the old guitarist slunk off again, defeated by the drone. By the time "Out on the Ocean" kicked in, Margie was rocking in her chair like a veteran sailor masterfully commanding her vessel.

Afterward, in a dewy field behind the auditorium, the band honored Win with a bottle of Jameson's. She passed it around. Karen played "Whiskey before Breakfast" on the fiddle, and everyone danced. It would be a long and well-deserved celebration. "What the hell—it's Happy Hour in France!" Win shouted.

In the late afternoon, wooden boats groaned mutedly in the water. The deer rested in the shade beneath the tree. The bees made loops among the limbs, intoxicated by sweet, sunny fruit. Soft light rayed through lace curtains in the cottage, giving the floors, the walls, the quilt on the bed, even Popeye, an amber glow as in an old photograph, preserving the rooms forever—where our friend would always be writing her novel.

That evening, Margie returned late, along with Karen and Bill and a pair of other friends she'd made at camp. We turned the cottage into an informal music hall, full of joyous noise. I brought out my bodhran. With pleasure, Margie danced to the beat of its heart.

Ever the expert, Bill promised to send her some sheet music. "You'll have to learn these tunes if you want to be considered a world-class player," he said. Margie smiled and thanked him. We are who we are.

Karen performed a song solo—a piece she'd written honoring her dead husband as well as her brand-new love. It was also a celebration of music: the beauty of fragile voices.

When she got ready to leave, I helped her carry her instruments to her car. We stood beneath the stars, next to the whispering marina. "Take care of that sweet girl of yours," she said, nodding at Margie through the glowing cottage window.

I promised her, "I will."

A day later, on the drive back to Oregon, Margie and I stopped at a place called the Hama Hama Oyster Saloon, on the banks of Hood Canal, a lovely long stretch of water tunneling through bee glades and pine-thick woods, through "limber broom," Virgil might have described it, "willow beds / Pale grey with silver leaves."

It was only noon, we'd eaten a grand breakfast, but . . . oysters! Margie couldn't resist, and I was happy to indulge with her.

Over white wine and Kumamotos at a cedar picnic table, we listened to the barking of sea lions on the shore of the canal, the crunch of children's steps on gray broken shells scattered across pebbles in the dirt. Flocks of kids ran, laughing, around covered fire pits. Lemons and salt lent a bittersweet tang to the air.

Margie picked a small delicacy from the bed of ice on the platter. She said, "I want to thank you again for encouraging me to play music with others." Juice dribbled between her fingers. "Earlier this week, on a CD by a band named Dàimh, I heard a special tune—a gorgeous Hebridean air called 'O Fair A-Nall Am Botal.' Can you remember that title?"

"Why?"

"I want it played at my funeral. No, no—before that. On my deathbed."

A child chased a dog past our table. "Why on earth are you talking like this?" I asked.

She plucked another oyster from the platter. "Because I think now I could die happy."

"You know, of course, I'm checking out before you do."

"You'd better not."

Wind rustled oak leaves, shook pine needles above us. In a flutter of feathers, a great blue heron rose from the sunlit canal. Margie pointed. Juice from her hands dazzled like lightning. "Look!" she said. "Oh, look!" The bird's wings cast a purple shadow on the water.

PART THREE
Dante's Shades

– 7 –

The water dimpled near the ledges of the land, yellow as a yellow onion except farther out to sea, where whale shadows appeared to rise from below, breaking the ruffled surface. Floes of frost floated round a larger slab of ice, a white mass as tall as a one-story office building, as evidenced, roughly, by the full-masted ship at its side . . . wide-based, tapering at the top—the shape of a human heart.

This image appeared in a book of early travel photographs. I shared it each term with my literature students at Oregon State. I wanted to show them how reality changed rapidly in the late nineteenth century with the invention of photography. "Just imagine walking down a city street one afternoon and coming across this picture of an iceberg in a shop window," I said. "This particular shot was taken around the time Mark Twain, our great American realist, died. Except for the very few travelers who'd made it to the Arctic, no one had ever witnessed icebergs. Imagine yourself confronted with this image as a swift crowd pushes past you on the sidewalk or as trolley cars clang behind you in the street—well, your world just got a whole lot bigger. Stranger. Much more dreamlike."

At the start of the twentieth century, certain novelists, such as Henry James, felt they couldn't compete with photography, I explained to my students. In terms of "realism," the camera had it all over the printed page. In one quick glance, the observer of a photograph could take in more of the world, more accurately and in more minute detail, than the reader of a paragraph. To keep narrative viable, James and his compatriots had to take it where the camera couldn't go: into the unlit recesses of pure mind.

Of course, this was history oversimplified. Every technique of what came to be James's modernism (stream-of-consciousness, self-referencing, etc.) appeared centuries earlier in the works of many writers, if from motivations vastly different from James's goals.

Dante, for instance. The constraints of sketching simple word pictures hindered the scope of his ambition, which was to "sail the small bark of his wit" on the mother-sea of existence. Depictions of the afterlife, of the unknowability of God, required a more flexible approach than realism allowed—more suggestive, less literally meaningful. As in dreams.

As in dreams, Dante's hell, his purgatory, and his heaven continually alter their dimensions. Perspectives are difficult to grasp. The most concrete images contrast with the obscurest abstractions. Powerful tropes repeat. Flying, morphing, masking. Sex and death. Shadows and light. Spirit guides—Virgil and Beatrice. St. Bernard. Thomas Aquinas.

Thomas was the thirteenth-century theologian whose ideas of mind and soul Dante recast, dramatically, in the *Divine Comedy*, as central pillars of his universe and as methods of expanding reality. Thomas's "reality" was populated by human beings composed of prime matter and substantial form, form being "that by which, or in virtue of which, a thing is what it is." And in human beings, he said, "what it is" is the soul.

Thomas thought about angels, too—quite a lot. They "combine" matter and not-matter in the makeup of their beings, he said. But more than mortals, they are "heavenly minds." Therefore, "[it] does [not] follow that an angel is ever contained by a place . . . an angel is in a place by acting there—provided that 'action' be understood in a sense which includes not only active movement . . . but also any kind of . . . connection with a body."

An angel may linger in one spot, vanish out of existence, then reappear in a completely different realm (in the quiet dining room of Henry James Sr., for example). According to Thomas, angels communicate by light, weaving web-like fields of energy throughout the cosmos, spreading grace as bees spread pollen.

One day near the end of the week in Port Townsend, while reading the *Comedy*, it occurred to me: to the modern mind, or minds of a certain bent, Thomas Aquinas's descriptions of angels echo William James's discussions of consciousness as a "much-at-once," a vast field continually melting and reappearing in various places, in multiple configurations.

Thomas's angel talk also accords with Stephen Hawking's terms and those of other scientists discussing quantum physics—at least those writing for general audiences.

Hawking stressed that electrons and photons (packets of discrete energy) hold no mass. They are incorporeal. Yet they can be localized through their actions. The electromagnetic field surrounding Earth, through which we become visible and through which things become visible to us, *contains* us. It acts on us and we on it. It is a field without a boundary.

Rupert Sheldrake, a practicing biologist, put it this way: "In quantum theory, in between one action and another, an entity such as a photon or electron exists as a wave function. And this wave function is spread out in space as a probability distribution. You can't say exactly where it is. It's only when it acts that it's localized."

Thomas Aquinas: "The whole universe is one thing; and similarly any part of the universe . . . is one thing. Since then an angel is in place inasmuch as his power is applied to a place, he is never simply everywhere at once, nor in several places, but in one place only at a given moment."

Angels and photons?

I suggest these teasing echoes just to affirm that, once again, in the preceding decades, our world got bigger, stranger, much more dreamlike.

In the end, photography did not destroy written narrative—though it *changed* writing, enhanced it, forced it in different directions, shading our understanding of how we grasp the world, how we order existence in our minds.

Similarly, the theology of Thomas Aquinas, the poetry of Dante, the physics of Hawking, mixing, intertwining. Together—to paraphrase Emily Dickinson—they help us dwell in possibility.

Photons and angels. Photons *as* angels?

Body and soul. Life and death. Surely dwelling in possibility requires us not to constrain ourselves with narrow definitions of reality.

It should not surprise us to discover that Dante's heroic struggles against the boundaries of realism turned him eventually toward music. For him, *music* was pure possibility.

It's through sound in the *Comedy* that he provides his most stirring examples of how human beings evolve through time, creating fresh avenues of inquiry, tweaking old terms, growing increasingly more complex in their awareness.

In hell, song is reduced to moaning. The body's suffering does not allow for subtle aesthetics. In purgatory, among the more enlightened souls saved for eternal life, harmonies begin to resound, supplied by angelic choirs. And in paradise, where individuals reach their peak potential, polyphony breaks out everywhere, along with bursts of blinding light.

Famously, it was percussion that led to the discovery of harmonic structure. Pythagoras, passing by a smithy's forge one day, heard the sounds produced by four hammers of unequal weight on the flattened heads of anvils. From this experience, he worked out musical scales mathematically—the octave, the intervals of fifths, fourths, and thirds.

Afterward, philosophers from Boethius to Thomas Aquinas speculated that (as Boethius said) "the state of our soul and body seems somehow to be combined . . . by the same proportions as . . . link together the modulations of harmony."

In purgatory, when Dante hears the noisy gate opening for him, clanging and groaning, on the path up the mountain toward paradise, he describes the sounds as "sweet." They are sweet because of what they promise—immortality—but also because medieval concepts of beautiful music emphasized harmony rather than individual notes. A drum and a hurdy-gurdy playing in concert, no matter how raucously, could produce *dulcis symphonia* ("sweet symphony").

Isadore of Seville, a medieval music theorist, wrote rapturously of drums struck "with small sticks": they create a "concord of low and high" notes, she said, resulting in "a most sweet song." She reserved her highest praise for "rhythmic music," for "various plucked stringed instruments, drums, and other percussion instruments, among them bells, the clapping of hands, and the creaking of hinges."

In early August, when we returned to Corvallis from Port Townsend—me a bit ghosty still—Margie rejoined a regular Sunday afternoon Celtic session at a downtown pub on the riverfront. She had gained substantial confidence at Fiddle Tunes, felt she was versatile enough and gifted with a fine enough ear to hold her own with more advanced players, and to learn from them. Most of all, she had a good time.

I went with her each week, sat and drank red wine and listened to the group. Eventually, at her urging, and encouraged by the players' unfailing generosity, I joined the sessions as well, unpacking my bodhran. (The musicians welcomed me because my curly gray hair and mustache reminded them of an amiable Mark Twain, one fellow said—how bad could I be?) Hierarchies were not as severe there. I remained convinced that my knowledge of the instrument was painfully limited. But I could always catch a tune's rhythm, and

I kept my flourishes simple, staying out of everyone's way. It was a sweet scene. In spite of my doubts, I felt warmly invited into the circle.

Glancing around the room one day, I remembered the gist of a passage in an old book on Dante's poetry: "The meaning of Purgatory . . . is a social one: the penitents must re-learn to act *a tempo* with a *communitas* of other human beings before they can reach beatitude."

The pub faced the lazy Willamette River on the east side of town. Its tree-lined bank sheltered many of the community's homeless. During any given weekday, doing business downtown, you'd rarely see these folks. They remained hidden in the shadows of underpasses or in alleyways beside greasy boxes stacked behind convenience stores. But on Sundays, especially if the sun was out, they'd gather by the water, sharing smokes and dumpster scraps, laughing, sometimes singing. Through the windows of the pub, as we played, we'd notice them, startled by their numbers. Big muddy boots. Massive overcoats, cloth hanging in tatters. Though I liked to imagine these stragglers as moving on the path to redemption, their resemblance to lost souls was more on the mark.

One afternoon, another bodhran player arrived at the pub, an older fellow, an ethnomusicologist by profession, he said. We traded off on tunes. All day, I felt extremely self-conscious under his expert eye, but at one point he said to me, "You know, you're terrific. You have no trouble with tricky rhythms that often give even the best drummers trouble."

I protested that I didn't even know how to hold the drum properly, that I was cheating by using my fingers on the back of the head.

"Doesn't matter," he said. "You've got your own style, your own feel for the instrument. Bottom line is, if it works, you're golden. And you're golden."

Dulcis symphonia. I'd taken a small step up the mountain.

ABACHTA: One of the seven angels of confusion.

CASTIEL: A Thursday angel.

ERIONAS: An angel invoked in the exorcism of Wax.

MEFATHIEL: An opener of doors.

SHAHRIVAR: An angel of August.

ZUHAIR: One of the ten angels that follow the sun on its daily course.

Sometimes at session, pounding out a heartbeat, I'd stare through the pub window at the riverside. Silently, I'd bestow angel names on the men and women huddled over paper-wrapped scraps of food because they vanished and reappeared with such ease each week. Yellow leaves fell all around them and onto the shoulders of their thick cotton coats.

FORCAS: an angel-teacher of rhetoric and mathematics—he can render people invisible.

PATROZIN: an angel of the fifth hour of the night.

I'm certain that part of what finally motivated Margie to cook for the homeless in our community was her photographs of Scotland.

For her, these were not just travel pictures like the ancient icebergs I used to show my students—though she *did* love sharing the photos with friends. She even used one of them as her computer's screen saver: a swirling fog-tunnel blowing across a hillside in the Highlands among gentle slopes of heather. The Cuillins, the Quiraing on the Isle of Skye, the ferries in the harbor at Mallaig—these images did not just hold warm memories for her; they composed a fragile record of places that might disappear the next time she traveled. The myth of Brigadoon was not false for her—in her bones, she felt the tenuousness of places and people she loved. She knew it might not be possible to return to Utopia. More than that: Utopia may be lost to us already.

Grief: the only response to so much beauty, such sweeping uncertainty.

With this fragility in mind, along with her awareness of the increasing numbers of drifters by the river, Margie realized a longstanding dream. Years earlier, before Ehud got sick, she had discussed with him her belief that a commitment to Judaism meant doing good in the world, performing mitzvahs. He agreed. Though he'd sloughed off formal religion, he still respected the Jewish tradition of social activism. As a result of these conversations, Margie, Ehud, and I volunteered one day, early in 2001, to serve meals at Stone Soup, the local soup kitchen operating out of St. Mary's Catholic Church, just a few blocks from our house. Margie captured that day in a journal:

> The three of us were stationed out on the gymnasium floor behind the milk, lemonade, and coffee, waiting for people as they came to the end of the food line. I love the big industrial church kitchen: all that stainless steel, the enormous burners, the walk-in fridges and freezers, the dishwasher square and silver and steaming. Such a big, good feeling there. When it's time to serve, someone in the kitchen presses a button, and voila, up lifts the slatted metal tambour door between kitchen and gymnasium, revealing the evening's casserole and soup in their steam pans, and also the food servers, spatulas and ladles aloft . . .
>
> At the long tables, people sat together in groups even if they weren't talking; an impression of momentary ease and sociability. There are clear solitaries, even in the midst of the groups: a man in a headband read an old-curled-up *McCall's* . . . An older gentleman . . . was overtaken by twitching: he crushed his hands between his legs, put his thumbnail to his mouth and bit hard, moved his arms in rapid sequence, then started over again, in order . . .
>
> People ate hard—how else to put it? Seriously bent over their plates of curly noodles and meat sauce, salad and bread and pea soup . . .

She told me that day she'd love to cook for Stone Soup—tacos for seventy! lasagna! a vat of pot pie!—but then came my long periods of recovery, Ehud's worsening illness . . . after that, trips to Scotland (noting the country's inevitable changes), deaths, deaths, and more deaths.

But Margie never lost sight of her commitment. Spurred by her resolve, eventually, in the fall of 2017, we began volunteering once a month to plan, coordinate, and cook a meal for the homeless at St. Mary's.

Margie was a whirlwind of determination and fierce organization. I built mountains of parsnips and chopped yellow onions. A sweet crew of friends from the local Jewish community met with us on the second Thursday of each month to fry, bake, stir, and simmer. Margie referred to us, collectively, as "Kitchens Brigadoon": here today, gone tomorrow.

At the wide tables in the gym, gulping down hot veggie soup: Halacho, genius of sympathies; Micheu, a minor angel wielding powers over the waters of life; Phanuel, archangel of penance . . .

Once, on a cold autumn afternoon in 2014, I drove Ehud to Portland for a chemo treatment. Afterward, groggy, he said he was hungry. "What would you like?" I asked. "Pizza," he said.

Gripping his arm, careful to avoid the spot where the IV needle had pierced his skin, I guided him through the door of a nearly deserted pizzeria a few blocks from the hospital. A teenage boy, clothes reeking of pot, tended the wood-fired oven. He stared at the flames and talked to himself. An elderly couple sat at a corner table glaring warily at the twists of green pepper strewn across their deep-dish pizza. The woman appeared to be drinking a pitcher of ale all by herself. Her head lolled. A second empty pitcher sat beside her. Her companion, a bald, toothless man with a smudgy mustache, did not seem to know where he was. Ehud stared into space. I realized with dismay that at the moment I was the only *functioning aware-ness* in the place. Perhaps that's overstating things, but loneliness overcame me, akin to the feeling I'd had as a kid (nine, ten?) when one day I'd stared at my parents' house and wondered how others saw it. Did they see the same things I did? The off-white paint on the eaves? The slant of the roof? The same front window? Did they hear birds in the trees, the humming of the power line?

Visiting my study one day before he got sick, Ehud glimpsed *A Dictionary of Angels* on my bookshelf. "Why do you have a copy of that?" he asked.

"Oh, I don't know. It's just a quirky little book I ran across one day." "Let me show you something," he said. He turned to Gustav Davidson's acknowledgments page, where the author praised the "counsel, knowledge, and help" he'd received from religious scholars in his effort to compile a list of angel references found in world literature. Ehud pointed to the bottom of the page, where Davidson had written, "I am . . . under obligation to Dr. Meir Havazelet of Yeshiva University, New York, who culled angels for me from the minor midrashim and who did not hesitate to ring me up in the middle of the night to spell out the names of winged creatures he had suddenly come across . . . and which, he feared, I might have overlooked."

"My father," Ehud said. "I remember those middle-of-the-night phone calls. I was a kid . . . I'd have a nightmare or something and I'd be yelling for him, but he'd be on the phone, talking angels. He was obsessed. So of course when I got older, I rejected his teachings. They were just awful memories for me." Gently, he ran his fingers across the ink on the page. "Sometimes, waking from sleep, I'd hear him on the phone . . . I thought he was talking *to* an angel . . ."

One day in late October, I stepped into St. Mary's gym to set up tables and chairs. In a far corner, beside a wall of sunny windows, the priests had erected a Day of the Dead altar for their Hispanic parishioners: collages of orange autumn leaves, pumpkins, a small wooden cross, a painting of Christ, postcards featuring winged cherubs. Among these delicate objects, Latino families had placed photographs of their dear departed, along with scribbled notes of love and devotion, and cans of food, in the spirit of breaking bread with the dead.

That evening, around the folding tables, sickness, hard luck, addiction, and grief huddled together, shivering over steaming plates of chicken and gravy, potatoes and peas.

Bells, the clapping of hands, the creaking of hinges.

My growing comfort with the bodhran at Sunday session, and the fun of learning new music along with my wife, made me ambitious to expand my repertoire, though I didn't know this until I walked into a music store to look at drums one day and found myself staring instead at a hammered dulcimer.

A hammered dulcimer looks a little like a piano after someone has performed an autopsy on it, the skin tossed away, leaving behind exposed sets of strings. Two lightweight sticks, curved like half-spoons, sound the notes.

References to dulcimers appear as early as the seventh century B.C. in Nineveh, I'd learn. Apparently, around A.D. 700, the Persians added bass and treble bridges to the board. From ancient manuscripts, we know the instrument was played throughout Europe in Dante's time, in cathedrals alongside massive organs rumbling like thunder. In describing angelic music, Dante often uses variations of the word *dulcedo*, "sweet," or *dolce suono*, "sweet dream."

In the spring of 1662, Samuel Pepys recorded in his journal: "Here among the fidlers I first saw a dulcimere played on with sticks knocking on the strings, and [it] is very pretty."

I stood in the music store, entranced, hefting the sticks, rolling, sliding, chittering, chiming. A percussion instrument singing melodies—for me, a charming musical evolution. Immediately, I felt attached to the thing.

I brought the dulcimer home, set it up in a closet in our guest bedroom upstairs, beneath a loose light bulb flickering off and on. With Margie's help, I taught myself to read simple music. I began with Beatles tunes—the Beatles had sparked my love of rock and roll as a kid. I knew the melodies; they made good starting points. After that, I ventured forth—"The Connaughtman's Rambles," the jig Margie had performed at Fiddle Tunes; meditative songs such as "Carol of the Bells."

Bells there were, and clapping and creaking. The dulcimer could sound like a choir or an a capella voice echoing across sharp, icy mountaintops. It had the resonance of a small piano, the crispness of guitar. Most of all, it evoked the strumming of a harp. It vibrated with qualities of sound we associate with angels: ethereality, delicacy, even silence.

– 8 –

When she was seven or eight years old, Hannah was an eager Beatles fan. I'd play the records for her, then sit her down at my drum kit to show her Ringo's tricks.

Until now, I've not mentioned Hannah. My stepdaughter. A major narrative error: never wait until the third act to introduce a crucial story element. The rules say the reader must be well prepared for all eventualities (*this wasn't supposed to happen to me*).

But here's a countervailing view, from Kierkegaard's journals: *Never speak of what you cherish most; as soon as you express your love, you have exposed it to the world's toxins.*

It is finally impossible not to speak of what you love. You'd like to believe that if your love is strong enough, the people you cherish will survive any poison. But in the case of a child, the first, the *overwhelming*, impulse is to protect. Protect at all costs.

Pity the poor child of writers. Once, when Hannah was little, Margie asked her what she'd like to be when she grew up. "Look at me!" she said. "I'm surrounded. I'll have to make books!"

"God forbid," Margie and I said in unison.

The child of writers does not ask to be made into subject matter. But that is an almost certain fate—even as late as Act Three—despite the writer's urge to protect. Besides flirting over oysters, when Hannah was four, Margie and I came together like Dante's Paolo and Francesca over books, a mutual love of reading and writing. Like the lovers in *Inferno*, we felt blown together by what seemed an irresistible force. It caused a rupture in Margie's marriage. Through it all, feeling guilty and scared, we did our best to protect Hannah from the consequences. We didn't move in together for over a year. I never stayed overnight at Margie's place when Hannah was with her. Hannah and I were friends—I didn't need to push the stepfather thing on her.

But inevitably we shook her world. In the months before Margie and I married, Margie took Hannah to a therapist, who tried to coax her to say what she felt. The doctor set up a tiny sandbox in her office and handed Hannah three dolls. She named the dolls Tracy, Marjorie, and Hannah. "Show me what you feel," the doctor said. At first Hannah buried the Hannah doll up to her neck in sand while Tracy and Marjorie lay together on a blanket. Then, like a skilled writer revising her ending, she reversed the scenario: Tracy and Marjorie went under, out of sight, while Hannah danced on the rim of the box. "Which of those two stories do you like best?" the therapist asked. "The second one," Hannah said. We felt immensely relieved. Killing us was a sign of her strength, her mental health.

I never really knew what worry was until a child slept beneath my roof. I was responsible for the child, responsible for the roof, responsible for keeping them both intact. Hannah was an uneasy sleeper. She'd toss, laugh, whimper, and talk through her athletic dreams. I often wonder if she'd have had an easier time of things if the ghost children Margie imagined—the brothers and sisters we never gave Hannah—had arrived. As it turned out, I was not destined for the version of immortality achieved through passing on genes.

"I'm not sure I believe in God," Hannah told me one night in the kitchen of the house Margie and I had bought together. She was twelve at the time. I was washing the dinner dishes, and Hannah was finishing her homework. Margie was away that night at an academic meeting. For some time, Hannah had been wrestling with her relationship to Judaism. She had many friends among the children of the Jewish families in town, and she liked the Passover feast and the colorful High Holiday rituals. She said she thought she'd like to have a bat mitzvah, but she admitted she was mainly interested in the party. "Judaism is a social thing for me," she said. "I'm not sure what else it is. What do Jews believe about life after death?"

I confessed I wasn't sure.

She thought hard. "Can I still be a Jew and not believe in life after death?"

I told her that if nothing else, Judaism could be a powerful cultural identity for her, if that was important to her, and she could be anything she wanted. I told her that for her mom, Judaism was a form of commitment to her community.

I didn't tell her I had no business telling her any of this because I didn't know what I was talking about. The responsibilities of stepfatherhood were getting more complicated.

Hannah was not alone among the Jews we knew in expressing confusion. I remember that at one Passover meal with some of our friends, just as we were listing the plagues—locusts and frogs—one of the children asked, "Is the Easter Bunny gonna come?"

Quite sensibly, Hannah longed for Christmas presents every year, and lights and a tree topped with golden angels.

Her religious perplexity reached a peak when she considered the problem of evil. "How can I believe in God when He let such awful things happen to the Jews?"

"Hmm," I said. "But on the other hand, there's your homework." She'd been poring over multiplication tables, sitting with our cat in her lap. "With numbers, we can understand how life is ordered and see that almost everything exists in some kind of harmonious relationship—"

"But the Jews!"

"Yes. I don't know, Hannah. I don't know." I admitted, "I don't have an answer for you."

"You had a bad dream."

Most of the time, Margie slept better than Hannah did. But occasionally I'd wake to a cry, turn, and see her twitching in the grip of a nightmare. She was falling (she had a terrible fear of heights) or trying to escape a predator. Or else it was some deeper mystery.

Of all the people I knew, she came the closest to possessing a sixth sense. It didn't happen often, but whenever a voice awakened her from sleep, or when a chill overcame her and she felt something had happened to someone she loved, I believed her.

Once, she confirmed after the fact that a friend of ours had died one day, thousands of miles away, at precisely the moment Margie broke into tears in a yoga class. "I *felt* her," she said. More than once while her mother was alive, she'd wake, startled, and say, "I need to call Mom," and always, we'd learn, for good reason.

She didn't consider this ability spooky or strange. She didn't consider it an *ability*. It was simply part of her consciousness.

She wrote, once, about a visitation she'd received from her father. He'd died of leukemia when she was nineteen. He appeared to her early one February morning in the hallway between her bedroom and Hannah's, in the rental house she'd moved into after leaving her husband. Hannah was six. She'd stay with Margie every other week. Before bed each night, Hannah put on a red and white striped nightgown. Together, the two of them drank hot chocolate in front of a woodstove. The place "felt like sanctuary but never quite home"; it "held the strange delights of the temporary bivouac but also the underbelly of fear," Margie wrote.

Then one morning, right before she woke Hannah for the day, Margie had a vivid dream. In the hall, standing on dark brown linoleum tiles, her father greeted her fervently. She wrote:

"I'm glad you're here," I began. "Hannah—"

"Listen, sweetheart, no time to talk," he replied in his old gruff way. "I need you at the hospital. I'm dying all over again."

"Oh, Dad, I can't," I said. "My little girl's sleeping—"

"Honey," he said. "Please—I don't want to bother your mother . . ."

"But I can't," I said.

"Are you sure?" he said . . . He knew how his story would go . . . He knew everything, and still could not resign himself to the way it had gone, the way it had to go.

"Well," he said with a sigh. "You can't blame me for trying. Goodbye."

At the time of his passing, Margie was living in Scotland, going to school in a study-abroad program. She felt guilty for not making it back to the States in time to speak with him. I've often wondered (so has she) if Scotland's enduring allure for her has something to do with this turbulent mix of emotions—delight with an underbelly of fear.

In the years since Hannah left us, going to college, moving to Portland, marrying, pursuing a career in transportation planning, Margie had become a lighter sleeper—anticipating a voice in the dark, telling her she'd better call her daughter? But then she began to play music. After weekly sessions on the river, she'd come home "totally high" from performing, she said. Hours would pass before she could settle. When she did, the sleep was profound.

"An absence, once announced, cannot be taken back," Margie wrote after her father's visitation.

Endorphins stirred my brain whenever I played the bodhran, but I didn't get "totally high." I was grateful to be drumming, to be socializing, to feel engaged with a friendly community, but grief had become ingrained in me. At random, in the middle of a tune, and for no reason I could discern, an image of my mother would crystallize in my head—her last days in the hospital. Or I'd see my father spasming in his bed.

In early autumn, when Margie and I learned of a chance to travel to Iceland, I resisted at first: our steady schedule, playing tunes, cooking for Stone Soup, hadn't eased my gloom, but it had focused me *away* from myself, made me less conscious, more purely active, and I was frightened of walking away, even briefly.

I knew Iceland would be splendid. We'd traveled there once before, on a quick stopover after one of our Scottish trips. One night, standing beside a still volcanic lake, we'd seen the Northern Lights: shimmering green fire blowing holes in the sky. I remember feeling I was going to be swept away in a vast electric field—dissolving, *becoming* motion and light.

It was thrilling to recall the place. Still, the timing of this new trip troubled me. What brief respite I got from depression seemed to depend on my recent habits. But an opportunity had come to us, a chance to fly cheaply—this time to see a glacier up close. It was hard to turn down. Margie said we should think about it, but we'd have to decide soon.

In the meantime, Karen, our friend from Fiddle Tunes, came to town. She passed through on her way back to Portland from a music festival on the Oregon coast. (Sadly, Bill and Carla, the other cool kids from camp, had fallen away from us, into the sweeping silence of the formerly known.)

Karen was accompanied by her lover, with whom she'd been testing a long-distance relationship. He was a guitar player. One afternoon they joined our Sunday session. During a break, Karen confided to Margie that she really loved the guy, but logistics and age and geography had defeated them. It wasn't going to work.

Later, Karen and her man sang a slow air together, sitting across from each other at a table banked with empty beer bottles and

THE LAND AND THE DAYS

half-cleared plates. Their rhythms locked fast. The miracle of harmony: two voices merging to become a single sound.

Lovers meet. Lovers part. Lovers pass away: Margie's deepest fear.

One night, she reminded me of the research she had done while preparing to write her modern myth. She'd learned that in certain versions of the Orpheus story, the singer's laments make the sun rise. This was the case in *Black Orpheus*, the 1959 Marcel Camus film. Camus set the story in Rio de Janeiro during Carnaval. Margie and I watched the movie for the third or fourth time on a home DVD shortly before leaving for Iceland.

In Camus's film, Orpheus is a young trolley driver. He is also a guitarist. Eurydice is a visitor to the city, fleeing a strange man. She says he wants to kill her. Orpheus falls in love with her. He vows to protect her.

At Carnaval, they dance in the streets to hypnotic samba beats. In the madness of swirling streamers, snowing confetti, incessant drumming, a lithe man wearing a skull mask pursues Eurydice. Finally he chases her into the hellish bowels of the trolley station. To escape him, she shimmies along a power line swaying high above him. Orpheus arrives, breathlessly calling her name. He can't see in the dark. He pulls an electric switch. Eurydice screams and falls to the ground. "Now she's mine," Death hisses.

Two children, Benedito and Zeca, follow Orpheus wherever he goes. Throughout the film, they delight in his morning arias, watching him strum his guitar while the sun rises. At the end, when Orpheus, crushed by grief, dies while carrying Eurydice's body up a hill, Zeca snatches up his guitar. Tentatively at first, then with growing confidence, he invokes the dawn. (Pity the children of artists— the responsibilities are many.)

A girl appears on the hill, as tiny as Hannah was when I first got to know her. The girl dances to Zeca's rhythm. The beat goes on, in a new generation.

Once, reading a history of the movie, Margie learned that several years after its release, and purely by coincidence, the actors who'd played Orpheus and Eurydice, Breno Mello and Marpessa Dawn, died of heart attacks less than two months apart.

– 9 –

According to *A Book of Bees* by Sue Hubbell:

> For centuries, beekeepers have been tanging—making a ringing noise by beating a metal spoon against a pot—under a swarm to bring it down . . . But bees do not have a sense of hearing in the way we do. Gilbert White, the eighteenth-century English naturalist, established this fact to his own satisfaction by roaring at [bees] through a speaking trumpet held near their hive. He reported they failed to show "the least sensibility or resentment." Modern authorities say bees are virtually deaf to airborne sound but moderately sensitive to sound waves that travel through other solid objects, which they can detect through sense organs on their feet.

Like Carnaval dancers sexily ignoring Death, the bees go about their sweet business, impervious to sound but vaguely aware of menacing vibrations. In this example, it's all too easy to dwell on our physical limitations—*our* limits as well as the bees'; easy to concentrate on the brute nature of our senses, on the little we perceive of the world. But if we reverse the focus, and think instead of the *effort* to grasp what lies beyond us, we reach the core of a certain kind of grief—longing to reconnect with those who've quit the physical. What persists of them, if anything, we cannot know. But occasionally, often in dreams, we believe we intuit them through some thin vibration.

In his vision of purgatory—of souls struggling to deserve eternal life—Dante celebrated human frailties. It's a provocative stance.

In a book called *Experiencing the Afterlife: Soul and Body in Dante and Medieval Culture*, Manuele Gragnolati notes the importance in modern Christian thought of shared limitations: "In the eleventh and twelfth centuries, Christian spirituality began to shift from a concentration on Christ's divinity to a strong focus on his humanity," Gragnolati says. Christian authorities, and Christian writings, looked to the possibility of suffering as the path to redemption (returning, perhaps, to Christianity's roots in Judaism, and the emphasis on worldly compassion). It was the capacity to feel bodily pain that bound individuals most closely to Christ. His gesture of physical suffering was his pact with us, a sign of love. According to Christian beliefs, pain, decay, and death entered the world through Adam's sin. Pain could only be conquered through pain.

During the late Middle Ages, the development of the cult of the Veronica increased the importance of Christ's humanity. The Veronica was a piece of cloth presumed to be imprinted with Jesus's tortured face. Pilgrims trekked for months across hard, dry plains to observe it in Rome: its very materiality (as well as its image of pain, preserved like a bee in amber) secured them to Christ and the mystery of salvation.

For worshippers of Mary, compassion and grief were holy forms of suffering. Though Mary was not nailed to the cross, she endured great agony during the crucifixion. Through her, grief became redemptive pain.

It was in this context—in the blessedness of grieving—that images of purgatory, silent shades hunched on a mountain, trudging toward immortality, took shape.

> I turned . . . with the confidence that
> a little child shows, running to its mother
> when something has frightened it or troubled it,
> to say to Virgil, "Not even one drop

of blood is left in me that is not trembling . . ."
But Virgil had left [me], he was no longer there
Among us, Virgil, most tender father,
Virgil to whom I gave myself to save me . . .

It seemed that at least one of my ghosts had not left me. Not entirely. But Ehud continued to age whenever he returned, growing physically frailer in death, in dreams, just as he had in life.

Exhausted after a day at Stone Soup tending bread or baking casseroles, Margie slept especially well if she drifted off in our bedroom while I stood in the room above it practicing my hammered dulcimer. The sounds vibrated through the floor, through the wood, shimmering, distant, like "heavenly harps," Margie said, or bells tolling sailors home from sea. They soothed her, and she'd nod out over one of the many books she kept by the bed: Edith Hamilton's *Mythology*, a history of Jewish diasporas, a recent biography of Colette.

According to Davidson's *Dictionary of Angels*, the angels' primary task is to praise. They do so mentally, with the power of their intelligence, Davidson writes—that is, they do so silently.

In trying, each day, to achieve heavenly sounds on the dulcimer, I aspired to near- silence, nearly pure vibration: the silence of praise, the silence of grief.

Dwelling in possibility must mean living like a midrashist, occupying the gaps, the silences *between* definitions. Embracing and welcoming the *opportunity* of silence.

A choked cry. "You had a bad dream."
I woke to Margie's hand on my shoulder.
Awful things had been happening to masses of people. In mud. Behind bloody barbed wire. I sprawled among the victims, gasping, gripping my chest.

And then I was lying comfortably in bed, clinging to my wife.

For a while after my parents died, it seemed that every night I dreamed of West Texas cow pastures, muddy and dark. The fields of my childhood.

Once, when I was thirteen or fourteen, I joined some friends in a pasture to watch a total lunar eclipse. As the earth's shadow fell across the moon's disc, turning it a rusty orange scored with rich red craters, the air grew chilly and still. The sky became a vast purple canvas. I tried to sketch the scene in a notebook, but pencil shadings could not accurately capture the event's fluidity. I vividly experienced the limits of my awareness.

I could observe. Yet I could not convey what I saw.

As soon as the moon's light reappeared from behind the earth's shadow, roosters began to crow; cows stirred among scraggly mesquite limbs, lowing, snuffling. They were unable to perceive the truth of the moment—fooled by a false dawn.

It was my habit on Thursday afternoons, before heading to Stone Soup, to stop by our local bookshop—an endless desire to augment my reading on immortality. In the bookshop one day, in the "Spirituality" section (where I lingered most often now), I picked up a curious volume titled *The Self-Aware Universe*.

In it, the physicist Amit Goswami discusses the impossibility of fully grasping existence—in essence, he says, we are forever chasing false dawns.

For example: "Watching electrons . . . is like watching fireflies on a summer evening. You can see a flash here and another twinkle of light there, but you have no idea where the firefly is between your observations."

The same principle holds for "macroscopic object[s]." For instance, the moon appears predictable in its orbital path only because our brute senses convince us that "deterministic trajectories" and "causal continuity" exist. But our reality is wrong. In fact, "initial conditions do not forever determine an object's motion."

Every time we observe something, there is "a new beginning . . . the world is creative at the base level": an evolving entity dazzling our untiring and restless consciousness.

In its final pages, as with most volumes on the nature and substance of the universe, Goswami's book did not conclude as much as devolve into a series of speculative mathematical equations—like Dante at the end of *Paradiso*, face to face with God: a great poet fumbling to express what he saw.

Which should have given me pause before I began thinking about immortality and grief.

Inevitably, approaching the end of writing a book, the feeling of urgency grows. The words get fewer, passages shorter. Language seems to have failed—or *you* have failed the language.

Silence seems desirable: silence in which the imperceptible may reveal itself.

Listen. Do you not believe I am still with you?

It was an unearthly landscape, Iceland, when we reached it late one autumn afternoon. A landscape tailored for dreams.

A place of crackling air—conveyed most effectively, perhaps, by saying little of it.

Imagine a fleeting glimpse of immensity. Then pass on.

Praise silence.

Our goal had been to float among icebergs. In a rubber raft one day, we motored out into the Jökulsárlón Glacier Lagoon. Among natural wind-carved cathedrals, we drifted in mist. In cold sunlight. The water melts the ice from underneath; in an instant, erosion can unbalance a giant crag and tip it. It's like a city block flipping over. Underwater ice looks crystalline, clear; ice forced above the surface hardens into a thick white coat, exposed to the toxins of the world.

Blue and lightly milky, the lagoon's beauty has come at a terrible cost. It grows more extensive, more impressive, every year, we learned, because the Jökulsárlón Glacier is rapidly diminishing, the result of climate change.

Several of our fellow visitors to the glacier that day bewailed the "evils" of corporate greed, of self-involved politicians hastening the earth's destruction. Others took a longer view. They wondered how *God* could allow such beauty to perish.

Shouldn't the earth be immortal?

My heart beat faster on the ice.

On a windy cliff overlooking the glacier, Margie asked me to hold her tight. Her acrophobia wasn't a fear of falling as much as worry that some irrational part of her brain might urge her to jump. As I understood it, it was a matter of the tiny self confronted with the emptiness of its surroundings, and recognizing how little kept them apart.

Back home, a week after the Iceland trip, I worked to recover my daily routines, my stays against grief: writing, practicing the dulcimer, attending sessions, cooking for the homeless.

The talk of evil from our afternoon in the lagoon stayed with me, though, reminding me of Hannah's long-ago questions concerning religious belief.

One day, I recalled reading, in Port Townsend, William James's discussion of a "finite god": not an all-seeing, omnipotent being with the power to eradicate evil, but a participant in the evolutionary struggle. I looked the passage up. Sure enough, James was convinced that only a "suffering god" could be intimately engaged in the ongoing process of creation. A god suffused with grief, his anguished cry like the sound of rending ice, a glacier cracking apart.

It occurred to me then: maybe the *Comedy* had it wrong. If James was right, the grieving *were* redeemed.

Grief as praise?

Grief as the angels' work, celebrating what is lost, what we're losing?

Grief as immortality, blurring time, extending every past into the present.

Rabindranath Tagore: "The immortal / does not boast of its length of years / but of the scintillating point of its moment."

A moment came one day when, pressed by grief, I needed to write this book. The moment is near—like a whisper from an unseen source—when I'll feel the need to finish.

One day the mounting pressure of grief prompted Margie and me to apply together for long-term care insurance policies so we would not wind up like my mother, enfeebled, adrift, and in need of emergency support.

Margie's application was swiftly approved. After an extended afternoon of cooking at Stone Soup, I learned that I had been declined because of my "history of coronary bypass surgery, in combination with asthma." From the company's point of view, I was already gone.

Naturally, the insurers were more interested in benefitting themselves than in helping me.

Society the redeemed form of man? I think not.

Margie without me.

Yes, I thought. I knew that. Who needs your damn actuarial tables?

Journalist Gina Kolata, writing in the *New York Times:*

> In a study that raises profound questions about the line between life and death, researchers have restored some cellular activity to brains removed from slaughtered pigs. . . . [B]lood vessels in the pigs' brains began functioning . . . certain brain cells regained

metabolic activity . . . [and] electrical activity [revived] in some neurons . . . [But] "What does it mean to talk about consciousness in a pig? What are we looking for?" [one of the doctors] wondered.

Consciousness moves through the universe, through dark matter, through solid objects, rippling into and out of our brains—like an electron's wave function, writes Amit Goswami. Moment to moment, with "every experience," our brains "collapse . . . the wave function." They do so "by acting self-referentially," making each one of our memories the equivalent of an electron's particle state, precisely locatable in time.

In this way, "*the universe is self-aware through us*. In us the universe cuts itself into two—into subject and object." Author and book.

Goswami: "What we are looking for is what is looking."

When the weather turned cold in late autumn, a few homeless men came early to St. Mary's gym and asked if they could slip inside to warm their hands and feet while awaiting the meal. They helped us set up tables and chairs, and the corkboard listing phone numbers for social services and emergency shelters. One young man, toothless, always ashen, insisted on signing his name to a piece of paper to prove that he'd been there, that he'd helped us, and to take responsibility, he said, in case anything he did caused a problem.

One of the regulars at the meals was a tall, lanky fellow with stringy white hair and a beard the length of his torso. The first time I'd seen him was the day Ehud, Margie, and I served food there, years earlier. He was rumored to have been a physics professor at Oregon State University who'd suffered a breakdown—the implication being that what he'd learned of the cosmos had overwhelmed him, dragging him into a vortex of confusion and silence.

He'd dance a little jig whenever he received a heaping helping of mashed potatoes and gravy.

To my unpracticed ear, the most beautiful songs for hammered dulcimer were composed by the blind poet and Celtic harper Turlough O'Carolan (ca. 1670–1738): ghostly, ringing—often a series of single-note runs up and down a scale, leaving grave silences in between. Facts about O'Carolan's life are scanty, but apparently he traveled across Ireland performing funeral airs and "planxties"—songs of praise for his patrons and hosts.

After a hectic day in St. Mary's kitchen, the most calming thing I could do was practice the dulcimer. My favorite piece was an air entitled "O'Carolan's Dream," rumored to be the final piece he ever wrote. In the book *Irish Minstrels and Musicians*, the music collector Francis O'Neill writes, "Shortly before his death, [O'Carolan] called for his harp, and with feeble fingers wandering among the strings, he evolved his last composition, [a] weirdly plaintive wail, 'O'Carolan's Farewell to Music.'"

For me, it was the musical equivalent of the end of Shakespeare's *A Midsummer Night's Dream*: "If we shadows have offended, / Think but this, and all is mended, / That you have but slumb'red here / While these visions did appear. / And this weak and idle theme, / no more yielding but a dream . . ."

"I think someday I'd like to have kids."
   "That's wonderful, Hannah."
   "I'm not in any hurry."
   "Well. But your kids may be."

One night—it was just a few nights ago—I dreamed that Ehud came to me as I was playing the hammered dulcimer: as if the tanging, or the silences between, had called him forth. From where? What can the dead hear? I was wearing an apron from St. Mary's kitchen as I struck the strings with wooden spoons. Frost coated the window of my practice closet. Ice etched crystalline shapes on the glass, recalling the intricate geometry of a beehive, of Dante's purgatorial mountain. Ehud sat in the little space, quietly listening.

The light bulb flickered. And then it occurred to me: he didn't know he was dead. In the mysterious, perfectly natural way of dreams, in my palms the sticks changed into a manuscript of typed pages. I understood it was my task to explain to Ehud what had happened to him—precisely the opposite of what had been true in my life ever since his passing.

In life, I had been seeking answers from him. Do you still exist somehow? Where? Visiting his grave, I waited for his voice on the wind, a finger-like leaf beckoning from a tree.

But in the dream, *I* had to provide the story. In the past, I'd said to my ghost, "I don't know if this is real," and he'd assured me it was. This time, I said to him he probably couldn't be here.

He looked at me: *Why not?*

I raised the manuscript. *The Land and the Days*. "These were the last words you ever wrote," I said.

Confusion crossed his face. He was aging right in front of me.

I ruffled the pages. "This is what's left of you," I said. "I'm deeply grateful for it . . ."

He began to recede. Like ink, the closet's shadows filled him in.

" . . . but, you see, you're no longer living."

He was gone.

The manuscript had become a pair of sticks again, delicate instruments for channeling pure rhythm. I flexed the muscles in my hands and resumed stroking the dulcimer, leaving longer silences than ever, aware that Margie, alone, slept below me in our warm and narrow bed.

ACKNOWLEDGMENTS

I am immensely grateful to Kent Calder at the University of Oklahoma Press for his patience, encouragement, and understanding, as well as his love of music and William James. Also at the Press, Stephanie Evans, Amy Hernandez, and Mona Springfield worked hard to make this a better book. Jane Lyle was a superb copyeditor. Michael Martone gave the manuscript an insightful early read. Jill Johnson granted me great forbearance.

For the life behind the stories, I am indebted to Terri and Ed Clarac; Anne, David, and J. C. Daugherty; Sue Jones; Martha Grace Low; Barbie and Ernie Martinez; Arlo and Hannah Mullin; Jo Beth Reeves; Noel Gene and Doris Ann Rodgers; Mark and Donna Rodgers; and Debra, Joey, and Charlie Vetter.

For friendship and support during the writing of this book, my deep appreciation to Ted Leeson and Betty Campbell, Creighton and Deborah Lindsey, Suzanne Berne, Kevin and Amy Clark, Bob and Mary Jo Nye, Keith Scribner and Jen Richter, Jon and Martha Lewis, Susan and Larry Rodgers, and David Turkel and Elena Passarello.

A spirited jig for the Corvallis sessioners: Shari Ame, Maria Blair, Beth Brown, Mina Carson, Kevin Craven, Michael Everett, Leslie Glassmire, Robbie Goetschalckx, David Greenberg, James Jordan, Bo Leydon, Katie Maxie, Erica Nagamoto, Jennifer Parke, Roy Rowland, and Mark and B. J. Tighe.

Finally, my deepest love and gratitude to the amazing Marjorie Sandor.

NOTES

Some names have been changed in these pieces to protect the privacy of living individuals, and certain events have been mildly altered for narrative clarity.

Epigraph

vi *Each of us finds*: C. S. Lewis, "Historicism," in *The Seeing Eye*, 141.

Preface: Obscure Destinies

ix *These two unaccountable freaks*: Mark Twain, quoted in Blum, *Ghost Hunters*, 314.

ix *vastation*: See Allen, *William James*, 18.

ix *One day . . . having eaten*: Henry James Sr., *Society the Redeemed Form of Man*, 45.

xii *I was shaped by the West*: Stegner, *Where the Bluebird Sings*, xv.

xii *implanted by divine act*: Wallace Stegner, "This I Believe," in *One Way to Spell Man*, 4.

xii *I simply do not know*: Stegner, "This I Believe," 3.

xii *sort of snug and homelike* and subsequent quotes: Willa Cather, "Neighbor Rosicky," in *Obscure Destinies*, 18–19.

xiii *May your days*: My wording of Deuteronomy 11:21.

xiii *Death is a convention*: Wallace Stegner, "Letter, Much Too Late," in *Where the Bluebird Sings*, 23.

xiv *stretch of dusty white road* and subsequent quotes: Willa Cather, "Two Friends," in *Obscure Destinies*, 229, 230.

Cotton County

2.

22 *As for me, I live in a small town*: Debo, *Prairie City*, 245.

4.

42   *She called for art*: Polito, *Savage Art*, 210.

9.

71   *One January day*: Cather, *O Pioneers!*, 133.
72   *I have cared too much*: Jewell and Stout, *Selected Letters of Willa Cather*, 561.

12.

98   *The light air about me* and subsequent quote: Cather, *My Ántonia*, 18, 15.

The Unearthly Archives

Epigraphs

102   *So far as we can see*: "The Strange Case of Mrs. Piper," 81.
102   *The question of immortality*: The original passage can be found in Kierkegaard, *Concluding Unscientific Postscript*, 154–55. I have chosen to use Eugene Fontinell's translation of the quote from his epigraph page in *Self, God, and Immortality*.

1.

107   *On August 12th at 8:23*: "Notes on the 1970 Perseid Shower," 326.
107   *The following poem was read*: "A Poem on Asthma."
108   *the "massacre" of aging*: Roth, *Everyman*, 156.
109   *reduced from a state of firm, vigorous, joyful manhood*: James Sr., *Society the Redeemed Form of Man*, 45.
110   *as nobody talking with nobody*: Henry James, "The Great Good Place," in *The Soft Side*, 17.

2.

120   *A route of evanescence*: Emily Dickinson, Poem 1463, in *The Complete Poems*, 619.
120   *We tarried by the seashore*: Dante Alighieri, *Purgatorio* II: 10–12, my translation.

121 *The broad sky and sea are whanging*: Allen, *William James*, 69.

122 *absence of everything* and subsequent quotes: James, "The Great Good Place," 7, 9, 10, 17.

123 *What makes the crops rejoice*: Virgil, *Georgics*, 3.

124 *What the laboratories and hospitals have lately been teaching us* and subsequent quote: William James, "Human Immortality," in *The Will to Believe*, 8, 7.

124 *Even though our soul's life*: James, "Human Immortality," 11–12.

124 *functions*: James, "Human Immortality," 12–13.

125 *Suppose . . . that the whole universe*: James, "Human Immortality," 15.

125 *air now comes through my glottis*: James, "Human Immortality," 17.

125 *James challenged his readers*: James, "Human Immortality," 23.

126 *I have had a dream*: Shakespeare, *A Midsummer Night's Dream*, IV.i.205–6, in *The Riverside Shakespeare*, 241.

126 *relevant to consciousness* and subsequent quote: Lindahl and Århem, "Consciousness and Neural Force Fields," 229.

127 *mental force field hypothesis* and subsequent quotes: Karl Popper, quoted in Lindahl and Århem, "Consciousness and Neural Force Fields," 239.

3.

128 *In its original form*: Sandor, "The Ram in the Thicket," 29.

128 *A midrashist, reading along*: Sandor, "The Ram in the Thicket," 29.

129 *And Sarah died*: Sandor, "The Ram in the Thicket," 30.

130 *the tremendousness of the idea of immortality*: Blum, *Ghost Hunters* 78.

130 *It must be now that he is reserved* and subsequent quote: Allen, *William James*, 279, 334.

130 *After long exile and martyrdom*: Allen, *William James*, 340.

132 *in possession of a power as yet unexplained*: William James, "Report of the Committee on Mediumistic Phenomena," 104.

132 *was strong [in her knowledge of] the events*: William James, "A Record of Observations of Certain Phenomena of Trance," 658.

132 *Our immediate family is a part of ourselves*: William James, *The Principles of Psychology*, 292.

132 *Did you get my messages?* and subsequent quotes: William James, "Report on Mrs. Piper's Hodgson-Control," 549, 550, 562.

134 *To explain a cognitive function* and subsequent quote: Chalmers, "Facing up to the Problem of Consciousness," 203, 204, emphasis in the original.

134 *James speculated that consciousness was a "field"*: For a discussion of James's "field" concept, see Fontinell, *Self, God, and Immortality*, 46–47.

134 *all shades and no boundaries*: William James, *A Pluralistic Universe*, 288.

134 *centres of reference and action* and subsequent quotes: William James, cited in Fontinell, *Self, God, and Immortality*, 109, 118.

135 *the hard problem of consciousness* and subsequent quote: Chalmers, "Facing up to the Problem of Consciousness," 201, 200.

135 *David Dennett*: For a discussion of Dennett, see Chalmers, "Facing up to the Problem of Consciousness," 208.

135 *neurobiological theory*: For a discussion of Crick and Christof, see Chalmers, "Facing up to the Problem of Consciousness," 205–6.

135 *Why should physical processing give rise*: Chalmers, "Facing up to the Problem of Consciousness," 202.

136 *Conscious minds result*: Damasio, *Self Comes to Mind*, 23.

136 *Unless the process*: Damasio, *The Strange Order of Things*, 188.

137 *grow in the direction of the terrain*: Damasio, *The Strange Order of Things*, 49.

138 *It's the past that tells us*: Overbye, "On the Other Side Now."

138 *the information will be re-emitted* and further discussion of Hawking's ideas: Overbye, "On the Other Side Now."

139 *he'd grown so "tired"*: Allen, *William James*, 456–57.

139 *Poor man*: James, *The Letters of William James*, 264.

139 *No pain at the last*: Dawidoff, *Making History Matter*, 73.

139 *He wanted to go*: Blum, *Ghost Hunters*, 316.

139 *he was still "safe and living"*: Blum, *Ghost Hunters*, 316.

140 *the grim refusal of the dead*: Blum, *Ghost Hunters*, 316.

4.

141 *that might be her "last"* and subsequent quotes from Colette: Colette, *Break of Day*, 8, 5, 6.

144 *I would not have thought*: Dante Alighieri, *Inferno* III: 55, my translation.

146 *The man lived from 70 to 19* B.C.: For a concise biography of Virgil, see Levi, *Virgil.*

147 *we need to watch the stars*: Virgil, *Georgics*, 12–13.

147 *living man or shade*: *Inferno* I: 66, my translation.

147 *No living man*: *Inferno* I: 67, my translation.

147 *The hides were useless*: Virgil, *Georgics*, 82.

148 *The world is like a chariot run wild*: Virgil, *Georgics*, 26.

149 *the enteric nervous system* and subsequent quotes: Damasio, *The Strange Order of Things*, 134.

150 *like a man carrying a flickering lantern*: See *Purgatorio* XXII: 67–69.

151 *Why are you . . . mistrustful?*: *Purgatorio* III: 25–27, my translation.

151 *It is already evening*: *Purgatorio* III: 25–27, my translation.

152 *It was the hour when a sailor's thoughts*: *Purgatorio* VIII: 1–6, trans. Musa (1985), 82.

5.

153 *How sweet it would be*: James Sr., *Society the Redeemed Form of Man*, 48.

153 *newspapers too many*: James, "The Great Good Place," 1.

153 *For the third year in a row*: Several U.S. newspapers reported the findings issued by the National Center for Health Statistics in Murphy, Xu, Kochanek, and Arias, *Mortality in the United States, 2017.*

154 *Plant laurels all around*: Virgil, *Georgics*, 86–87.

155 *perfect, model state* and subsequent quote: Virgil, *Georgics*, 85, 91.

155 *some [people] draw the implication* and subsequent quote: Virgil, *Georgics*, 94, 95.

155 *The fourth* Georgic *is farthest of all* and subsequent quote: Royds, *The Beasts, Birds, and Bees of Virgil*, xiv.

155 *On certain matters . . . Virgil* did *hit the mark*: Royds, *The Beasts, Birds, and Bees of Virgil*, 58–60.

156 *obscure bee lore*: Royds, *The Beasts, Birds, and Bees of Virgil*, 61–64, 71.

156 *the sound of a "sleeping" hive*: Royds, *The Beasts, Birds, and Bees of Virgil*, 81.

156 *the sum and total of all bee experience*: Royds, *The Beasts, Birds, and Bees of Virgil*, 73.

156 *it will die of "loneliness"*: Royds, *The Beasts, Birds, and Bees of Virgil*, 73.

156 *awake craniotomy* and subsequent quote: de Greef, "A South African Jazz Musician Strums His Way through Brain Surgery."

157 *at once / distinct from matter* and subsequent quotes: *Purgatorio* XVIII: 49–59, my translation.

157 *luminous white rose* and subsequent quote: *Paradiso* XXXI: 1–12, my translation.

159 *"Can a Delicate Little Creature of the Sea Unlock the Secret of Immortality?"*: All quotes from Rich, "Forever and Ever."

160 *thou must not be unchaste and uncleanly*: Samuel Butler, quoted in Royds, *The Beasts, Birds, and Bees of Virgil*, 89.

160 *Bees sustain vicissitudes* and subsequent quotes: Virgil, *Georgics*, 96, 97–98.

160 *narrow site* and subsequent quotes: Virgil, *Georgics*, 98.

160 *Within the corpse / The fluids heat* and subsequent quote: Virgil, *Georgics*, 99.

161 *rag[ing] . . . with grief*: Virgil, *Georgics*, 106.

161 *failed to see / The monstrous serpent*: Virgil, *Georgics*, 106.

161 *a nightingale concealed* and subsequent quotes: Virgil, *Georgics*, 108, 109.

161 *sacrifice / A calf* and subsequent quote: Virgil, *Georgics*, 110.

161 *deceptive calm* and subsequent quotes from Marjorie Sandor: Sandor, "Orfeo's Oyster," in *The Late Interiors*, 96–99.

164 *Physics will permit the resurrection*: Tipler, *The Physics of Immortality*, 1.

165 *Earth [was] doomed*: Tipler, *The Physics of Immortality*, 18.

165 *died in the hope of the Universal Resurrection* and subsequent quote: Tipler, *The Physics of Immortality*, dedication page, 11.

6.

166 *for most of history* and subsequent quote: "Pioneers of Heart Surgery," *Cut to the Heart*, NOVA, https://www.pbs.org/wgbh/nova/heart/pioneers.html.

166 *According to current medical knowledge*: van Lommel, *Consciousness beyond Life*, vii.

167 *every piece of equipment I touched*: van Lommel, *Consciousness beyond Life*, 60.

167 *Consciousness may be nonlocal* and subsequent quotes: van Lommel, *Consciousness beyond Life*, 241.

168   *electronic and molecular oscillating states*: van Lommel, *Consciousness beyond Life*, 277.

168   *biological luminescence* and subsequent quotes: van Lommel, *Consciousness beyond Life*, 272.

168   *reception . . . for certain aspects of our consciousness* and subsequent quote: van Lommel, *Consciousness beyond Life*, 277.

168   *The red surface of an apple* and subsequent quote: Churchland, *Matter and Consciousness*, 15. See also the discussion in Charles Taliaferro, "The Soul of the Matter," in Baker and Goetz, *The Soul Hypothesis*, 26–39.

170   *Death should never be something public*: Thurman, *Secrets of the Flesh*, 498.

171   *Regarde!*: Thurman, *Secrets of the Flesh*, 498.

172   *limber broom*: Virgil, *Georgics*, 29.

7.

176   *sail the small bark of his wit*: *Purgatorio* I: 1–2, my translation.

176   *that by which, or in virtue of which*: Thomas Aquinas, cited in Kenny, *Aquinas on Mind*, 27.

176   *They "combine" matter and not-matter*: Thomas Aquinas, *Summa Theologiae*, vol. 9, 1a, q. 61, a. 3.

176   *heavenly minds*: Thomas Aquinas, cited in Fox, *Sheer Joy*, 185.

176   *[it] does [not] follow*: *Summa Theologiae*, vol. 9, 1a, q. 52, a. 1.

176   *an angel is in a place by acting there*: *Summa Theologiae*, vol. 9, 1a, q. 52, a. 1, fn. a.

177   *much-at-once*: William James, cited in Fontinell, *Self, God, and Immortality*, 118.

177   *In quantum theory*: Rupert Sheldrake, cited in Fox and Sheldrake, *The Physics of Angels*, 103.

177   *The whole universe is one thing*: *Summa Theologiae*, vol. 9, 1a, q. 52, a. 2.

178   *the state of our soul and body*: Boethius, cited in Heilbronn, "Concentus musicus," 6.

179   *he describes the sounds as "sweet"*: Heilbronn, "Concentus musicus," 2.

179   *with small sticks* and subsequent quotes: Heilbronn, "Concentus musicus," 4–5.

180   *The meaning of Purgatory*: Ciabattoni, *Dante's Journey to Polyphony*, 110.

181 *Abachta* and other names of angels: Davidson, *A Dictionary of Angels*.

182 *The three of us*: Sandor, *The Late Interiors*, 165.

184 *counsel, knowledge, and help* and subsequent quote: Davidson, *A Dictionary of Angels*, xxvii.

185 *References to dulcimers*: See Thompson, *Beginning Hammered Dulcimer*, 11.

185 *Here among the fidlers*: Pepys, *Diary*, May 23, 1662.

8.

186 *Never speak of what you cherish most*: My paraphrase of an entry found in Kierkegaard, *Papers and Journals*, 154–55.

189 *felt like sanctuary*: Sandor, *The Late Interiors*, 15.

190 *I'm glad you're here*: Sandor, *The Late Interiors*, 16.

190 *An absence, once announced*: Sandor, *The Late Interiors*, 16.

9.

193 *For centuries, beekeepers have been tanging*: Hubbell, *A Book of Bees*, 129.

194 *In the eleventh and twelfth centuries*: Gragnolati, *Experiencing the Afterlife*, 93.

194 *I turned . . . with the confidence*: *Purgatorio* XXX: 42–48, trans. Merwin (2000), 295.

195 *the angels' primary task*: Davidson, *A Dictionary of Angels*, xvii–xviii.

196 *Watching electrons . . . is like watching fireflies*: Goswami, *The Self-Aware Universe*, 42.

196 *macroscopic object[s]* and subsequent quotes: Goswami, *The Self-Aware Universe*, 42.

197 *a new beginning*: Goswami, *The Self-Aware Universe*, 42.

198 *finite god* and *suffering god*: William James, cited in Fontinell, *Self, God, and Immortality*, 152, 216.

199 *The immortal / does not boast*: Rabindranath Tagore, cited in Goswami, *The Self-Aware Universe*, 250.

199 *a study that raises profound questions*: Kolata, "Study Blurs the Line."

200 *every experience* and subsequent quotes: Goswami, *The Self-Aware Universe*, 190.

200 *the universe is self-aware*: Goswami, *The Self-Aware Universe*, 190.

200 *What we are looking for*: Goswami, *The Self-Aware Universe*, 96.

201 *Shortly before his death*: O'Neill, *Irish Minstrels and Musicians*, 76.

201 *If we shadows have offended*: Shakespeare, *A Midsummer Night's Dream*, V.i.423–28, in *The Riverside Shakespeare*, 246.

BIBLIOGRAPHY

Alighieri, Dante. *Inferno*. Translated by Robert Hollander and Jean Hol-
lander. New York: Doubleday Anchor Books, 2002.
———. *Paradiso*. Translated by Robert Hollander and Jean Hollander.
New York: Anchor Books, 2008.
———. *Purgatorio*. Translated by Robert Hollander and Jean Hollander.
New York: Doubleday Anchor Books, 2004.
———. *Purgatorio*. Translated by W. S. Merwin. New York: Alfred A.
Knopf, 2000.
———. *Purgatorio*. Translated by Mark Musa. New York: Penguin Books,
1985.
Allen, Gay Wilson. *William James: A Biography*. New York: Viking Press,
1967.
Baker, Mark C., and Stewart Goetz, eds. *The Soul Hypothesis: Investiga-
tions into the Existence of the Soul*. New York: Continuum Interna-
tional, 2011.
Blum, Deborah. *Ghost Hunters: William James and the Search for Scientific
Proof of Life after Death*. New York: Penguin, 2006.
Cather, Willa. *My Ántonia*. New York: Book-of-the-Month Club, 1995.
First published 1918 by Houghton Mifflin.
———. *Obscure Destinies*. New York: Vintage Books, 1960. First pub-
lished 1932 by Alfred A. Knopf.
———. *O Pioneers!* In *Early Novels and Stories*, 133–290. New York: Library
of America, 1987. First published 1913 by Houghton Mifflin.
Chalmers, David J. "Facing Up to the Problem of Consciousness." *Jour-
nal of Consciousness Studies* 2, no. 3 (1995): 200–219.
Churchland, Paul. *Matter and Consciousness: A Contemporary Introduction
to the Philosophy of Mind*. Cambridge, Mass.: MIT Press, 1988.
Ciabattoni, Francesco. *Dante's Journey to Polyphony*. Toronto: University
of Toronto Press, 2010.
Colette. *Break of Day*. Translated by Enid McLeod. New York: Farrar,
Straus and Giroux, 1961.
Damasio, Antonio. *Self Comes to Mind: Constructing the Conscious Brain*.
New York: Pantheon Books, 2010.

———. *The Strange Order of Things: Life, Feeling, and the Making of Cultures*. New York: Pantheon Books, 2018.

Davidson, Gustav. *A Dictionary of Angels, Including the Fallen Angels*. New York: Free Press, 1967.

Dawidoff, Robert. *Making History Matter*. Philadelphia: Temple University Press, 2000.

Debo, Angie. *Prairie City: The Story of an American Community*. 1944. Reprint, Tulsa, Okla.: Oak Council Books, 1985.

de Greef, Kimon. "A South African Jazz Musician Strums His Way through Brain Surgery." *New York Times*, December 22, 2018, A4.

Dickinson, Emily. *The Complete Poems of Emily Dickinson*. Edited by Thomas H. Johnson. Boston: Little, Brown, 1960.

Fontinell, Eugene. *Self, God, and Immortality: A Jamesian Investigation*. Philadelphia: Temple University Press, 1986.

Fox, Matthew. *Sheer Joy: Conversations with Thomas Aquinas on Creation Spirituality*. San Francisco: Harper, 1992.

Fox, Matthew, and Rupert Sheldrake. *The Physics of Angels: Exploring the Realm Where Science and Spirit Meet*. Rhinebeck, N.Y.: Monkfish, 2014.

Goswami, Amit. *The Self-Aware Universe: How Consciousness Creates the Material World*. New York: G. P. Putnam's Sons, 1993.

Gragnolati, Manuele. *Experiencing the Afterlife: Soul and Body in Dante and Medieval Culture*. Notre Dame, Ind.: University of Notre Dame Press, 2005.

Heilbronn, Denise. "*Concentus musicus:* The Creaking Hinges of Dante's Gate of Purgatory." *Rivista di Studi Italiani* 2, no. 1 (1984): 1–15.

Hubbell, Sue. *A Book of Bees . . . and How to Keep Them*. Boston: Mariner Books, 1988.

James, Henry. *The Soft Side*. New York: Macmillan, 1900.

James, Henry, Sr. *Society the Redeemed Form of Man, and the Earnest of God's Omnipotence in Human Nature: Affirmed in Letters to a Friend*. Boston: Houghton, Osgood and Company, 1879.

James, William. *Human Immortality: Two Supposed Objections to the Doctrine*. 1898. Reprint, New York: Cosimo Classics, 2007.

———. *The Letters of William James*. Edited by Henry James. 2 vols. Boston: Atlantic Monthly Press, 1900.

———. *A Pluralistic Universe: Hibbert Lectures at Manchester College on the Present Situation in Philosophy*. London: Longmans, Green, 1909.

——. *The Principles of Psychology*. 2 vols. 1918. Reprint, New York: Dover, 1950.

——. "A Record of Observations of Certain Phenomena of Trance," pt. 3. *Proceedings of the American Society for Psychical Research* 6, nos. 15–17 (1889–90): 651–59.

——. "Report of the Committee on Mediumistic Phenomena." *Proceedings of the American Society for Psychical Research* 1, nos. 1–4 (1885–89): 102–6.

——. "Report on Mrs. Piper's Hodgson-Control." In *Proceedings of the American Society for Psychical Research*, vol. 3, pts. 1–2, 470–589. New York: American Society for Psychical Research, 1909.

——. *The Will to Believe, Human Immortality, and Other Essays in Popular Philosophy*. New York: Dover, 1956.

Jaynes, Julian. *The Origin of Consciousness in the Breakdown of the Bicameral Mind*. New York: Mariner Books, 2000.

Jewell, Andrew, and Janis Stout. *The Selected Letters of Willa Cather*. New York: Vintage Books, 2014.

Kenny, Anthony. *Aquinas on Mind*. London: Routledge, 1993.

Kierkegaard, Søren. *Concluding Unscientific Postscript*. Translated by David F. Swenson and Walter Lowrie. Princeton, N.J.: Princeton University Press, 1941.

——. *Papers and Journals: A Selection*. Edited by Alastair Hannay. London: Penguin Books, 1996.

Kolata, Gina. "Study Blurs the Line between Life and Death." *New York Times*, April 18, 2019, A19.

Levi, Peter. *Virgil: His Life and Times*. New York: St. Martin's Press, 1998.

Lewis, C. S. *The Seeing Eye: And Other Selected Essays from Christian Reflections*. New York: Ballantine Books, 1986.

Lindahl, B. I. B., and Peter Århem. "Consciousness and Neural Force Fields." *Journal of Consciousness Studies* 23, no. 7–8 (2016): 228–53.

Murphy, Sherry L., Jiaquan Xu, Kenneth D. Kochanek, and Elizabeth Arias. *Mortality in the United States, 2017*. NCHS Data Brief no. 328. Hyattsville, Md.: National Center for Health Statistics, 2018. https://www.cdc.gov/nchs/products/databriefs/db328.htm.

"Notes on the 1970 Perseid Shower." *Sky and Telescope* 40, no. 5 (November 1970): 325–27.

O'Neill, Francis. *Irish Minstrels and Musicians*. Chicago: Regan, 1913.

Overbye, Dennis. "On the Other Side Now, but Still Spurring Debate." *New York Times*, October 30, 2018, D6.

Pepys, Samuel. *Diary of Samuel Pepys, 1662: Transcribed from the Shorthand Manuscript in the Pepysian Library Magdalene College Cambridge by the Rev. Mynors Bright*. Edited by Henry B. Wheatley. London: George Bell & Sons, 1893.

"A Poem on Asthma." *Annals of Allergy: Devoted to the Interests of the Practicing Allergist* 43, no. 1 (July 1979): 68.

Polito, Robert. *Savage Art: A Biography of Jim Thompson*. New York: Vintage, 1996.

Rich, Nathaniel. "Forever and Ever: Can a Delicate Little Creature of the Sea Unlock the Secret of Immortality?" *New York Times Magazine*, December 2, 2012, 32–39, 66, 68, 70.

Roth, Philip. *Everyman*. Boston: Houghton Mifflin, 2006.

Royds, Thomas Fletcher. *The Beasts, Birds, and Bees of Virgil: A Naturalist's Handbook to the Georgics*. Oxford: B. H. Blackwell, 1918.

Sandor, Marjorie. *The Late Interiors: A Life under Construction*. New York: Arcade, 2011.

———. "The Ram in the Thicket: Midrash and the Contemporary Creative Writer." *Writer's Chronicle* 51, no. 2 (October/November 2018): 28–39.

Scott, A. O. "Wallace Stegner and the Conflicted Soul of the West." *New York Times Book Review*, June 7, 2020, 1, 14–16.

Shakespeare, William. *The Riverside Shakespeare*. Edited by G. Blakemore Evans. Boston: Houghton Mifflin, 1974.

Simon, Linda. *Genuine Reality: A Life of William James*. Chicago: University of Chicago Press, 1998.

Slocum, Joshua. *Sailing Alone around the World*. 1898. Reprint, New York: Dover, 1956.

Stegner, Wallace. *One Way to Spell Man*. Garden City, N.Y.: Doubleday, 1982.

———. *Where the Bluebird Sings to the Lemonade Springs: Living and Writing in the West*. New York: Penguin Books, 1992.

"The Strange Case of Mrs. Piper" (book review). *Saturday Review of Politics, Literature, Science and Art*, July 16, 1898, 81.

Thomas Aquinas. *Summa Theologiae*. Vol. 9, *Angels (1a. 50–64)*, translated by Kenelm Foster. New York: Blackfriars, 1968.

Thompson, Linda Lowe. *Beginning Hammered Dulcimer*. Denton, Tex.: Linda Lowe Thompson, 1995.

Bibliography

Thurman, Judith. *Secrets of the Flesh: A Life of Colette*. New York: Alfred A. Knopf, 1999.

Tipler, Frank J. *The Physics of Immortality: Modern Cosmology, God, and the Resurrection of the Dead*. New York: Doubleday, 1994.

Tymn, Michael E. "The Case for the Return of Richard Hodgson." *The Ground of Faith*, February 2011. http://thegroundoffaith.net/issues/2011-02/The%20Return%20of%20Richard%20Hodgson.pdf.

van Lommel, Pim. *Consciousness beyond Life: The Science of the Near-Death Experience*. Translated by Laura Vroomen. New York: HarperOne, 2010.

Virgil. *Virgil's Georgics: A Modern English Verse Translation*. Translated by Smith Palmer Bovie. Chicago: University of Chicago Press, 1956.

Wild, John. *The Radical Empiricism of William James*. New York: Doubleday Anchor Books, 1970.

CPSIA information can be obtained
at www.ICGtesting.com
Printed in the USA
LVHW040545140122
708425LV00011B/1226

9 780806 176239